Leadership and Musician Development in Higher Music Education

Leadership and Musician Development in Higher Music Education informs, challenges and evaluates the central practices, policies and theories that underpin the preparation of future music leaders and the leadership of music in higher education. In higher education, it is often presumed that preparing for professional work is the responsibility of the individual rather than the institution. This anthology draws on the expertise of music practitioners to present the complexities surrounding this topic, exploring approaches to leadership development while addressing prevalent leadership issues from multiple standpoints.

Leadership is an inherent part of being a musician: from the creative act through to collaborative engagement, it is fundamental to creating and sustaining a career in music. To expect musicians to develop these necessary skills "on the job", however, is unreasonable and impractical. What support might be given to those looking to negotiate a career as a musician? In 14 essays, contributors from around the globe explore this question and more, questions such as:

- How might leadership be modelled for aspiring musicians?
- How might students learn to recognise, appraise and extend their leadership development?
- How might institutional leaders challenge curricular and pedagogical norms?

Effective leadership development for musicians is vital to the longevity of the profession – *Leadership and Musician Development in Higher Music Education* is a likewise vital resource for students, educators and future music leaders alike.

Dawn Bennett is John Curtin Distinguished Professor of Higher Education and Director of the EmployABILITY and Creative Workforce Initiatives with Curtin University in Australia.

Jennifer Rowley is Associate Professor and Program Leader of Music Education at the Sydney Conservatorium of Music, The University of Sydney, where she coordinates the professional placement programme for students into the arts industry, regional conservatoriums and schools.

Patrick Schmidt is Associate Professor and Chair of Music Education at Western University in Canada, where he specialises in critical pedagogy, urban music education and policy studies.

ISME Global Perspectives in Music Education Series

Senior Editor: Margaret Barrett

Leadership and Musician Development in Higher Music Education
Edited by Dawn Bennett, Jennifer Rowley and Patrick Schmidt

Leadership of Pedagogy and Curriculum in Higher Music Education
Edited by Jennifer Rowley, Dawn Bennett and Patrick Schmidt

Leadership and Musician Development in Higher Music Education

Edited by
Dawn Bennett
Curtin University, Australia
Jennifer Rowley
The University of Sydney, Australia
Patrick Schmidt
Western University, Canada

NEW YORK AND LONDON

First published 2019
by Routledge
52 Vanderbilt Avenue, New York, NY 10017

and by Routledge
2 Park Square, Milton Park, Abingdon, Oxon, OX14 4RN

Routledge is an imprint of the Taylor & Francis Group, an informa business

© 2019 Taylor & Francis

The right of Dawn Bennett, Jennifer Rowley, and Patrick Schmidt to be identified as the authors of the editorial material, and of the authors for their individual chapters, has been asserted in accordance with sections 77 and 78 of the Copyright, Designs and Patents Act 1988.

All rights reserved. No part of this book may be reprinted or reproduced or utilised in any form or by any electronic, mechanical, or other means, now known or hereafter invented, including photocopying and recording, or in any information storage or retrieval system, without permission in writing from the publishers.

Trademark notice: Product or corporate names may be trademarks or registered trademarks, and are used only for identification and explanation without intent to infringe.

Library of Congress Cataloging-in-Publication Data
Names: Bennett, Dawn. | Rowley, Jennifer (Professor in music education) | Schmidt, Patrick K.
Title: Leadership and musician development in higher music education / [edited by] Dawn Bennett, Jennifer Rowley, Patrick Schmidt.
Description: New York ; London : Routledge, 2019. |
Includes bibliographical references.
Identifiers: LCCN 2018039407 (print) | LCCN 2018042217 (ebook) |
ISBN 9780429503924 (ebook) | ISBN 9781138587465 (hardback) |
ISBN 9781138587472 (pbk.)
Subjects: LCSH: Music in universities and colleges. |
Music–Instruction and study. | Leadership.
Classification: LCC MT18 (ebook) | LCC MT18 .L43 2019 (print) |
DDC 780.71/1–dc23
LC record available at https://lccn.loc.gov/2018039407

ISBN: 978-1-138-58746-5 (hbk)
ISBN: 978-1-138-58747-2 (pbk)
ISBN: 978-0-429-50392-4 (ebk)

Typeset in Minion
by Newgen Publishing UK

Contents

List of Figures and Tables — x
Series Foreword — xi
Preface — xiii

Foreword: A Call for Care in the Development of
   Musicians as Leaders — 1
DAVID LINES

   Becoming a Musician — 1
   Connecting Music and Life — 2
   A Call for Care — 3
   Implications for Leadership — 4
   References — 5

I How is Leadership Developed in Higher Music Education? — 6
JENNIFER ROWLEY, DAWN BENNETT AND PATRICK SCHMIDT

   Leadership in the Musician's Practice — 6
   Institutional Leadership — 9
   Conclusion — 11
   References — 12

II Leaders and Leadership in Higher Music Education:
    Meeting the Challenges — 14
GLEN CARRUTHERS

   The Nature of Leadership — 14
   Cyclic Reviews — 16
   Case Study Background — 17
   Case Study Data — 18
   Case Study Discussion — 19
   Review Findings — 22
   Further Research — 30
   Conclusion — 30
   References — 32

III Leadership in the Midst of Higher Education   33
ANNA REID

    Being a Musician and a Leader   33
    Understanding Variation for Leadership   36
    Understanding Musician Identity for Leadership   37
    Understanding Leadership Theories for Leadership   39
    The Real World and Work of Higher Education
        Music Educators   41
    References   42

IV Leading Institutional Change through Better Policy Thinking 44
PATRICK SCHMIDT

    Policy, Leadership and a Framing Disposition   45
    Redefining Policy and Moving Away from Incredible
        Certitude   48
    From Advocacy to Counsel: Policy as Leadership   50
    Stories of Practice: Current Action and Food for
        Future Thought   54
    Final Thoughts   58
    References   59

V   Educating Professional Musicians: Gender Equality,
Career Creativities and Strategies for Change in
Institutional Leadership   62
PAMELA BURNARD

    Higher Music Education and Gender   62
    The Challenge of Gender Bias   63
    Gender Messaging, Career Creativities and the Insidious
        Human Capitals Divide   65
    Gender, Professional Capital, Career Creativities and
        Institutional Change Matters   67
    The Research Study   68
    Leadership and Institutional Change   72
    Developing Passionate Leadership for the 21st Century   77
    References   79

VI Student Commentary: Institutional Leadership from the
Point of View of a Latin American Student; Being
Aware of the Wall   81
EURIDIANA SILVA SOUZA

	The Context	81
	Policy, Curriculum and Community	83
	Final Words	85
	References	85
VII	Developing Leadership Capacities with Generation Z Students in Higher Music Education SUSAN A. O'NEILL	87
	Generational Issues in Higher Music Education	87
	Who are Generation Z?	89
	Being a Change Agent	91
	Affordances and Constraints to Developing Leadership Capacities with Generation Z	95
	Allies in Generation Z Leadership Development: Towards a Pedagogical Practice	97
	Conclusion	99
	References	100
VIII	Leadership as an Essential Graduate Attribute for Musicians ANNA REID, DAWN BENNETT AND JENNIFER ROWLEY	103
	Approach and Context	106
	Results and Discussion	107
	Concluding Comments	111
	References	113
IX	Educing Leadership and Evoking Sound: Choral Conductors as Agents of Change MARTIN BERGER	115
	Choral Conducting in Context	115
	Leadership Theory	117
	Leadership and Choral Conducting	119
	Towards the Education of Choral Conducting Students	121
	Conclusions	126
	References	127
X	The Tapestry of Leadership, Creativity and Advocacy: Weaving Musicians' Core Abilities into the Curriculum PAMELA D. PIKE	130
	Leadership, Creativity and Advocacy	131

	Transformational Leadership, Indirect Leadership and Following the Leader	132
	Creativity	133
	Music Advocacy	137
	Method	139
	Findings and Synopsis of the Results	140
	Discussion and Implications for Music Education	143
	Conclusions	145
	References	146
XI	The Leadership Role of Instrumental Teachers in Students' Career Development: Negotiating Professional Identities CHRISTINE NGAI LAM YAU	149
	Leadership and the Master–Apprentice Model	149
	Method and Context	152
	The Institution	154
	Findings	155
	Dreams, Reality Checks and Possibilities	156
	Guidance and Reassurance from Instrumental Teacher	157
	Emerging Professional Identity	160
	Discussion	160
	Power Dynamics Invested in Leaders	161
	Recommendations	162
	Conclusion	164
	References	164
XII	Leadership and Conducted Improvisation: Connections and Opportunities in Undergraduate Music Programmes JANIS F. WELLER	167
	Framing 21st-Century Musician Careers	168
	Leadership Roles	170
	Intersections of Composition and Improvisation	172
	Conducted Improvisation: Liminal Musical Spaces	174
	Case Study: Aaron and Improvestra	176
	Summary and Recommendations	179
	References	181
XIII	Student Commentary: Leadership at the Undergraduate Level; Cultivating Collective Ownership KELLY BYLICA	184

	The Initiative to Lead	184
	Why Does Leadership Matter?	185
	The Roles of Teacher and Curriculum	186
	Collective Ownership	188
	References	189
XIV	Institutional Leadership and Musician Development in Higher Music Education	190
	DAWN BENNETT, JENNIFER ROWLEY AND PATRICK SCHMIDT	
	Leading the Development of Student Musicians	191
	Leading Faculty Engagement	193
	Leadership and Policy Thinking	195
	Leading for Today and Tomorrow	197
	Concluding Comments	199
	References	200

The International Society for Music Education (ISME)	202
The ISME Commission on the Education of the Professional Musician	204
Contributors	205
Index	209

Figures and Tables

Figures

4.1 Leadership as a centrifugal force   53
5.1 The fields within the fields of power   75
10.1 Three skill sets required to demonstrate creativity, based on Amabile (1996)   135
10.2 Overview of skills employed regularly by professional musicians   142
10.3 Interwoven connection between leadership, creativity, teaching and advocacy among professional musicians   144

Tables

2.1 Institutions (pseudonyms) included in the analysis   17
2.2 Recommendations from 2015 external reviews of universities   19
11.1 Themes and subthemes for the dyad   153

Series Foreword

The **ISME Global Perspectives in Music Education Series** is one of two book series partnered by Routledge and the International Society for Music Education (ISME), with Senior Editor, Professor Margaret Barrett from the University of Queensland. The collection reflects topics of broad and critical interest to music education. The themes are fluid, changing with time and responding to the contemporary issues and need of music educators worldwide.

The **ISME Specialist Themes in Music Education Series** with Senior Editor, Associate Professor Jennifer Rowley from Sydney Conservatorium of Music, The University of Sydney, explores specialist themes addressed by the ISME commissions, forum and standing committee. The designated areas are well established within the Society, with leading experts already leading cutting-edge research, scholarship and educational change.

Each series offers a focused conduit through which members of ISME and their colleagues can publish scholarly and instructional work.

Professor Dawn Bennett, Curtin University, Australia
Series Editor-in-Chief

More Information

To be included in, contribute to and/or submit a proposal, authors must be, or must become, a member of ISME. The collaboration with the Canadian Music Educators' Association (CMEA), with Senior Editor, Professor Susan O'Neill, Simon Fraser University, Vancouver, also encourages and enables contributions from CMEA members for inclusion in either of the two series.

Proposals are welcome. For more information please refer to the guidelines at www.isme.org/isme-routledge-series.

Preface

This is the first of two volumes concerned with leadership and leadership development in higher music education. The anthologies mark the launch of two new Routledge series: *Global Perspectives in Music Education* and *Specialist Themes in Music Education*.

A central focus of the new series, produced in partnership with the International Society for Music Education (ISME), is to understand and enhance the processes by which music in all its forms is accessed, experienced, utilised, connected, communicated, learned and taught. Consequently, it is fitting that leadership should form the topic of the first volumes in the *Global Perspectives* series. Musicians – and both series will emphasise the holistic and non-hierarchical view of musicians as people who practise in one or more specialist fields – are leaders in and through their communities. Whether or not these communities include higher education, musicians must lead not as solitary leaders of the past but as collaborative facilitators of the future.

The authors of the two leadership volumes first presented and discussed their work at the ISME Commission for the Education of the Professional Musician (CEPROM) in St Andrews, Scotland, in July 2016. Leadership as a competency was discussed from theoretical and practical perspectives, yet a common theme was that the preparation of musicians rarely addresses the qualities required to lead – to create and sustain – a meaningful career in music.

It is insufficient to expect that musicians will develop their leadership "on the job" as part of what is often referred to as lifelong learning. This is not to suggest that higher music education programmes should partition vital curricular time for formal leadership training. Far from it; as the authors in these volumes illustrate, leadership is an inherent part of being a musician from the creative act through to collaborative engagement and creating and sustaining a career.

How, then, might leadership be modelled for aspiring musicians? How might students learn to recognise, appraise and extend their leadership development? How might institutional and curricular leaders challenge extant structures and processes to enable more distributed and transformative leadership approaches? Where are the examples and the lessons through which music educators might extend their practice within the constraints of time, resources and energy? The authors agree that leadership development for musicians is vital for the longevity of the profession. It is through their contributions that these volumes will make their mark.

Dawn Bennett, Jennifer Rowley and Patrick Schmidt
June 2018

Peer Review Statement

All published chapters in this volume have undergone rigorous double-blind peer review based on initial editor screening, anonymous refereeing by independent expert referees, and consequent revision by chapter authors when required. The published chapter constitutes the final, definitive, and citable Version of Scholarly Record.

Foreword: A Call for Care in the Development of Musicians as Leaders

DAVID LINES

Becoming a Musician

What does it mean to become a musician? For me, music was a distinct and real part of my childhood, mainly due to the fact that I grew up in a family that valued and loved music of all kinds: classical piano, orchestral, rock guitar, jazz, folk, pop songs, musical theatre, church music and much more. But it was in my teenage years and early twenties when I started to think more seriously about becoming a musician and I then became more focused on the reality of what that meant.

During that period, a number of converging musical events, relationships, challenges and discoveries came together in such a way that a "becoming in music" happened. I was a reasonably serious piano student who enjoyed learning the classic keyboard compositions of Chopin, Haydn, Beethoven, Bach and 20th-century piano pieces like Bartók's *Mikrokosmos*. But at the same time, I found plenty of enjoyment in the acoustic guitar, mainly through a process of self-learning and social connections that were aurally focused and associated with the mainstream rock music of the 1970s. This all occurred alongside a period of very active musical listening to all kinds of eclectic musical styles, a listening process that was stimulated, no doubt, by the dual experiences of formal piano learning and informal guitar learning. Having this element of difference in the formative years of my musical development allowed me to move outside conventional listening experiences and be open to different kinds of musical experiences and approaches.

As a result, it is very hard to pinpoint or narrow down my musical development to a particular influence, linear direction or conscious decision; and in this sense it could be said that my emergent life as a musician was "rhizomatic" (Deleuze & Guattari, 1987) – the directions of change came from a fusion of different stylistic, social and material impulses, in no particular linear order. Of course, you could say this account of my life experience of becoming a musician is anecdotal at best, but as a tertiary music educator with 30 or more years of experience I can look back and reflect on what happened with confidence and with a tacit understanding that also connects with the experiences of others.

Connecting Music and Life

Becoming a musician is one thing, but discovering and experiencing how music connects with life is another. The act of learning music can involve a great deal of serious investment in time and concentrated energy. It is a labour of love, a dedication and investment in an ongoing process of self-control and self-discipline. Consequently, a musician's journey can be insular and removed from other experiences in the wider world. But music is not an art that exists in a vacuum; it thrives on its connections and intersections with diverse forms of cultural life. Musical sound is ephemeral and expressively connected with life; the vibrancy and communicative impulse of music comes from its metaphoric and imaginative association with the "non-musical", or what is outside the immediacy of playing an instrument or singing.

The ironic thing is that as a musician, it is through a connection with the world outside music where you can find the opportunity to express the power of music through its living relations with things like language, technology, care, love, freedom, individuality and community. This gives us a hint as to what kind of music and music leadership programmes can be implemented at the university level.

I discovered this outside element through teaching. Following a performance degree in classical piano and a year playing professionally in jazz and rock bands, I decided on a change of career direction and became a primary school teacher. This change forced me into the unfamiliar territory of constant interaction with children in the classroom and the teaching of a broad curriculum across all subjects.

I recall the primary classroom as being a space filled with an assortment of many different personalities and needs, and dealing with this was a challenge. I was, after all, a friendly "muso" who, up to that point, was used to socialising with like-minded friends in bands, not with adolescent children. But the intensity and difference afforded by this new working experience led to a whole new range of interesting experiences and possibilities. This eventually included a very interesting career pathway in tertiary music education, research and creative musical performance.

In my new job as a primary teacher I started to make connections between my musical passions and my personal desire for the children in my care to experience something exciting and educative through the arts. This evolved into a series of musical shows based initially on New Zealand children's novels, which then morphed into annual collaborations of entirely new shows composed and authored with other teacher colleagues and the children themselves. These shows created a place for the children to experience the richness of a living community with music and other arts.

A Call for Care

Professional experiences like these have made me realise how important it is to challenge the normative ways of teaching and learning music at the tertiary level. How can we prepare students for these kinds of future musical and extra-musical connections? I feel strongly that tertiary music learning should not be too innocuous or mundane. It should not be overly formulaic or regulated, for in doing so it runs the danger of becoming insular, stale and repetitive. Tertiary music education should be structured in such a way that diverse learning directions are possible alongside more regular kinds of music learning, so that the potential for rhizomatic connections remains possible. When we fail to structure our programmes in this way, we limit music's potential by restricting music learning to tired old forms of training and nihilistic repetition.

In recent decades the economic paradigm of what has become known as neoliberalism has infiltrated many sectors of society, including areas traditionally connected with the arts and education. By neoliberalism I refer to the rise of marketisation and the intensification of the logic of the market in all areas of society. Under neoliberalism, all things are judged according to their market worth; for anything to be possible it must first be fiscally viable. In this paradigm everything is a potential market opportunity where an ethic of self-interest and individual consumer choice trumps other values (Wren & Waller, 2017, p. 498). Under neoliberalism what was known as the "public good" – that is, the beneficial and ethical character of public institutions such as the benefits of universities, schools, early childhood centres, health organisations and arts and cultural organisations – has become increasingly privatised and subject to the logic of individualism, profit and efficiency. These processes are occurring in front of our very eyes in tertiary education spaces.

University faculty and others know how the economic realities of student class numbers influences tertiary education values. In the past 20 years or so, tertiary education has developed a market-orientated and competitive approach to the provision of both undergraduate and postgraduate study, perpetuated by competition for student numbers and research. Results have been mixed. From where I see it, the increased competitiveness for students in the tertiary sector has resulted in some disappointing and negative outcomes; it has disrupted the quality of many academic programmes, lessened student choice and, in some instances, led to the loss of competent music staff. Further, atomistic research auditing systems have encouraged individual research over and above more collaborative, team-based research.

As arts educators we need to take stock of the influence of neoliberalism and other disabling ideologies that affect our artistic work and pedagogy. To what degree should the neoliberal economic paradigm completely dominate our lives, our artistic and musical values and our concepts of pedagogy, teaching and learning? And to what extent can arts educators take up a counter-narrative or dialogue with neoliberalism that offers artistic and humane outcomes for students?

While the realities of neoliberalism prevail, tertiary music education must also take care not to become too wedded to the modern neoliberal university code, which presents itself as commodity-driven education and performativity. Music, as a discipline within the university, can become restrained and defensive through having to conform to the regulatory demands of systematic education and the associated economic pressures of educational cost. In such circumstances, music departments can become diluted and it can become increasingly difficult for music students to experience a meaningful connection with their studies.

Perhaps part of the solution to these concerns comes not from the musical act itself but from an alternative way of thinking about it. While a "care-less" ethic of self-interest may prevail in neoliberal tertiary education, the notion of music-as-care could be positioned as an alternative. I would argue that a notion of care underpins both music and education as a pedagogical concept and as a real process between teachers, students and communities. Music is a relational activity involving performers and audiences; it is an act of communication and sharing (Cobussen & Nielsen, 2012). Music-making or *musicking* (as Christopher Small calls it, 2011) in its various modes (performing, composing, improvising, recording, listening, writing and reading…) is therefore an ethical act; it is utterly human, communicative and expressive. In this sense music-making is also an act of care – a mindful practice that involves the care of the music itself along with a care for the act of musical creation with others (be they co-musicians or listeners).

Implications for Leadership

A call to care necessitates a new kind of tertiary music education leadership that can negotiate these real challenges and seek creative solutions to help music be the vital and powerful creative force that it is. This book is an excellent introduction to new and challenging thinking and research about how institutional leadership in tertiary music education can respond to thinking about music curricula, music careers and music leadership in the 21st century. Editors Dawn Bennett, Jennifer Rowley and Patrick Schmidt, and the chapter authors, have done a wonderful job of presenting an array of different perspectives and angles on this topic. Like my own career, future careers in music will be diverse and substantively different than the perceived norm; these new musicians will need to embrace an ethic of care, be agile, make connections and find space for new ways of communicating through musical action. This important book is a step in that direction.

References

Cobussen, M., & Nielsen, N. (2012). *Music and ethics*. London: Ashgate Publishing Ltd.
Deleuze, G., & Guattari, F. (1987). *A thousand plateaus*. Minneapolis: University of Minnesota Press.
Small, C. (2011). *Musicking: The meanings of performing and listening*. Middletown, CO: Wesleyan University Press.
Wren, M., & Waller, W. (2017). Care and the neoliberal individual. *Economic Issues, 51*(2), 495–502.

I

How is Leadership Developed in Higher Music Education?

JENNIFER ROWLEY, DAWN BENNETT AND PATRICK SCHMIDT

Leadership and Musician Development in Higher Music Education is the first of a two-volume edited anthology dedicated to leadership and leadership development in higher music education. The volume presents compelling arguments in support of leadership development as a core component of student musicians' development. Authors from diverse countries and contexts explore the broader dimensions of leadership, musicians' work, institutional policy and music in higher education. The authors, who include two students, define the diverse qualities required by graduate musicians if they are to create and sustain their lives in music. With a focus on leading institutional change, they suggest how these qualities might be developed so that the next generation of musicians and leaders is equipped to succeed.

Leadership in the Musician's Practice

Over the past 20 years, higher music education has been both the subject of increased scrutiny and the innovator of substantial reform. Within the innovative and diverse higher music education settings are seen many examples of distributed, collaborative and transformative leadership. Questions remain, however, as to how leadership is developed among students and faculty, the extent to which leadership is understood by participants, and the degree to which it is supported and sustained within a performance-centric culture.

This volume exposes the practice of musicians engaged in a diverse range of roles. It highlights the demands on individual workers to lead their own work, careers and professional learning and it considers the implications for music education. Drawing his context from the practice of choral singing, Martin Berger (Chapter IX) explores the development of leadership skills and musician identities among choral conducting students. Central to Berger's thesis is that choral conductors lead music-making in multicultural contexts for which they must combine musicality, creativity and social citizenship. As Berger argues, the multifaceted societal role of choral conductors presents a challenge to practitioners and educators. Indeed, to Durrant's (2005, p. 89) list of necessary music graduate attributes, "philosophical underpinning, music-technical skills and interpersonal skills", he adds the need for transformational leadership, transcultural understanding, creativity and expanding awareness of the contexts within which music work takes place.

Pamela Pike (Chapter X) continues the creativity and citizenship themes, adding that musicians have an essential role to play in advocating for the intrinsic value of music and creative experiences. Beyond this, Pike's study illustrates, yet again, that musicians are more than performers and that creating and sustaining a career in music requires music-technical skills alongside the ability to run a small business, to teach and to provide high-level leadership roles within diverse societal settings.

Like Berger, Pike emphasises the role of transformational leadership; however, she also points to indirect leadership and the role of the mindful follower. To illustrate her point, Pike conveys leadership in terms of the creative convergent and divergent thinking that underpins the creative phases of preparation, incubation, illumination and verification. Pike contends that curricular space must be made for the exploration of these phases, not necessarily through whole-scale curricular change but through meaningful practice, explicit discussion and critical reflection on problem-based, team-based challenges.

In her chapter, Janis Weller extends Clarke and Doffman's (2017) discourse about distributed creativity and autonomous zones. She explores leadership through the theoretical lens of transformational leadership and the metaphorical lenses of musical improvisation, composition and performance.

Weller (Chapter XII) emphasises that musicians have been responsible for leading their practice and careers – in whole or part – for centuries. Drawing on recommendations made in 2014 by the United States College Music Society Task Force (CMS) in its manifesto on the undergraduate music major (Sarath, Myers & Campbell, 2016), Weller presents compelling evidence for higher music education to prepare students for the *practice* of being a musician. Musicians' practice involves diverse musical genres, collaboration, business capabilities, teaching and coaching abilities and an entrepreneurial mindset. Transformational and shared leadership theories are used to tease out the spontaneous and yet strategic leadership demonstrated by a musician whose practice mirrors many of Berger's points about the musician as an agent of social change. In framing leadership both *of* and *within* the musician's practice, Weller suggests a way forward for the CMS manifesto recommendations and the thinking of higher music education elsewhere in the world.

One of the most intensive and influential relationships in higher music education is that between a student and the vocal or instrumental music teacher, described by Burwell (2012, p. 150) as a relationship of "businesslike intimacy". In Chapter XI, Christine Ngai Lam Yau draws readers inside the undergraduate student experience to see how the leadership of instrumental teachers informs or disrupts students' complex identity work. Articulating the thinking of incoming performance students who encounter equally talented peers and become increasingly aware of the fierce competition for work (see also Burland & Pitts, 2007; MacNamara, Holmes & Collins, 2008), Yau emphasises the influential leadership role of instrumental and vocal teachers. As argued previously by Gaunt (2008), Yau finds that the power relationships between teacher and student, coupled with the relative isolation of the teaching studio can inhibit learners' emerging sense of artistic autonomy (Gaunt, 2008). The findings of Yau's study will inform strategies for explicit identity work with students. They should also be considered in the development of reflexive thinking as a leadership trait among both teachers and learners.

Susan O'Neill (Chapter VII) presents as her subject the challenge of developing leadership capacities among students born after 1995: students identified as "Generation Z". Mindful of that generation's preferred learning styles, which include practice-based learning, O'Neill emphasises the benefits of educator investment in creative opportunities for leadership development. In line with Berger (Chapter IX), she also signals the efficacy of using an ally approach to help students realise their potential as change agents.

Two music students provide commentary on the chapters in this volume. The commentator for the leadership development in musicians' practice group of chapters is Canadian graduate student, composer and pedagogue Kelly Bylica (Chapter XIII) who summarises the leadership types expressed by the five authors presented above. In line with Yau's focus on identity, Bylica homes in on the development of self-concept and critical thinking. She observes that transformational leadership is an essential part of higher education, given that its goal "is to prepare the student to become the teacher: to lead in performance, studio and classroom". Leadership, she attests, is at the centre of every musician's practice, regardless of career phase or activity. The inherent nature of leadership within the practice of musicians is illustrated by several of the authors (see for example Pike, Chapter X; Reid, Chapter III; and Weller, Chapter XII). It is unsurprising, then, that one of the most immediate opportunities for curricular reform relates to positioning student musicians' leadership development as a reflexive and developmental component of their studies. Leadership should be learned, and the responsibility lies equally with student and teacher. This is a theme to which we return in the concluding chapter.

By looking at the chapters about leadership development in musicians' practice, then, we introduce many of the complexities that surround the topic of leadership in and through higher music education. We acknowledge the complexity of higher music education, but we do not absolve its leaders of the responsibility to lead effective change.

Institutional Leadership

Susan O'Neill's chapter provides a logical bridge from the development of institutional leadership to that of leadership in musicians' practice. O'Neill (Chapter VII) presents multiple and complex insights into the nature of leadership in higher education. The intersection of experiences and concepts helps to set the agenda for change and renewal. Anna Reid, Dawn Bennett and Jennifer Rowley (Chapter VIII) extend the agenda to encompass the needs of students when they transition from student to professional. The authors establish the rationale for leadership to be a core graduate attribute and an essential element in the identity formation of emerging music professionals. Reid, Bennett and Rowley explore students' experiences of the liminal spaces between formal study and internship work experiences. Their exploration reveals the positive outcomes of industry exposure and points to the need for multiple venues where exploration, transformation and continuous identity renewal can occur, not in isolation but as a core component of musicians' development.

As Reid, Bennett and Rowley propose in Chapter VIII, the movement of expert student to novice professional is a complex transition. Not only do students need to navigate the practicalities of creating a career in music, they can "experience a significant period of personal and professional identity uncertainty as they attempt to move into the world of work" (Bennett & Bridgstock, 2015, p. 264). Overcoming these challenges demands that educators and institutional leaders support leadership development opportunities for students and the delivery of leadership opportunities by staff.

Glen Carruthers (Chapter II) shares an interesting Canadian case study of institutional leadership practice by analysing data from four cyclical programme evaluations in which he was one of the reviewers. Carruthers begins by highlighting the exponential growth in the impact and consequence of accountability measures. He emphasises that priority setting and external response have become an integral and pervasive aspect of higher education in North America, as is the case in many other settings; these realities consume a substantive part of the time and efforts of those in formal leadership positions. Carruthers ends by providing data in the form of findings. These serve as guidelines for thought and action within higher education.

If leadership is to be impactful it must also address structures and the manner in which these structures can facilitate or prevent change. The review process is a central and "structural" element through which academic leadership is recognised and through which institutions of higher learning either maintain the status quo or are pushed to engage in adaptive or even transformative practice. The chapter by Carruthers provides a clear and practical way to consider such issues. It adds a music dimension to broader disciplinary arguments that leadership development within the student population is crucial, not just as an "employability" attribute but because leadership "can enrich the undergraduate experience, and because it can empower students and give them a greater sense of control over their lives" (Astin & Astin, 2001, p. 28).

Anna Reid borrows from the distributed leadership literature to discuss the ways in which musicians and their milieu, particularly the orchestra, have much to contribute to the understanding of collaborative forms of leadership. Reid (Chapter III) provides examples from her own work environment, highlighting the challenges for leadership model enactment for conservatoires that operate within larger universities. She presents examples and metaphors as to how distributed leadership is a common and befitting model for musicians and she describes how the need for autonomy, collaboration and careful and precise skill development, among other attributes, position musicians as critical contributors who are naturally adept to this model of leadership.

Pamela Burnard (Chapter V) addresses the important issue of gender as a significant and underrepresented element in higher education leadership discussions, particularly in music. She uses Pierre Bourdieu's concepts of habitus, capital and field to problematise and theorise how academic institutions can and must enable more equitable opportunity structures for women. Burnard argues that "career preparation and support for girls in practices such as sound producing, sampling, resampling, mixing, mashing, coding, DJing, sonic art and song-writing are as important as composing, arranging, improvising and performing".

Burnard asks the reader to consider the lack of institutional models of leadership other than those which preserve the typical conservatoire tradition of music education. Such concepts are supported by extant leadership literature and present a thought-provoking if controversial argument for contemporary leaders to consider the role of higher music education in equipping students for equitable careers in music. As argued by Bennett, Macarthur, Hope, Goh and Hennekam (in press):

> Only if they develop their critical understanding will students will be equipped to challenge inequality as deliberate professionals. Acknowledging that change will take time, the most important recommendation is for all composition students and music educators to be made aware of gendered behaviours and under-representation, and to be empowered to create change from within their own practice.

We accept that inequity in music goes beyond gender to include cultural background, socio-economic circumstances and age. We contend, however, that students' awareness of inequity lies at the core of their ability to create change.

Patrick Schmidt approximates leadership and policy thinking, arguing in Chapter IV that a policy frame disposition is critical to the development of more robust, pervasive and effective leadership development in higher education. He uses the metaphor of policy as art and craft, generated by Aaron Wildavsky (1988), to highlight that policy can be seen as a "form of leading change". Schmidt's conceptual thinking is in line with Carruthers' practical analysis (Chapter II) in that both are concerned with ways in which higher education leadership needs to contend with constantly changing environments that demand *recurrent adaptability*. This is seen in the three elements that Carruthers asserts must be identified in those who are considered leaders: namely, the ability to facilitate interaction, to create spaces for shifts in conversations, and to optimise environs where risk taking is welcomed.

Graduate student Euridiana Silva Souza (Chapter VI) offers a summation of institutional leadership through the lens of a PhD student in a music education programme in Minas Gerais, Brazil. She uses Raymond Williams's (1989) metaphor of the wall to remind us that

> democratisation is not limited to expanding access to the curriculum, or, ultimately, access to higher education itself. Democratizing is related to values of politics as art and to look straight to the other. It is related to the vivid meaning of the neighbouring term typical of communities.
> (Souza, Chapter VI, this volume)

Souza reminds us that leadership that is committed to democratic engagement must strive not only to achieve fairer outcomes but to adopt a more apt and equitable process. This is critical, not only if we strive to be innovative and creative, addressing the challenges framed by the liquidity of our current world (see Bauman, 2011), but also if higher education scholars are committed to creating leadership that is less vertical, hierarchical, bureaucratic and based on stale understandings of authority.

Conclusion

This volume is the first of two volumes which bring together higher music education scholars, teachers, students and practitioners to create an authoritative overview of leadership in and through higher music education by challenging the central practices and theories that underpin musicians' preparation and practice. Within the contemporary frameworks of higher education globally, in this volume we are exposed as consumers to the various policies and practices that dictate educational nuance. It is only by continued research and collegial collaboration that we advance education for the greater good and produce musicians who are effectively ready to create and sustain their lives in music.

The second of the two leadership volumes focuses on pedagogical and curricular leadership in higher music education. This is an extension of how the capacities created by proactive institutional reform might be developed and exercised by educators and students alike.

Today, as in historical times, a musician's life offers many more options than teaching and performing. Encouraging students to recognise, develop and transfer their capabilities to the real world of practice necessitates opportunities to broaden, indeed, to question and define, their definitions of success and their awareness of self, music, community and society as a whole.

Throughout history, musicians have been revered by society as they entertain, inform, connect, delight and disrupt a diverse range of stakeholders. What we need to protect is the integrity surrounding the development of future leaders inside the discipline of music so as to ensure professional longevity. Protecting the integrity of higher music education through a united voice will ensure that music graduates are ready to create and maximise their opportunities for work at the completion of their degrees. It will also enable the reform of current leadership models. Here, change management and regulatory practice offers enormous potential to scaffold the changes required to produce a new era of social citizens who are not only globally aware but self-aware, and who are prepared to negotiate the changes and opportunities that characterise a life in music.

We encourage readers to think beyond the modularised curriculum, beyond the dominant perceptions of success in music and beyond the traditional models of leadership. Music graduates tell us that they want to work in partnership with institutional leaders, academic mentors and one another in order to realise a valued community of practice. We suspect that were this to occur, a groundswell of interest would also engage many student musicians and music educators. How, then, do we encourage this community to flourish? There is much to be discussed, shared and reworked together if we are to arrive at a place of agreement. We are hopeful that the leadership volumes will highlight some of the common ground on which we might begin.

References

Astin, A. W., & Astin, H. S. (2000). *Leadership reconsidered: Engaging higher education in social change*. Battle Creek, MI: Kellogg Foundation.

Bauman, Z. (2011). *Culture in a liquid modern world*. Malden, MA: Polity Press.

Bennett, D. (2008). *Understanding the classical music profession: The past, the present and strategies for the future*. Aldershot, UK: Ashgate.

Bennett, D., & Bridgstock, R. (2015). The urgent need for career preview: Student expectations and graduate realities in music and dance. *International Journal of Music Education, 33*(3), 263–277. doi.org/10.1177/0255761414558653.

Bennett, D., Macarthur, S., Hope C., Goh, T., & Hennekam, S. (In press). Creating a career as a woman composer: Implications for higher education. *British Journal of Music Education*. Accepted February 2018.

Burland, K., & Pitts, S. (2007). Becoming a music student: Investigating the skills and attitudes of students beginning a music degree. *Arts and Humanities in Higher Education*, 6(3), 289–308. doi: 0.1177/1474022207080847.

Burwell, K. (2012). *Studio-based instrumental learning*. Farnham: Ashgate.

Clarke, E., & Doffman, M. (Eds). (2017). *Collaboration and improvisation in contemporary music*. Oxford: Oxford University Press.

Durrant, C. (2005). Shaping identity through choral activity: Singers' and conductors' perceptions. *Research Studies in Education*, 24, 88–98. doi: 0.1177/1321103X050240010701.

Gaunt, H. (2008). One-to-one tuition in a conservatoire: The perceptions of instrumental and vocal teachers. *Psychology of Music*, 36(2), 215–245.

Hope, J. (2016). Get your campus ready for Generation Z. *The Successful Registrar*, 16, 1–7. doi: 10.1002/tsr.30216.

MacNamara, A., Holmes, P., & Collins, D. (2008). Negotiating transitions in musical development: The role of psychological characteristics of developing excellence. *Psychology of Music*, 36(3), 335–352.

Perkins, R. (2013). Learning cultures and the conservatoire: An ethnographically-informed case study. *Music Education Research*, 15(2), 196–213. doi: 10.1080/14613808.2012.759551.

Reid, A., Abrandt Dahlgren, M., Petocz, P., & Dahlgren, L. O. (2011). *From expert student to novice professional*. Dordrecht, Netherlands: Springer.

Sarath, E. W., Myers, D. E., & Campbell, P. S. (2016). Transforming music study from its foundations: A manifesto for progressive change in the undergraduate preparation of music majors. In E. W. Sarath, D. E. Myers, & P. S. Campbell (Eds.), *Redefining music studies in an age of change* (pp. 59–99). New York: Routledge.

Wildavsky, A. (1988). *Speaking truth to power: The art and craft of policy analysis*.

Williams, R. (1989). Communication and community. In R. Williams (Ed.), *Resources of hope: Culture, democracy, socialism* (pp. 19–31). London and New York: Verso.

II
Leaders and Leadership in Higher Music Education: Meeting the Challenges

GLEN CARRUTHERS

Institutional success is predicated on visionary leadership that provides the framework and infrastructure to address the evolving challenges of student recruitment, curricular reform, and program relevance. Priority setting and accountability provide the backdrop against which decisions regarding recruitment, reform and relevance are made. To these ends and in this context, leaders set goals and objectives and are measured against them. What is theoretically simple, however, is pragmatically complex. Institutions of higher learning have multiple stakeholders whose vested interests may not readily align. Priority setting presents enormous challenges such as determining whose priorities matter most, as does determining the metrics by which "success" is defined and measured. By collating and analysing data from recent case studies – cyclical reviews of undergraduate and graduate music programs in Canada – this chapter interrogates the practice of institutional priority setting. The chapter weighs the outcomes of cyclical review processes and assesses the roles leaders play in realising review recommendations. If, as review outcomes suggest, curricular reform is of paramount importance in fostering inclusion and diversity and in adapting music schools to societal needs, this chapter asks what kinds of reform must institutional leaders undertake and facilitate to remain accountable to their most important stakeholders – the students themselves?

The Nature of Leadership

I have spent more than 20 years in leadership roles at Canadian post-secondary institutions and one of the most dramatic changes, and one that has spiked in the past five years, concerns accountability. Public institutions, especially in health care, education and the arts, but in other sectors as well, are held to increasingly high standards of accountability. Institutions are called upon to demonstrate, via metrics determined internally by consensus or imposed by governing bodies (at the two extremes), how they are accountable, in terms of everything from programming to budget, to their stakeholders. University programmes, for example, are accountable to governments, donors, students, parents, the disciplines, the professions and the industries, whose interests may complement or contradict one another. Furthermore, these various interests may or may not accord with an institution's own core values or principles.

Leadership, by its very nature, implies independent thinking, in combination with experience, knowledge, good judgement and intuition. Some of these qualities are more readily measured than others. Some factors that contribute to an institution's success are easily quantifiable and others are not: for example, enrolments can be quantified more reliably than morale. Qualitative and quantitative markers are provided to assess success and leaders are held to account. Periodic reviews determine which goals and objectives have been met, not met, abandoned and those that remain in process. Prescribed time periods are provided so that progress can be determined to be on schedule, ahead of schedule or behind schedule.

In the past few years, the present author has been directly involved in more than a dozen departmental or institutional prioritisation processes. These have included:

- A review of my own performance at the end of a renewable five-year term as dean of the Faculty of Music.
- Reviews of three of four degree programmes under my purview – BMus (Bachelor of Music), BMT (Bachelor of Music Therapy) and MMT (Master of Music Therapy).
- Development of an institution-wide integrated planning and resource management plan (IPRM).
- Development of an institution-wide Strategic Academic Plan (SAP).
- Development of a unit-specific (Faculty of Music) Strategic Plan (FOMSP).
- Development of a Strategic Mandate Agreement (SMA). These agreements are negotiated between universities and the provincial government (Ministry of Advanced Education and Skills Development) and set the university's course for the next three years regarding new programming, new buildings and other initiatives that require provincial approval and/or support.

At the same time as these processes were underway, I agreed to review music programmes at several sister institutions and, after much preliminary work, I authored or co-authored substantial review reports.

In connection with these prioritisation processes and reviews, the call for data was constant, the analysis of which would determine strategic priorities and review outcomes. A staggering number of hours was required to amass data and for long stretches of time the production and analysis of data precluded doing much else.

There is not space here to delve into each of these prioritisation and review processes. Of these processes, the cyclic review is most pervasive (some would say invasive) and so will be the focus of the remainder of this chapter.

After collecting, collating and processing data has occurred, generally by support staff, leaders must respond to – or oversee the response to – input from sources as disparate as students and faculty, and donors and governments. As described later in this chapter, the onerous task of data collection and analysis is only a beginning. Instinct, knowledge, wisdom and pragmatism must guide decision-making, and the relationship between inputs and outputs is frequently non-linear and non-causal. This is where the subtle art of enlightened leadership comes into play. While inputs may point in one direction, leaders may pursue another direction. Leaders would, in fact, be unnecessary if outputs were determined by doing nothing more than processing inputs. A computer could do this. Although effective leaders must be committed to consultative processes, once all positions have been heard and potential outcomes have been debated thoroughly, leaders must sieve and filter inputs before reaching a final decision. Policies, procedures, data and opinions are the starting point, not the end point of informed, intelligent and progressive decision-making.

Cyclic Reviews

The cyclic review is a popular instrument of assessment and priority-setting in North American universities. Generally, the names and credentials of possible arm's-length reviewers are supplied by the unit under review to the Provost, who selects one or more people from the list to be approached to serve as external reviewers. One or more internal reviewers join the external reviewers and this team will conduct an in-depth review to assure the quality of the programme and its alignment with the institution's vision and mission. A self-study is provided by the unit, with various appendices, including faculty curriculum vitae, course syllabi and new programme proposals.

The review report, usually due a few weeks after a site visit, will address such areas as programme objectives, admission requirements, curriculum, teaching quality and assessment methods, human and physical resources, equity and diversity, academic integrity and quality indicators such as research productivity and other achievements of faculty members, student and alumni satisfaction, and employment rates after graduation. The review report will conclude with a set of recommendations, which will sometimes address specific questions posed in the self-study.

Case Study Background

This following case study compiles outcomes from four cyclic reviews (involving three institutions) in which the author participated during the 2016–2017 academic year. In some instances, the author was a review team member assessing programmes at another institution. In other instances, programmes for which the author has academic and fiduciary responsibility were under review. It should be stressed that none of these reviews was occasioned by problems or misgivings, but were part of a normal institutional life cycle.

By analysing more than 100 recommendations in the four review documents, themes were identified and ranked in order of the frequency with which topics arose. Because only parts of the reports are public documents, all review outcomes and findings are presented anonymously. The three institutions have been renamed North, South and East Universities. Of the four separate reviews analysed here, one was undertaken at North University, two at South University, and one at East University (see Table 2.1). At North University one programme was reviewed and at South and East Universities, several programmes were reviewed.

The 124 recommendations in these reviews were not weighted in any way. A recommendation to build a new building was accorded as much importance as a recommendation to improve signage. This is clearly one limitation of the study; others are noted later in this chapter.

The recommendations were grouped into eight categories and each recommendation was counted only once. If a recommendation spanned several categories, it was assigned to the category with which its objective most closely aligned. For example, if outreach to another university was recommended, but the point of that outreach was to establish online programming that could be shared between institutions, the recommendation falls under curriculum (the objective), not outreach (the method). The eight categories are shown below.

Table 2.1 Institutions (pseudonyms) included in the analysis

University Name	Programme(s) under review
North University	Bachelor of Arts (Music)
South University	Bachelor of Music (with several specialisations)
South University	Bachelor of Music Therapy; Master of Music Therapy
East University	Bachelor of Music (with several specialisations); Master of Music (Performance); Master of Arts (Ethnomusicology)

1. **Curriculum.** This category includes revisions to extant curricula and development of new curricula. It includes all courses and programmes offered on a for-credit basis.
2. **Outreach.** This category includes marketing and recruitment, community projects, work placements, concert series and ensemble tours. It also includes all courses and programmes offered on a non-credit basis.
3. **Leadership and governance.** This category includes academic and administrative units and sub-units, reporting structures, chains of responsibility, and internal policies and procedures.
4. **Facilities and equipment.** This category includes physical structures and the musical instruments and other equipment and technology housed within them.
5. **Staff complement.** This category includes support positions such as administrative managers, financial analysts, recruitment officers, development officers, career counsellors, facility managers and office assistants.
6. **Faculty complement.** This category includes full- and part-time instructors, adjunct professors, visiting professors, artists-in-residence and graduate students engaged in teaching.
7. **Budget.** This category includes operating funds, capital reserves, special initiative funds and donations (including one-time gifts, endowments and bequests). The allocation of these funds is also included here.
8. **Miscellany.** This category includes a wide range of other topics from library holdings to building security that were cited three times or less across all four reviews.

A category conspicuous by its absence is research. Since none of the recommendations in the four reviews concerned research, the category could be omitted entirely. In many universities, research productivity would be captured in reviews, not of academic programmes (for example, Bachelor of Music), but of academic units (for example, Faculty of Music).

Case Study Data

In Table 2.2, the number of review recommendations under a single heading is broken out by institution (recall that South University includes two separate reviews) and expressed as a percentage of the total number of recommendations in that review. East University had significant challenges related to facilities, equipment and leadership, and data for that institution skewed the aggregate

Table 2.2 Recommendations from 2015 external reviews of universities

Region	Curriculum	Outreach	Leadership	Facilities	Staff	Faculty	Budget	Miscellaneous
North (n=65)	49	18.5	7.5	5	0	11	0	9
South: A (n=19)	47.5	16	10.5	5	0	16	0	5
South: B (n=18)	61	17	0	0	11	0	0	11
Totals								
Without East: (n=102)	51	17.5	7	4	2	9.5	0	9
With East: (n=124)	47	14.5	8	8	2.5	8	1	11

results somewhat. Accordingly, aggregate percentages were calculated twice, once excluding and once including East University.

Case Study Discussion

It is evident that, on average, more recommendations concern curriculum than outreach (including marketing and recruitment), leadership (including governance), facilities (including equipment), staff/faculty complement, and budget combined. The percentage of recommendations concerning curriculum ranges from an anomalously low 27 per cent at East University to 61 per cent in the second review at South University. The percentage at North University and in the first review at South University hovers just below 50 per cent. In total, excluding data from East University, 51 per cent of all recommendations concern curriculum. When East University is included, the total drops a little to 47 per cent. Embedded within recommendations on curriculum are industry partnerships, online and blended learning, the curricular core and specialised courses.

The topic with the fewest number of recommendations was budget. Budget was not mentioned in the reviews of North and South Universities and was mentioned only once in the review of East University. More recommendations regarding the budget necessary to support curriculum development might reasonably have been expected; for example, budget should be reallocated from an extant course in medieval music history to a new course in digital media. Although the reviews were filled with recommendations that could not be cost-neutral, reviewers were content to leave the means by which new courses and programmes would be funded to the institutions themselves. The vast majority of recommendations concerned the curriculum itself.

Ironically, a systemic preoccupation with prioritisation and review processes draws considerable time and energy away from curriculum development. This is true for deans and other administrators who are responsible for holding units accountable to internal and external stakeholders. Administrators are also increasingly called upon to fundraise and the cultivation of donor prospects and stewardship of past donors is important but time-consuming. Because of the weight of these and other responsibilities, curricular reform is usually off-loaded to associate deans or department chairs, who oversee curriculum development committees.

A quotation from Robert Fowler, who headed the Commission on Broadcasting in Canada over 50 years ago, is relevant here. Fowler famously stated that: "The only thing that really matters in broadcasting is program content; all the rest is housekeeping" (Fowler, 1965, p. 3). Pierre Juneau, who served as chair of the Canadian Radio-television and Telecommunications Commission (1968–1975) and president of the Canadian Broadcasting Corporation (1982–1989) invoked Fowler's words when he reflected on his own role at the CBC:

> Philosophically, Fowler was right, at least as far as the CBC or public broadcasting is concerned. Everything we do … is done in order to provide good radio and television programmes. That is the only goal that matters ultimately. …
>
> Unfortunately, we in the CBC sometimes have the impression that the reality is different…, [that] the only thing that really matters in this world is housekeeping and all the rest is programming!
>
> (Juneau, 1996, p. 197)

Fowler's quotation and Juneau's response could easily be reworked to apply to the teaching (as distinct from research) mission of universities:

> The only thing that really matters is curriculum; all the rest is housekeeping.
>
> Everything we do … is done in order to provide good curriculum. That is the only goal that matters ultimately …
>
> Unfortunately, we in universities sometimes have the impression that the reality is different …, [that] the only thing that really matters in this world is housekeeping and all the rest is curriculum!

This situation, whereby curriculum development is not central to the role of senior administration, is reinforced by professional development opportunities. The Centre for Higher Education Research and Development (CHERD) at the University of Manitoba, for example, offers three courses annually for academic administrators, shown below.

1. **Senior University Administrators Course.** This course is intended for "experienced administrators responsible for making institutional policy, including presidents, rectors, principals, vice-presidents, provosts, associate vice-presidents, treasurers, comptrollers, registrars, chief librarians, deans and senior directors of services". Topics covered include "legal issues and institutional policies, power and influence in the organization, restructuring issues, resource management, negotiation and conflict management, and the changing leadership role".
2. **University Management Course.** This course is intended for "administrators of academic and administrative units with direct responsibility for recommending and implementing policy, including department heads, chairs, associate deans, managers, directors of services and executive assistants". Topics covered include "human rights, administrative and contract law, financial management and planning, human resource management and conflict resolution".
3. **Heads and Chairs – Challenges in Academic Leadership.** This course is intended to help "Chairs/Heads reflect together on the challenges, opportunities and responsibilities of this critical role in universities and colleges". Topics include "the changing academic culture, leadership in a collegial environment, faculty development, the legal structure of the university … and fostering a teaching culture".

This emphasis on everything but curriculum for academic administrators is reflected in conferences and meetings across North America. The Canadian Association of Fine Arts Deans (CAFAD), for example, is an autonomous organisation that holds a conference annually. In 2015, for the first time in several years, the CAFAD conference programme included a session devoted to curriculum. The session, entitled "Curriculum Reviews/Redesign and Opportunities of Alternative Streams of Revenue Generation for Creative Arts Programs", took the form of a panel discussion that, as noted by its title, linked curriculum development to revenue generation. The implication that curriculum is most relevant to senior administrators when it generates income reflects pragmatic exigency. Curriculum and the revenue it generates are conjoined in the resource management model of many universities. This model rewards entrepreneurship by linking revenue to class enrolments, such that curriculum, budgets and enrolment become inextricably bound up with one another (Dickeson, 2010).

Having determined that curriculum is, nonetheless, the greatest focus of cyclical reviews and that, by extension, curriculum constitutes a seminal challenge to music schools today, is it possible to isolate commonalities among the review recommendations? What directions do recent academic reviews recommend curricular reform take?

Review Findings

Finding 1 – Flexibility

Curricular reform must take into consideration the dynamic interaction of core courses, specialist courses and electives. The curricular core cannot be so prescribed as to limit specialist choices in years one and two, and core and specialist offerings together cannot be so prescribed as to preclude choice, in the form of music and free electives, in upper year levels. Although this seems self-evident, it is a finding of the reviews that programmes are too packed with required courses to allow for the flexibility students want and need to acquire skills for personal fulfilment and professional breadth.

One institution received commendation for reforming its curriculum to include more choice, noting that students could now pursue interdisciplinary, cross-disciplinary and cognate interests and achieve a minor in another discipline. Permitting and, ideally, facilitating double degrees – music and kinesiology, for example – was cast in a particularly positive light. Flexibility could also be used as a marketing and recruitment tool, in light of the inflexibility of sister institutions. The reviews were explicit that degree programmes with the greatest flexibility were apt to appeal most to incoming students.

At one institution, the message was received loud and clear from the students that flexibility in course selection was of paramount importance. The reviewers agreed. As one reviewer remarked, "the sum total of many good ideas is often a bad idea". In this case, well-intentioned course additions over time had resulted in curricular gridlock. Reviewers were confident that curriculum renewal already underway would lead to more flexibility, especially in terms of free electives, and that this would serve current and future student needs. At another institution, the review acknowledged that a curricular rebuild from the bottom up, which had been completed just prior to the site visit, had been an appropriate and timely initiative. Whether achieved by cumulative reforms or a disruptive rebuild and relaunch, curriculum renewal that afforded greater choice and student autonomy was applauded and encouraged.

It was noted in two of four reviews that certain courses were required of students because they always had been part of the core curriculum. One review recommended that longstanding upper-year requirements in music history and theory be eliminated. This would not only allow students more choice, but the department would not be required to mount courses solely because they needed to be offered to fulfil degree requirements. Faculty could teach to their strengths and budget would not be expended offering redundant, unnecessary or low-enrolment courses. In this way, students, faculty and administration would all reap the rewards of increased flexibility.

Finding 2 – Relevance to a Wider Constituency

All four reviews recommended new courses be designed and scheduled (in evenings, for example) to cater to non-music students. Increased enrolment in service courses can bolster comparatively small numbers of declared music majors. High-enrolment courses can provide substantial income to music programmes in responsibility-centred budgets. Increasing the relevance of course offerings to the wider student body need not involve dumbing down extant offerings. If music is important to the population at large, and we know that it is, then it follows that music programmes have responsibility to offer as much musical opportunity, both credit and non-credit, as possible to students and community members who are not music majors. From economic (these courses generate revenue), political (these courses assert the discipline's relevance), sociological (these courses integrate music and non-music students) and other perspectives, music schools must look beyond their own cohort to generate enrolments. For publicly funded institutions this is an ethical issue too; it is not appropriate to serve elite populations only. It was proposed, as one example, that music therapy expand its on-site clinic, offer programming to campus counselling services, and collaborate with other programmes within music, like community music, and with programmes outside music, such as social work or psychology. This recommendation was received with enthusiasm by students and administrators who recognised that revenues from such initiatives could support new course offerings and other programme enhancements.

Finding 3 – Learning Outcomes

Many curricula were designed when the delineation of learning outcomes was not part of the course approval process. General aims were considered – the desire to familiarise students with a wide range of repertoire specific to their instrument, for example – as was the manner in which individual courses would support general learning outcomes. However, wider aims – to help students to think critically about received information, for example – were addressed summarily, if at all. Often, courses were created because they reflected the teaching and/or research interests of faculty members, and these courses would align with the interests of students by chance rather than by design. Which courses should be maintained, eliminated, introduced or transformed, and which deserve enhanced funding or human resources, cannot be determined unless the connection between course outcomes and degree-level expectations is clear.

The valuation of current courses and programme offerings cannot be achieved without in-depth knowledge of national and international trends in teaching methodologies and curriculum. Reviews were adamant that there needs to be oversight, by a knowledgeable committee, of new course creation. One review recommended that current degree-level expectations be determined collectively and that the unit's success in meeting these expectations be evaluated course by course before curricular reforms were undertaken. While new programming is a viable means of attracting students, a clear alignment of learning outcomes with degree-level expectations ensures that courses and programmes are introduced strategically.

Finding 4 – Diversity

As noted previously, the reviews cited the need to reach beyond the current student base to attract new populations for pragmatic reasons – to keep student numbers strong – and for altruistic reasons – to reflect the make-up and interest of the community. All the reports contained ideas for expanding the breadth and scope of course offerings to appeal to a broader demographic. Such expanded programming can require new or redistributed financial resources and this was acknowledged, but programmes that addressed multiple genres and styles and, in one instance, a new purpose – Community Music – were encouraged in all the reviews. Many suggestions were cost-neutral or revenue-positive and limited financial resources does not mean limiting course offerings to particular student populations. On the contrary, limited resources can be countered with burgeoning enrolments.

Students, faculty and reviewers were in agreement that better representation of the diverse interests of music and non-music students would ensure a sustainable future. A boost in enrolment would often offset new programme costs. Providing students with learning experiences across several genres often requires hiring new faculty to teach in these areas. One university was ahead of the curve in this regard, having made several recent hires in areas outside current curricular offerings. New faculty had developed new courses, so the new hires could teach in their areas of interest and students could be afforded more course choices. The result was that extracurricular musical interests of students and faculty were now incorporated into the curriculum.

At another institution, where several positions were likely to become available because of retirements, the unit was encouraged to make hires in areas different from the ones in which vacancies would occur. Course offerings, after a long period of stasis, could be updated. There was consensus that an appropriate and inevitable step towards providing students with learning experiences that were not restricted to a single genre or style would require not only new course creation but extensive revisions to existing courses. The expertise of current faculty must take a backseat to the needs of current and future students; hence, the need for new hires to teach new or substantially modified courses.

As challenges posed by diversity are addressed, some courses will need to be eliminated, truncated or consolidated to make room for new courses within the curriculum. At my home institution, a legacy course in medieval and renaissance music history was replaced by a new course called "Music in its Contexts", which examines the relationship between music and, for example, philosophy, commerce, film, gender, dance, power, religion and ritual. It would not have been possible to incorporate this course into the core curriculum without consolidating two extant courses into one.

Finding 5 – Streamlining and Consolidation

Concern over the proliferation of new courses and programmes, resulting in curricular congestion and in too many courses with too few faculty to teach them, was a common thread in all the reviews. A balance between old and new programming, core and elective courses, major and service teaching can only be achieved if each and every course is measured against degree-level expectations. Is this course essential? Can its content be incorporated elsewhere? Pragmatic considerations are also at play. Can this course be cycled every two or three years? Are there sufficient resources to support this course?

The proliferation of degree programmes is also a concern. I once reviewed a unit (not included in these case studies) that had as many programmes as it had full-time faculty members. The programmes ranged from poor to good, but none was outstanding. That university subsequently eliminated a number of programmes, as recommended by the review, and the remaining programmes are now academically strong and flourishing.

Another university, one that was part of the current research sample, offered more degree credentials than other schools six or eight times its size. The reviewers had difficulty understanding the need for so many programmes or even distinguishing what the differences between them were. Prospective students were likely to be confused, too. Less is often more and any move that streamlines and simplifies programmes and course offerings was, by agreement among the reviewers, a step in the right direction. Three reviews identified programmes that had very few students enrolled in them. A first step towards streamlining and consolidating programmes is to eliminate programmes not attracting a minimum number of new students each year or that attract students only by default and not by choice.

It was noted that curricular reforms at two institutions should continue, but a cautionary note was also sounded. Expansionary programming should not be detrimental to existing programming. Revisions to the current curriculum should be completed before new curriculum is introduced. Further, new programmes should only be introduced after extensive market research. Much useless effort can be expended developing new programming to generate increased enrolments that do not materialise.

Finding 6 – Experiential Learning

There was consensus that experiential learning was appropriate in all programmes, but that grafting placements and outreach opportunities onto existing programmes could be problematic. Fundamental change is sometimes necessary to align the theoretical and practical components of the curriculum. It was also recognised that partnerships are a key element of experiential learning (see Finding 7, and also Souza's observation (Chapter VI, this volume) that such partnerships, often teacher-driven, need institutional leadership to ensure quality and sustainability). Students could be given instruction in pedagogy, for example, not only by faculty members, but by experts in the internal offices of teaching and learning as well as by external experts active in the field. Opportunities for experiential learning in music are limitless and occur informally all the time. Accordingly, consideration could be given to incorporating a practicum into the fourth year, if not all years, of all programmes.

Experiential learning also fosters important community connections. At my home institution, the opening of a conservatory for non-university students (discussed later in this chapter) and development of undergraduate and graduate programmes in community music were successful attempts to broaden the reach of the Faculty of Music.

Internships were cited in three reviews as means of fostering career preparedness, and such internships could occur in conjunction with courses in music entrepreneurship. Blended formats, especially online courses with on-site placements, were encouraged in several instances. Online offerings were also suggested as a practical way of rationalising courses between institutions. There is, for example, no reason why multiple universities should be offering a Western art music history survey when one course, shared among many institutions, would serve the same purpose. Online delivery is also advantageous for comparatively small and/or geographically isolated institutions, whose students can benefit from a wider range of courses and from interaction with a national and international cohort of students.

Finding 7 – Partnerships

Experiential learning most often involves partnerships, which were cited as increasingly important in environments where funding for higher education is static or decreasing. Multiple recommendations stressed the importance of both internal and external partnerships. Alliances with other disciplines on campus and between institutions, including colleges, other universities and industry partners, are crucial to the success of university fine and performing arts programmes.

In the Canadian system, among external partners, colleges are an obvious choice. Efforts should be made to strengthen ties with colleges to avoid redundancies in course offerings and to allow access to more courses. Formal articulation agreements are an option but, even without such agreements, generous provisions for transfer credits will benefit students and faculty budgets. There is little point in developing new courses in the business of music, contemporary commercial music or sound recording, for example, when many colleges already offer them.

Finding 8 – Targeted Programmes

Differentiation between university programmes is necessary and appropriate – necessary to attract students to smaller programmes and appropriate to avoid unnecessary duplication across the system. Each review focuses on programme differentiation and on the demography of potential students. At one university, as enrolments in arts programmes were declining, as were conversions from applicants to registrants in music (although, interestingly, audition numbers remained relatively stable), two populations were largely overlooked – Indigenous Canadian students and Franco-Ontarian students.

Given current and anticipated demographics in the catchment area, a direct appeal to these populations is advisable. While international students may drive enrolments upwards in some arts programmes, the music programme was unlikely to attract significant numbers of out-of-country registrants. However, since approximately 13 per cent of arts students at this university are Indigenous, intentionally indigenising the curriculum and offering targeted service courses makes a great deal of sense. Other than in the concurrent education programme, there was little to no Indigenous content in any of the music courses and this was flagged as a serious concern.

Although courses need to be developed with direct appeal to Indigenous students, it is more important that Indigenous content be incorporated across the curriculum. Likewise, although French-speaking students at this university constitute a minority, it is a population the university is committed to serving. It would be entirely appropriate to incorporate Franco-Ontarian content into many of the courses already offered. Similar examples of targeted programming and marketing, involving local populations and/or music, occurred in the other reviews. For example, East University was encouraged to build, at the undergraduate level, on its graduate success in folklore studies and to take advantage of its unique location to develop programming focused on the music and culture of maritime regions.

It was recommended that North University concentrate on music education and that regular meetings with the School of Education and local and regional school boards occur to ensure that the curriculum remains current. By focusing on teacher education and bolstering its commitment to service teaching, the programme could suspend or delist courses that support neither of these areas so that the remaining courses could be cycled more frequently.

New courses could also be developed that reflect current trends and interest. An asset highly valued by music teachers is the ability to improvise. There is also widespread agreement that improvisation should play a greater role in music programmes generally. Peer tutoring can play a role here, in that jazz students could provide guidance and assistance to classical students. A more symbiotic relationship between these two cohorts was recommended in any event.

South University was urged to find ways to consolidate its long-established programme in music therapy with its new programme in community music to achieve innovative synergies at the doctoral level. It was also suggested that music therapy courses be offered to the student population at large and that a minor in music therapy be available to non-music students.

Even though the universities reviewed are geographically remote from one another and there had been no attempt historically to avoid programme duplication, there were no redundancies in the curricular emphases recommended by the various review committees. Implicit differences between institutions could be made explicit in their curricula. Although at one time most undergraduate music programmes in Canada resembled one another closely, there is great opportunity to develop distinct programmes by building on inherent differences from one institution to the next.

Finding 9 – Approvals Processes

The reviews pointed repeatedly to the need for clarity in new course and programme approval processes. Who initiates, who develops and who approves new proposals? A curriculum committee must be satisfied that learning outcomes reflect degree-level expectations before new programming can move forward. Students repeatedly expressed a desire to be actively involved in curriculum design by serving on programme development committees. Any committee that lacks meaningful student representation is overlooking its key stakeholder.

At more than one university, it was observed that curricular responsibilities were so widely distributed that, at times, the left hand was unaware what the right hand was doing. This concern extends beyond a single department or faculty. At one institution, it was found that a research methods course offered by another faculty was, with few modifications, appropriate for use by the music faculty. Approvals processes that encourage (and budget models that reward) such efficiencies serve everyone's interests.

Finding 10 – Student Health and Well-Being

An area not limited to curriculum but closely allied to it is student success. It is obvious that programme requirements must be reasonable and paced realistically, but two pervasive challenges remained in play at more than one institution: 1) scheduling, in that everything seems to happen at once; and 2) barrier courses, which present too great a challenge for too many students.

On the first point, concern was expressed in all four reviews that bottlenecks occurred when term assignments, concerts, rehearsals and tests in several courses occurred within a one- or two-week period. Some professors rarely look beyond their own courses to see what student life looks like at a given point in time. Coordinated scheduling of tests, assignments and the like is a recurrent review theme, although definitive action is rarely taken. This inaction fails to address a growing concern among students.

Specific courses that make unreasonable demands on students were identified at each institution. Such courses should be revamped (if the issue is content) or assigned to other faculty members (if the issue is teaching). Course content quickly becomes stale. This often results from inattention, so that course material requirements remain static, despite changing pedagogical or real-world landscapes. The assignment of workloads, which is a key challenge at the unit level, must ensure that the most up-to-date professors, who practise current teaching and learning methodologies, are assigned to instruct core courses at all year levels.

Some courses demand too much work and the time and effort required to succeed in them is incongruent with their credit weighting. This is especially true of large ensembles. In smaller programmes, students are frequently called upon to participate in more than one ensemble, sometimes for credit and sometimes not. This places unreasonable demands on some students.

These issues reflect a general concern for student wellness and well-being. At one institution, 40 per cent of music students reported facing significant mental health challenges during their studies. Wellness initiatives were underway at each of the institutions, including the development of dedicated wellness spaces within two music buildings. At one university, students could access massage therapy, Alexander lessons, lifestyle counselling and nutrition information in a central location, administered by the music student association. Such services were offered on a drop-in or by-appointment basis. It was stressed in the reviews that student well-being is not only the concern of centralised student support services, but is the responsibility of instructional units and sub-units, course instructors, studio teachers and the students themselves.

Further Research

The sample in the foregoing case study encompasses only review processes in which the author participated. It is, therefore, limited and quite possibly biased. A far larger research sample would be necessary to determine with certainty national or international trends arising from prioritisation and review processes. Further research into internal and external reviews, undertaken with more checks and balances for bias has potential to pinpoint more accurately key challenges facing post-secondary music schools. A longitudinal study that plots review recommendations over time would help identify emergent and regressive trends. Further research could also link recommendations to outcomes, and thus help determine whether the review system is working. The cyclic review process has not changed substantively in the 30 years I have been involved in higher education. Reviewing the review process is crucial to ensuring its continuing efficacy.

Conclusion

Corporate management models are destined to flounder in academic milieu. The double jeopardy of tenure and collective bargaining creates a power dynamic absent in the corporate sector. A collegial governance model empowers the professoriate in ways not mirrored in the business world. Despite this collegial model and the manifold planning exercises that arise from it, senior academic and administrative leaders are ultimately responsible for institutional goal-setting. This is accomplished in conjunction with senates and boards of governors or their equivalents, the members of which are more often elected than appointed.

Institutional goals are then reflected in personal goals. Goals for chairs and deans are negotiated with their immediate supervisors, usually deans and vice-presidents, respectively. Deliverables are determined jointly and outcomes are assessed in face-to-face meetings on an annual basis. Another layer is added to this process periodically whereby, in the course of a cyclical review, colleagues from other institutions are engaged in goal-setting at the programme level. This triggers new personal goals, since leaders are not "held harmless" if agreed-upon goals remain unrealised. Cyclical reviews serve two important purposes: they encourage innovation and hold leaders accountable. If, as the foregoing case study indicates, curriculum is the key deliverable, then leaders must be held accountable for curricular relevance and reform above all else.

The aims of the reforms highlighted in the foregoing study can be subsumed under two broad headings, altruism and pragmatism. The altruistic aim is to provide a learning environment – for example, programmes, courses, assessment tools – relevant to students today and tomorrow. Whether relevance implies career-readiness or not is a separate issue, but it is easily argued that critical thinking and intellectual agility are essential attributes for all music graduates, whatever their career choice might ultimately be. Altruistic aims cannot be separated from institutional pragmatism. Curricular relevance encourages healthy enrolments. There are many possible ways to stabilise or increase enrolment by creating attractive curricula and no single answer applies to all institutions. On the contrary, the answer may lie in differentiation between institutions, so that all programmes are not fishing in the same applicant pool.

It is appropriate to end this chapter on a somewhat cautionary and personal note. The solution to the challenges identified in this study will be achieved, not only by setting priorities and realising them efficiently, but by responding quickly and decisively to emergent opportunities. To a great extent, leaders need to be reactive in pragmatic terms but proactive in ideological terms. Let me explain. Despite efforts to plan carefully and to review results frequently, institutions must be free to evolve organically, not prescriptively. They are dependent on the political, social and economic contexts in which they operate. True leadership is, by its very nature, opportunistic. This presents leaders with a significant challenge when it comes to markers, metrics and accountability. Metrics may assess with what was intended at one point in time but may fail to account for what actually happened. What happened might require an entirely new set of metrics to determine success or failure.

I'll give one example from each of the three institutions at which I have held leadership roles. At Lakehead University I was chair of the Department of Music for two terms beginning in 1988, at Brandon University I was dean of the School of Music for two terms beginning in 1998, and at Wilfrid Laurier University I am currently completing my second term as dean of the Faculty of Music. My first term began in 2010.

At Lakehead University, Ministry funding to retrofit our off-campus facility – a renovated public school – was reallocated to allow for construction of an entirely new on-campus building. This building did not appear on the campus masterplan, which was hastily redrawn to include this purpose-built facility. The building, opened in 1992 and named the William H. Buset Centre in 1995, continues to house Lakehead's music and visual arts programmes.

At Brandon University, since jazz is an important part of Manitoba's public school curriculum and music education is a leading programme at the School of

Music, a new position in jazz music education was introduced in 2001. Within weeks of filling this position, prospective students began to enquire about our new "jazz studies" programme. There was no such programme – we had hired one individual to oversee jazz within music education. The Strategic Planning documents for the School of Music had included no mention of jazz studies. But the persistence of enquiries led me to solicit the provincial government for funding for two expansionary positions to create a jazz studies programme with three full-time faculty members. The request was granted and a flourishing jazz studies programme continues to this day at Brandon University.

At Wilfrid Laurier University, a local businessman decided to divest himself of a private music school that had been functioning locally for 35 years. The faculty had no aspirations to operate a community-based conservatory of music, but when opportunity arose to rethink our community outreach plans, the path forward became clear. After hastily renovating an unoccupied student residence, the Faculty of Music assumed operation of the Laurier Conservatory of Music in 2015. There are well over 1,000 students enrolled in the Conservatory, ranging from toddlers to seniors, in a wide array of ongoing programmes supplemented by one-off workshops, master classes and community events.

The disparity between what leaders intend and what they achieve underscores the limitations of review processes and the goals and objectives that arise from them. Nonetheless, these processes provide important direction and, as has been shown, point resoundingly to the importance of curricular reform. Curriculum must reflect student wants and needs and the success of any music school depends on the programmes it offers. Curriculum and all that goes with it must remain in a state of constant development, informed by student, alumni and industry input. It is this challenge, to maintain curricular relevance in light of evolving technologies, fluid student expectations and changing industry requirements, that higher music education first and foremost must address.

References

Canadian Association of Fine Arts Deans. (2015). Conference program. Retrieved from www.cafad.ca/pdfs/2015Conference/CAFAD%202015%20-%20Final%20Conference%20Program.pdf.

Dickeson, R. C. (2010). *Prioritizing academic programs and services: Reallocating resources to achieve strategic balance*. San Francisco: Jossey-Bass.

Fowler, R. M. (1965). *Report of the Committee on Broadcasting*. Ottawa: Queen's Printer.

Juneau, P. (1996). The CBC: From need to necessity. In G. Carruthers & G. Lazarevich (Eds.), *A celebration of Canada's arts 1930–1970* (pp. 197–210). Toronto: Canadian Scholars' Press.

Organisation for Economic Co-operation and Development (OECD). (2003). Proceedings of *Managing Arts Schools Today*, Paris, France. Retrieved from www.oecd.org/edu/imhe/32997195.PDF.

University of Manitoba. (2015). Extended education – Centre for Higher Education Research and Development (CHERD). Professional development programs. Retrieved from http://umanitoba.ca/centres/cherd/programs/index.html.

III
Leadership in the Midst of Higher Education

ANNA REID

Leadership in music higher education is a dynamically contested space. It could be argued that all musician educators are leaders with a focus on student learning, instrumental pedagogy, cultural awareness, technical development, communication, business skills and so on. But many of these areas of leadership are also predicated on the roles that individuals have inside organisations. Borrowing established ideas, this chapter will examine the notion of "distributed leadership". This concept will enable us to appreciate how musician educators understand and work with the affordances of their sites of work and also their personal experience. It explores essential ways of thinking and acting as musicians and how this impacts on their exercise of leadership capability. The experience of being a musician can generate concepts of leadership that are appropriate to the specific situation, and perhaps appropriate in wider domains.

Being a Musician and a Leader

This chapter will explore the notion of leadership from the perspective of a professional musician who has experienced formal higher education leadership positions (outside of music) and now experiences it within a conservatoire. I suggest that leadership in musical institutions is based in part in the experience that we have had of music-making, and that it is essentially a distributed leadership model. Even the word "leader" has a possibility to be contested because our experience, in a dominant paradigm of performance activity, implies personal autonomy in collaboration to realise a joint aesthetic.

The idea of leadership in higher music education is one that is contested in both the areas of philosophy and leadership. The majority of thinking about leadership activity and capability comes from the area of business (Senge, 2005; Wenger, 1998) and research in those areas has made a profound difference to the way that higher education leaders see themselves. However, the concept of disciplinarity lends a different way of experiencing and understanding leadership. From inside a particular community, leadership can be understood in quite specific and quirky ways, and enacted in a kaleidoscope of patterns.

Leadership theorists often take the image of an orchestral conductor as the epitome of good leadership (Bennis & Nanus, 1985; Carnicer, Garrido, & Requena, 2015; Koivunen & Wennes, 2011). Under a single, usually male (Hall, 2001) baton an entire group of players of different instruments agree (against a common brief – the score) to make a nuanced performance in "harmony" with each other. The outcome of this is a moment of pleasure and catharsis for the audience, where the audience is usually unaware of leadership or cooperation dimensions (Hall, 2001).

Using a sample of 334 musicians from 30 German orchestras, Boerner, Krause and Gebert (2004) showed, empirically, that directive-charismatic leadership positively affected the quality of ensembles' performances. However, players in these forms of conducted ensembles will recognise instantly that there are a lot of problems with a simplistic description of the conductor as conjointly directive and charismatic (not the least of which is that some conductors can be seen as simply tyrants). This particular discussion is directed then to what leadership means to musicians, and how that understanding of leadership manifests when musical education is also involved. The idea of an orchestra will be used as a device to explore different issues.

Bathurst and Ladkin (2012) have explored leadership as an emergent process using the specific case of musical ensembles. They identify the role of formal leaders of ensembles and contrast that with "leaderless" ensembles. Importantly they recognised that look, gesture and movement all contribute to musicians' sensitivity in music-making where the music produces a real-time negotiation. Bandino, Li, Tokay, Craighero & Canto (2012) postulate that coordinated action is a very human activity that has its origin in evolutionary behaviour. They suggest that "action coordination" and "joint action" require sharing a single goal, such as expressing the aesthetic of music. Sharing a goal can encourage working relationships that business leaders often describe as "working in harmony" (Johnson & Geal, 2015).

The *Oxford Dictionary* suggests that harmony is "the combination of simultaneously sounded musical notes to produce a pleasing effect" and provides statements from literature to show how it is used: "the piece owes its air of tranquillity largely to the harmony". Every musician, however, will know from experience that "harmony" is largely about tonal dissonance and resolution, rhythmic disjunction and conjunction, textural variation and unity. In other words, the idea of "pleasing" is simply a culturally derived idea where listeners (the musical outcome in essence) have learned what sounds good to them. Musicians, however, are adept at making much of the variation found in the practice of music, deliberately changing the colour of their instrument for maximum impact. This ability is acquired and developed through contact with other experienced musicians, through playing experience, exposure to a range of different compositions, years of deliberate practice and the textural indications in the score. It is only after such a set of experiences that the conductor comes into the act.

The conductor's job is to conceive of the work as a coherent whole in order to be able to present it to the listeners. To do the job well, the conductor needs all the same performance experiences of the player: an in-depth understanding of the musical and social aspects of the work, an appreciation of the capabilities of the players, and a personal arsenal of meaningful gestures and articulations. All being well, the orchestra will combine their diverse talents, work with the conductor, and create musical works that are satisfying to an audience. However, if the conductor is ill-prepared, the orchestra will probably be able to continue, despite the instructions of the conductor. Many if not most in the audience will be unable to tell the difference. Fellow musicians in the audience – expert practitioners – will probably be able to discern what is going on. Working harmony, then, has a much more sophisticated nuance to those who are musicians. Musicians can work through situations that are extremely complex, when playing music *and* when working towards non-musical goals (teaching, for instance) and bring with them a long experience of recognising the importance of variation to bring about a positive result.

Consequently, the conductor as a metaphor for leadership, and an orchestra as a metaphor for an organisation, can provide different perspectives on our understanding of leadership. There are functional, managerial, activities that pervade organisations. As Koivunen and Wennes (2011, p. 62) say, "some structural agreements also make words unnecessary: seating plans and rehearsal plans are organized similarly in almost all symphony orchestras to help musicians and conductors orientate their sense perception". In every organisation there is tacit knowledge that requires little or no discussion. In an orchestra, tacit knowledge also comprises each musician's relationship with their particular instrument and historical genres. However, musicians involved in orchestral playing have a wide variety of aesthetic and musical views that must, in some way, cohere to create a performance.

Musical leadership then involves people who have diverse experience and desires, who may be in the centre or periphery of the activity, may be early or late in their careers, and who may have many ideas that compete with each other. This may be described as a form of distributed leadership. Being in a position that enables distributed leadership to occur successfully in any organisation requires an understanding of the essential qualities of individuals; how they – and the organisation – react to (and learn from) difference; how theories from other areas inform our immediate practice; and how the "real politick" of the specific situation enables or restricts activities. Musical leadership cannot be described simply, rather there is variation in the matters that musicians attend to (based on their previous experiences) and specific goals that afford a situation where they must work together. This essential activity for musicians can be linked to the manner in which musicians teach in higher education.

Understanding Variation for Leadership

In the 1970s, a group of Swedish researchers in education explored the very interesting notion of variation for learning (Marton & Saljo, 1976). In their first exploration they described two different approaches to learning, namely a deep approach and a surface approach. Basically, if a person found something meaningful they were more likely to understand and remember it. If they found something trivial, they would focus on atomistic aspects of the task and be unlikely to remember after some time. For this discussion, the important fact is that people can understand and experience the same thing differently. In the 21st century this research has extended beyond the field of education, with researchers now focusing on the idea of variation as a means of understanding the world around them (Marton & Pang, 2009). Returning to our orchestra, each member has the ability to focus on the things they find meaningful and also pay little attention to the things they find trivial. Being professional musicians, they are able to distinguish these moments as they occur. The interesting thing about musicians is that, despite their particular approach to a task, the group as a whole can still manage to produce an outcome that communicates.

This brings up some further connections to leadership. Even when there is a common goal (such as the preparation and performance of a symphony), there is huge variation in the way that people engage with that goal. Understanding the nature of such variation seems critical when considering leadership. Whereas members of an orchestra have clearly defined parts, how they understand the importance of that part for the whole is critical. Each member's appreciation of the difference is critical. However, when approaching their own organisational structures and approaches to leadership, many higher education organisations do not mirror the situation of an orchestra. How are the roles in a conservatoire defined? What are the goals of the conservatoire? Do the members agree and work towards those goals? Is there a score (strategic plan) to follow? Do the educational members appreciate each fellow teacher's or researcher's contribution to the overall outcome? What is the role of a director?

Using variation theory (Marton & Pang, 2009) we can come to appreciate that it is the inherent ways that people understand, experience and approach things that enables complex forms of distributed leadership to flourish. The notion that a conductor controls all aspects of a performance is erroneous. She may be singly responsible for providing shape to a vision, but the shape will only work if there is confidence in the members to do their bit creatively and responsibly. As someone in a position of leadership at a conservatoire, I am conscious of variation theory as it provides a means of my appreciating the different ways people engage with their work, the different contributions they each make to the pedagogical, the musical, and the research environment, as well as to the institution as a whole. Being conscious of this variation also demands that I appreciate the affordances of the difference. I need to create a space for people to explore different solutions to problems, different ways of working, different relationships between people, and have different developmental activities. In other words, I must consider the shape but allow for variation in its execution.

This approach fosters distributed leadership (Chambers, Burchell, & Gully, 2009) through the organisation to flourish. Each music higher education practitioner has a personal narrative that enables the person to link past and current events together. Their musician identity contributes to the solutions that they find for complex situations. Music teachers will interpret situations in the light of experiences they have had. Appreciating individual differences and experiences allows music educators to set up learning situations that are analogous to an orchestral score.

Understanding Musician Identity for Leadership

Like most musicians, the creation of music has simply entranced me from an early age. I loved discovering how instruments worked, how they could be played for my own pleasure and with others, how manuscripts (or their absence) enabled me to understand composers' ideas, and how music could make an impact on everyone around. At this stage I also had the (erroneous) idea that everyone thought the same way that I did about most things: for instance, thinking that everyone (including my brother) must enjoy practising (I found out later that my brother really didn't like it!). As I grew older, I came to realise how much music there was, and how different that music could sound. There was the thrilling day when I listened to something "new" and noted that it sounded a bit like Bach (having had the experience of playing something by him earlier).

I came to realise that the sounds and forms of music said something about the time and place that it was first made, and that the same music continues to say something even when the era, country, venue and instrument selections change. The more music you encounter, the richer your understanding of individual works, and the entirety of your musical experience. Playing music with others developed an appreciation of the complexity of music, the subtle, nuanced sounds that could be made through different acoustic elements, harmony, rhythm and duration. And, most excitingly, you could hear how your friends were also encountering that sound and that it miraculously all worked together. Importantly, it takes time to appreciate the differences in music and also the ability to play different forms of music. Focusing intently on the development of expertise on one instrument is also the key to understanding a whole range of others. From the perspective of my research and that undertaken by others, all these experiences comprise musician identity (Bennett, Reid, & Petocz, 2015).

Musician identity has two entwined central components that are also shared across disciplines. They are "a sense of being" and "a sense of transformation" (Solomonides & Reid, 2009, p. 117). In essence, there is an element of self that totally identifies with the complex attributes that "make" a musician and, concurrently, these attributes change over time as we learn. Musician identity is hence rather fluid as time passes, as one focuses on the aesthetic of music, and as one has different life and musical experiences.

Leadership is much the same. Thinking and working as a musician provides a basis to consider both the point of leadership and its associated activity. A commonality in all workplaces is complexity. Everyone's own professional experience prepares them uniquely for the work that they do. Taking the example of the orchestra, it is simply not possible to replace the horn solo with a violin – if this was done, the integrity, texture and intention of the musical work would be lost. Simply put, musicians understand that each voice makes a specific contribution to the work and that all voices are needed to create the composer's vision. Similarly, each workplace has a set of internal characteristics and is also subject to external pressures. Within each workplace there are distinct sub-groups that work together on specific problems, and there are also distinct cultural sub-groups (such as those who do Sudoku for relaxation, or those who discuss different media for their next digital composition). Each of these groups offers specific enhancements to the group as a whole. These enhancements can be small- or large-scale in their influence, or they can be positive or challenging, or they can be conservative or innovative, and this diversity is what leaders work with.

Continuing with the orchestral analogy, my conservatoire recently performed Mahler's 2nd symphony. While the conductor has known the work for a very long time, it was the first encounter for most of the students. They had to work hard on their individual parts, to find their own voice inside the parts, to collaborate to blend sound, to be aware of the intent of the music, to concentrate in rehearsals and to respond to instruction, to understand why that music was created in the first place, and finally had to communicate all of this social and aesthetic understanding meaningfully to an audience. These students focused on the heritage aspect of music-making where sincere homage is paid to the music of the past in order to make it alive for today.

Even more recently, our composition students made a digital mash-up of the recording of Mahler's 2nd symphony – in essence, reimagining the music to suit a 21st-century aesthetic and using 21st-century tools to do so. Each set of students was equally focused on the task and produced valid interpretations of the music. In the end, the communicative and educational objects were the same. Similarly, a leader will provide scope for this level of variation inside their organisation. It seems vitally important to allow complex ideas and relationships to flourish. And our musician identity provides just such an appreciation of complexity that then lends itself to positive and empathetic leadership. Developing expertise in music can be the foundation of expert leadership. Consequently, music higher education can be seen as a complex amalgam of characteristics that relate to individuals, their professional musical experience, the learning environments in which they teach, and the leadership approaches that are fostered through the delegated leaders (deans, directors, chairs, for instance).

Understanding Leadership Theories for Leadership

Beyond the idea of variation and musician identity, there are many theories of leadership that contribute to our understanding of what happens in musical institutions. Each view of leadership rests inside its own epistemological position. For instance, leadership can be seen as a process of influencing people. This implies particular hegemonic practices and sophisticated linguistic and emotional devices. In this paradigm, a leader may seek consensus on various matters, may initiate discussions that allow agreement and dissent, may initiate projects in which educational companions are invested in the outcomes. This type of leader understands that difference can lead to strong, creative solutions to problems. Leadership, however, can also be seen as controlling events, implying that the leader has certain forms of power over others. Both of these views could be seen as having paternalistic or even colonial epistemologies. Alternatives to this are when leadership is seen to be democratically decided (although this implies that once decided the followers will implicitly follow). Or, leadership could be socially constructed and based on mutual respect and trust. These latter views seem (to me) to bear the closest relation to the distributed leadership implied in music-making.

Previously I have anchored my discussion on a musical format that is known to most Western art music musicians. However, different musical types, genres and cultures also show how musician identity contributes to our understanding of leadership. The majority of leadership theories (at least in the English-speaking literature) have come from different professional discourses and can help us understand what goes on inside musical institutions.

Harris (2014) suggests various foci for leadership activity. First, the basic point of leadership can be seen as to foster change and improvement across an institution. This seems a common concept often married to quality assurance. However, with an improvement there is the possibility that common good practice is ignored as "improvement" becomes an end in itself. Similarly, designed changes to systems can alter institutional activity hugely. In my own institution, a change to technical infrastructure intended to streamline student enrolment experiences also forced the centralisation of many activities. This has caused confusion in the academic workspace as people have adapted to new responsibilities generated through the technology.

Moving aside from centrally controlled institutional activities, Harris (2009) focuses on the future of leadership where the attention is on providing opportunities for emerging leaders. This reorientation allows attention on the real situations in which people find themselves. Learning how to develop and enhance future leadership skills for earlier career colleagues also makes a change in their social capital. In my own practice, I keep a deliberate eye on early and mid-career faculty to ensure that they have important formative experiences and that through those experiences their colleagues develop trust in their work. This, in turn, leads to workplace emancipation where colleagues are able to take control of their creative, performance and teaching roles.

Harris (2009, p. 14) suggests that distributed leadership influences organisational outcomes and change and that it is the nature of the distribution that can have positive effects on change. She writes, "the evidence highlights that the role of 'leader' is not one imposed upon teachers, it is usually selected". Although much of Harris's commentary is focused on distributed leadership in primary and secondary school settings, she has noted that there are positive learning outcomes for students. Explorations of distributed leadership in higher education settings are scarcer, and even more so in the specific area of music higher education.

Gronn (2002) provides an interesting window on the concept of distributed leadership, where he recognises that it can be wildly uncoordinated, or consciously managed. In this case, leadership can be seen as rather more than one would expect if there were only a tight leadership team. More people can be influenced and supported by leaders when there is a wider group. Gronn (2002) indicates that there are three possible forms of distributed leadership: *spontaneous collaboration, intuitive working relations* and *institutionalised practice*. These attributes of distributed leadership are related to specific forms of problems that require resolution. For instance, spontaneous collaboration usually occurs where there is a finite problem that needs solving (in my conservatoire context this could mean the artistic programming required for the following year and, consequently, the student resources required to activate the plan). More intimately intuitive relationships normally arise when individuals see the need to collaborate on something of mutual interest (again, within my conservatoire context this could mean the exploration of research ideas in order to bid for external funding or the writing of collaborative papers).

Institutionalised leadership follows more the formal structures that are imposed for functional reasons. The challenge for my own conservatoire is that we share managerial functions with a large university, consequently the institutional leadership structures do not necessarily support the needs of our complex musical environment. Harris (2014) rightly indicates that the concept of distributed leadership can lead to collective capacity building, but can also support "misleading" activity as well. Davison and colleagues, however, suggest that distributed leadership:

> resists representations of heroic leaders and passive followers, and implies that boundaries of leadership are inclusive rather than exclusive. Distributed leadership is a fluid potential held be a group that enhances the capacities of individuals to take the lead and that aligns this capacity with specific challenges and organisational environments.
> (Davison et al., 2013, p. 100)

This group also makes the pertinent point that distributed leadership can extend beyond a specific institution and provide influence and support for other institutions, usually through the use of critical friends.

Bolden, Petrov and Gosling (2009) extend the idea that distributed leadership has characteristics that are somewhat beyond specific institutions. Of interest is their analysis of data from 12 UK universities where they noted two key principles: that of devolved leadership, which is symptomatic of top-down approaches, and that of emergent leadership, which they associated with horizontal and bottom-up influence; these two forms of influence are manifest across institutional boundaries. In my conservatoire context, I can appreciate these two approaches as they are simultaneously manifest as the conservatoire plays the role of supporting its own students and faculty, is a part of a large research-intensive university, is funded by the government with specified reporting requirements, supports other conservatories for curriculum development and quality assurance, and also contributes to the cultural landscape of Australia and beyond.

The Real World and Work of Higher Education Music Educators

The work of musicians, the specialised world they inhabit, and the way they go about teaching and creative research combine to build leadership styles that could be considered inherently musical. A characteristic that I have observed is respect for music specialisations and what those specialisations can contribute to a joint event. This specialisation is embedded within musical cultural practices but is also open to new cultural perspectives. These specialisations lead to personal confidence and autonomy when colleagues are asked to contribute to familiar and unfamiliar problems. Musicians seem to be able to segue between authentic work situations quite smoothly. This is reminiscent of transitions described by Wenger (1998), when people move from being the centre of an activity to the edges, when required. It acknowledges legitimate peripheral engagement as essential to the developing health of a field. Most importantly, musician identity forms a picture of variation theory in practice.

In recent years, my own university has dramatically shifted its student and academic support services. The implementation of student support systems caused a radical shift in the ways that we had to undertake our teaching and organisational work. We had our own internal culture built over 100 years of experience. Many of us were (are) orchestral musicians of various genres, and also composers, music educators, musicologists, jazz or contemporary musicians, or digital music or technology experts. In common we had a musician identity and experience of high-level teaching and performance practice. We needed to understand what possibilities were now available due to the university-wide systems change.

One of our biggest challenges was moving away from an "orchestral" model, where each instrumental area was considered a cognate group. Instead, we needed to move to a degree model where individuals had autonomy over a specific curriculum, but understood how that curriculum fitted into the overall construction of a student's programme of study. This led to robust discussions relating to the mix of performance, ensemble, musicology, languages and liberal arts studies – which is the most important thing for students. From our own experiences, we all held strong and well-articulated views. However, the contemporary world of musical work is somewhat different from when we were young.

We needed to change our thinking to focus on what students needed to prepare for the professional world as it is now. Taking on board the discussions above in this chapter, we noted that we all held expertise in a range of areas that were musical and non-musical. We realised that to move forward, we needed to combine our range of different experiences and views to make the mandatory university changes work in meaningful ways for us and for our students. I have to admit that this is still a work in progress, but by adopting a distributed leadership approach where individuals have autonomy to invent, criticise, change and mould processes, we have progressed far towards our goal of enhancing our students' learning experiences and preparing them for future work.

Leadership that is distributed throughout an organisation where each member is recognised for their real musical skills, and is able to work in ways that are authentically musical, seems to work!

References

Bandino, l., Li, Y., Tokay, S., Craighero, L., & Canto, R. (2012). Leadership in orchestra emerges from causal relationships of movement kinematics. *PLoS ONE, 7*(5), 1–6.

Bathurst, R., & Ladkin, D. (2012). Performing leadership: Observations from the world of music. *Administrative Sciences, 2*, 99–119.

Bennis, W., & Nanus, B. (1985). *Leaders: The strategies for taking charge.* New York: Harper and Row.

Bennett, D., Reid, A., & Petocz. P. (2015). On the other side of the divide: Making sense of student stories of creativities in music. In P. Bernard & E. Haddon (Eds.), *Activating diverse musical creativities: Teaching and learning in higher music education* (pp. 21–37). London: Bloomsbury.

Boerner, S., Krause, D., & Gebert, D. (2004). Leadership and cooperation in an orchestra – an empirical study. *Human Resource Development International, 7*(4), 465–479.

Bolden, R., Petrov, G., & Gosling, J. (2009). Distributed leadership in higher education: Rhetoric and reality. *Educational Management, Administration and Leadership, 37*, 257–277.

Carnicer, J., Garrido, D., & Requena, S. (2015). Music and leadership: The role of the conductor. *International Journal for Music and Performing Arts, 3*(1), 84–88.

Chambers, P., Burchell, H., & Gully, T. (2009). Different ways of knowing and telling. *Reflective Practice: International and Multidisciplinary Perspectives, 10*(1), 65–66.

Davison, A., Brown, P., Pharo, E., Warr, K., McGregor, H., Terkes, S., Boyd, D., & Abuodha, P. (2013). Distributed leadership: Building capacity for interdisciplinary climate change teaching at four universities. *International Journal of Sustainability in Higher Education, 15*(1), 98–110.

Gronn, P. (2000). Distributed leadership. In K. Leithwood & P. Hallinger (Eds.), *Second international handbook of education leadership and administration* (pp. 653–696). Dordrecht: Kluwer Academic Publishers.

Hall, V. (2001). Management teams in education: An unequal music. *School Leadership and Management, 21*(3), 327–341.

Harris, A. (2009). Distributed leadership: What we know. In A. Harris (Ed.), *Distributed leadership: Different perspectives* (pp. 11–21). Studies in Educational Leadership 7, Springer Science+Business Media B. V.

Harris, A. (2014). *Distributed leadership matters: Perspectives, practicalities, and potential.* London: Corwin Press.

Johnson, B., & Geal, M. (2015). Working in harmony. *Training Journal*, September, 34–38.

Koivunen, N., & Wennes, G. (2011). Show us the sound! Aesthetic leadership of symphony orchestra conductors. *Leadership, 7*(1), 51–71.

Marton, F., & Pang, M. (2009). On some necessary conditions of learning. *Journal of the Learning Sciences, 15*(2), 193–220.

Marton, F., & Saljo, R. (1976). On qualitatively difference in learning. Outcome as a function of the learner's conception of the task. *British Journal of Educational Psychology, 46*(1), 15–127.

Oxford Dictionary online. https://en.oxforddictionaries.com/definition/harmony

Senge, P. (2005). *Presence: Exploring profound change in people, organisations and society.* London: Nicholas Brealey Publishing.

Solomonides, I., & Reid, A. (2009). Variation in student engagement: A design model. *Prime, 3*(2), 115–128.

Wenger, E. (1998). *Communities of practice: Learning, meaning and identity.* Cambridge: Cambridge University Press.

IV
Leading Institutional Change through Better Policy Thinking

PATRICK SCHMIDT

In this chapter, the process of leading institutional change from a policy standpoint is addressed using the seminal work of Wildavsky (1988, p. 389) to frame policy "as a process of leading change" that is both art and craft. The notion of craft places policy as we know it traditionally, as justification and rule making. This stance facilitates "stake claiming" and emphasises relations through procedures focused on solutions. Policy as art emphasises discovery by placing greater emphasis on processes, where the aim is to find an intersection between what is feasible and desirable. This policy framing constitutes individuals' dispositions, supporting their inclination to adapt and uncover. The art metaphor opens up a new space for reframing traditional conceptions of policy while presenting innovative policy thinking as a guide for institutional change. Two cases are offered as examples.

At a time in which the idea of leadership has become a commoditised ideal sold in "ten steps" or through workshops, and fetishised as a highly desirable attribute or even an innate talent, leadership in higher education has become a serious matter. This is particularly so given that institutional leadership, "which is a major agency of cultural, spiritual, moral, intellectual and political education in society, is [often] reduced to a set of technical maneuvers" (Grace, 1995, p. 236). Just as important, the ways in which we come to see policy and its aims has a palpable impact on the practices we choose and the processes we make legitimate.

Expanding on earlier work on policy framing capacity (Schmidt, 2017), I argue that traditional policy thinking, just as traditional efforts towards institutional change, tends to focus on the map when it should focus on the territory. Developing a policy-framing disposition around the metaphor of territory might help facilitate stronger process-based leadership in music and a greater alignment between the change leadership literature (Herold, Fedor, Caldwell & Liu, 2008) and music education. If leadership in music and music education were to place greater emphasis on its own milieu and work-environments as territories – as constantly changing environments that demand recurrent adaptability – it might more easily commit to institutional, organisational and community action aimed at generating interaction, shifting conversations and taking risks.

In North America, as elsewhere, many higher education faculty and programmes have resisted change as if their lives – and livelihoods – depended on it. While historical and internal issues remain, an extensive literature has articulated the challenges of modernising the contemporary university-based school of music, making it more complex and less reliant on its original conservatoire model (see Jones, 2017; Nettl, 1995). What is readily visible today is an expansion of the original enterprise, with schools of music adding programmes such as jazz, popular music, production and film. This points to the old policy as craft strategy, which looks for solutions by expanding the map. If recent discussions fomented by the College Music Society's Curriculum Manifesto (Myers et al., 2014) are any indication, this approach has tinkered with the edges and has under-delivered. It has created greater economic feasibility – mainly to the established, innovative or endowed few – but has also incentivised stake claiming and entrenchment. As importantly, it has not generated wide institutional diversity, curricular creativity or pedagogical innovation, nor has it facilitated space for leadership development.

In this chapter, I argue that without a renewed approach to policy thinking, higher music education's capacity to shift conversations, generate greater inter- and cross-disciplinary interaction and take programmatic risks will remain limited. This will prevent the significant and necessary change capacity that music education must develop in order to more aptly educate college-age students (Myers, 2016) and to contend with contemporary economic, social and cultural challenges (Jenkins, Purushotma, Weigel, Clinton & Robison, 2009; Latham & Ewing, 2018; Moldavanova & Goerdel, 2018). In what follows, I present a conceptual argumentation of how and why an approximation between policy framing dispositions and change leadership can be beneficial to change in higher music education. I end by presenting cases from North America, inviting readers to consider whether, how and to what extent these ideas and frameworks might emerge in practice.

Policy, Leadership and a Framing Disposition

A policy disposition can impact leadership capacity and become a trigger for work in higher education, particularly the work that seeks to create sustainable curricular, pedagogical, ethical and equitable change that is mindful and not just expedient. A way forward implies an understanding of policy as an intrinsic part of, and contributor to, deliberative democracy (Gutmann &

Thompson, 1996, 2004) and thus a way to focus efforts on learning how to adapt and contest.

At the centre of productive policy and leadership is deliberation; that is to say, the capacity to interact, shift conversations and take risks. This requires the development of a framing disposition, but not just by those in traditional leadership positions; rather, working to develop it to a larger part of the organisational whole. Traditionally, the notion of framing is one of establishing a clear picture: an immutable "slice in time" that provides insight for action. The challenge is that traditional strategic planning is not only based on a singular vision, which is promoted, incentivised or enforced, but also on the systematic suppression of alternatives. As Lees-Marshment (2016) suggests, deliberation is eschewed and has little to do with communication and collaboration.

If ideas such as wide-range leadership development are important, potential structural impediments to this kind of practice become significant. Current notions of strategic planning might form one such impediment. As Davies and Ellison (1999, p. 12) explain, strategic planning in education is often understood as "the process of matching the school/organization's activities to the emerging environment, bearing in mind what can feasibly be achieved with the resource base which can be generated". If looked at more critically, however, Davies and Ellison suggest that the optimal way to lead is to create a clearly defined and easily (at times simplistically) communicated picture for future action: to create a map to be followed. This notion is commonly adopted but has often been ineffectual. Davies and Ellison (1999, p. 2) provide one such example as they explain the problems caused by "inspections" as a manifestation of the escalation of strategic planning in United Kingdom schools.

> The inspection process has resulted in reports that encourage schools to extend short-term plans into a strategic framework and to produce three- or five-year costed plans. Planning is seen as desirable, necessary and (often, but mistakenly!) as a solution for poor management practice. Much of this planning work has, however, been linear and incremental in nature and no longer meets the needs of schools.

Critical to this passage is not simply that "a reliance on strategic planning assumes a rational and predictable process which, in practice, may not be possible in the current turbulent environment" (p. 15), but that these leadership processes do not foster a framing disposition within a representative portion of school community. In reality, they discourage it by further exacerbating policy processes that are not deliberative, thus also restricting interaction, shifts in conversations and risk-taking. This is also meaningful in higher education, particularly as schools of music can be contentious, ideological and at times non-participative working environments. The important message is that both serious and methodical thinking is necessary, as is a renewed and redirected sense of what participation in decision-making looks like.

One way forward might be an expansion of current structural spaces for action in leadership and policy work that draws from current and traditional understanding and attempts to create continuums: to generate change that feels familiar but still "moves the needle". This approach acknowledges the map but superimposes onto it territory ideas and ideals. Mintzberg, Ghoshal and Quinn (1995) offer an interesting way to schematically see the potential for change while using well-known notions of strategic planning. What they show is a way to move from the most traditional strategy as a "ploy" to the more collaborative strategy as a perspective. The first three points legitimise outcomes, while the latter two incentivise process and outcome in greater balance.

1. Strategy as a ploy, such as taking a position to outwit an opponent.
2. Strategy as a position: a means whereby the organisation orientates itself to a specific location in its market or field.
3. Strategy as a plan, incorporating a consciously intended course of action, thus strategies are made in advance and are consciously taken.
4. Strategy as a pattern. By this definition, strategy is consistency in behaviour.
5. Strategy as perspective: a way of perceiving the world. A shared way in the organisation of looking at its role and position.

An emphasis on framing dispositions might be another important space for action. Music educators familiar with Rein and Schön (1993, p. 148) will understand framing as a way of "making sense of a complex reality to provide guideposts for knowing, analysis, persuading, and acting". I go a step further, arguing that framing is a creative disposition rather than a perceptual sorting skill (Schmidt, 2013) and thus should be seen as a schema *for* interpretation and not as schemata *of* interpretation. Thus, framing capacity is akin to Boisot's (1995, p. 37) concept of strategic intent, the goals of which are to "build capability ... to meet major challenges in the future when precise plans are not available [or desirable] but where capability to respond in a dynamic environment is necessary".

Nagel (2010) makes a similar claim, linking creative skills and framing disposition and emphasising their importance once we come to understand that policy is first and foremost a process. Policy as a thing – a piece of legislation, rules for action or an organisational strategic plan – is only a temporary segment of a larger policymaking process, which must also include implementation, enactment, adaptation and re-evaluation. This is why leaders should not miss the territory – the constantly changing – by focusing on the map and what is immediately solvable.

Key in all the above is the notion that ideas and agendas alone are insufficient in leading institutional change, particularly in highly diverse spaces such as higher education. How, then, might music education leaders foster policy leadership that is willing to move away from singularly focused, delimited strategic planning? How might the actors involved in "leadership" be deepened and expanded? Central to the argument so far is that higher music education would benefit if it were to amplify a process-based understanding of leadership, which places high value on interaction, risk-taking and shifts in conversations by matching it with a policy-framing disposition at the individual level. The potential outcome is a stronger grassroots movement predicated by greater positive engagements with adaptation and re-evaluation. In the next section, I address some of points to structural resistance to these aims and illustrate how embedded these structures are to extant conceptions of policy and leadership.

Redefining Policy and Moving Away from Incredible Certitude

Resistance to change can be significantly located in the fact that both policy and leadership have traditionally been portrayed as spaces of certainty: clear vision, certitude and avoidance of "soft" choices all link traditional policy action and power-directed leadership. It follows that if higher music education leaders are interested in different leadership we also must re-conceptualise our understanding of policy, as the two are often entwined.

Leadership and policy are imbued by similar challenges and historically have been beholden to the same mix of patriarchy, cults of personality and over-reliance on data. The result is what Majone (1989, p. 15) calls "decisionism", in which policy is defined as "instrumental rationality under a resource constrain" (p. 15). Majone's term encapsulates a critique of policy and of leadership as precise, controllable and objective: dependent on a "unitary decision maker". By arguing that policy is always formed by "a complex blend of factual statements, interpretations, opinions and evaluations" (p. 31), Majone turns the table, legitimising the notion of policy as a deliberative practice and laying out the argumentative turn in policy research (see also Fischer & Forester, 1993; Stone, 2011). Majone's critique is directed at an "analycentric" mode of thinking, which Dunn (1981) considers to be based on instrumentally rationalistic techniques such as cost–benefit analysis, decision analysis, multi-attribute utility analysis and systems modelling. Central to the robust criticism he and others have laid out is the charge that verifiability, or empiric certitude, is oversold.

The trouble is that there are many incentives to "strong" leadership based on unitary decision-making and the kind of perceived certitude present in analycentric policy thinking. Economics professor at Northwestern University, Charles Manski, expresses concern with what he calls "incredible certitude", which clearly intersects with the kind of deliberate leadership and framing capacity advocated here. According to Manski (2007, p. 7):

> the scientific community rewards those who produce strong and novel findings. The public, impatient for solutions to its pressing concerns, rewards those who offer simple analyses leading to unequivocal policy recommendations. These incentives make it tempting for researchers to maintain assumptions far stronger than they can persuasively defend, in order to draw strong conclusions.

Manski's (2007, p. 12) point is that policy analysts, like leadership in general, face a dilemma centred on the ethical decision of what assumptions to maintain, given that "stronger assumptions yield conclusions that are more powerful but less credible". In economic terms, Manski's central argument is that, just as decision-making, policy analysis should operate under a "range and not a point" (p. 12). In other words, scientific data – in social science and political environs – cannot aptly inform or predict point outcomes. Manski uses this case to illustrate the challenge:

> A perhaps apocryphal, but quite believable, story circulates about an economist's attempt to describe his uncertainty about a forecast to [US] President Lyndon B. Johnson. The economist presented his forecast as a likely range of values for the quantity under discussion. Johnson is said to have replied, "Ranges are for cattle. Give me a number."
> (Manski, 2007, p. 8)

This example illustrates that leaders and policy makers often operate under arbitrary criteria, preferring a strong assumption over uncertainty. Haussman and Wise (1985, p. 23) go further, writing that policy leadership has a history of being "either psychologically unwilling or cognitively unable to cope with uncertainty". Such leadership tends to "argue that pragmatism dictates provision of point predictions even though these predictions may not be credible" (p. 23).

Pretending that certitude is an absolute necessity or assuming that point data are indeed both reliable and highly predictive has formed a vision of leadership that projects confidence, but in fact works to actualise ideological agendas; is primarily outcome-focused; dismisses or simply tolerates participative work; and is, more frequently than not, wasteful. One of the challenges is that a tactical culture of planning and leadership has been developed that often projects collaborative or shared dispositions, but, in reality, is in full service of directed decision-making.

Higher music education is not immune to these social, cultural and political realities and it too has been traditionally framed by forms of scientificism that have generated – and been further supported by – the leadership decisionism described by Majone. The conundrum or opportunity here is one Hamel and Prahalad (2010, p. 63) articulated, dating back nearly 20 years, and which is still slowly and surely unfolding that:

> concepts such as strategic fit (between resources and opportunities), generic strategies, (low cost vs. differentiation vs. focus) and the strategy hierarchy (goals, strategies, and tactics) have often abetted the process of competitive decline. Marginal adjustments to current orthodoxies, however, are no more likely to produce competitive revitalisation than are marginal improvements in operating efficiency.

On the one hand, there is a clear interest and a more open realisation that adaptation and change are the new constant and require careful and multi-pronged work. On the other hand, resistance, denial and peripheral work remain a clear strategy in many music higher education programmes.

What can be learned from the more innovative ways of understanding policy and leadership? The literature in these areas of study helps to reveal that disrupting conventional wisdoms is not simply about replacement, but replacement that establishes new processes alongside new outcomes. Healey (1993, p. 242) offers conceptualisations of planning that are more fluid and adaptable, underlining expectations of a process that "should involve recognizing, valuing, listening to, and searching for translative possibilities between different discourse communities". Healey sees good policy and good leadership emerging not simply from the craft – tactics, guidelines and criteria – but also from the art – adaptable framing, capable listening and informed translation capacity. She assumes, as does Wildavsky (1988), that policy and leadership environs are diverse, fluid and overlapping.

It seems critical that attention be paid to how higher music education leaders might translate possibilities and distinctions between communities. A critical step is to consider how language can restructure existing conceptions and trouble the tendency to hold on to and generate conventional wisdoms in policy and leadership. This seems to be an important and worthwhile area of investigation and exploration.

From Advocacy to Counsel: Policy as Leadership

The educational policy work developed by Ball (1993, 2005) over the past 25 years carries with it a similar message to the argument made above: namely, that change in action is preceded by change in thinking, which requires change in language. This argument also follows policy thinkers such as Stone (2011), who sees policy and leadership as the intersubjective interpretation of common experiences and the conceptual framing of ideas that guide the ways people create the shared meanings that motivate them to act. Fischer and Forester (1993, p. 1) explain this in simpler terms while also noting the consequences.

> If analysts' [or other leaders'] ways of representing reality are necessarily selective, they seem as necessarily bound up by relations of power, agenda setting, inclusion and exclusion, selective attention, and neglect. If analysts' [or other leaders'] way of representing policy and planning issues must make assumptions about causality and responsibility, about legitimacy and authority, and about interests, needs, values, preferences, and obligations, then the language of policy and planning not only depicts but constructs the issues at hand.

The aim of this chapter is to bring policy and leadership together, suggesting that both function at their best but also more equitably when they avoid highly constrained and insensitive normative approaches. Fischer and Forester (1993, p. 12) concur with this stance, writing that policy and leadership directly benefit when there is an understanding that "the interplay of competing frames is a source of new knowledge rather than an impediment to it". The urgency of policy thinking and leadership that is educated through a framing disposition lens is the growing need for practice that is capable of "exposing and counteracting manipulation of agendas, illegitimate exercises of power, skewed distributions of information, and attempts to distract attention" (Dryzek, 1993, p. 228). But beyond this critical approach, the point of a framing disposition is to facilitate the expansion of this same disposition in others.

Torgerson (1985) suggests that this becomes noticeable when leaders reject their roles of leaders-as-adjudicators and start asking questions about deliberation. For instance, leaders might ask how action goals for curricular reform in higher education can not only change the structure of knowledge delivery, but also impact pedagogical conversations. Could it be that, in the process, they can, for example, help the community to deliberate more openly and critically?

Another way to think about this might be to consider the distinction between leadership that sees itself as counsel and that which sees itself as advocate. While advocates tend to present a formed, established and delineated argumentation in defence of a position or initiative and on behalf of a community, counsel as described by Jennings (1991, p. 448) suggests action that starts by seeing community as purposive agents and thus is "attentive to the moral sensibilities, vocabularies, and forms of life that comprise the ethos of the political community it serves". The shift is to see both processes and outcomes emerging out of leadership not as "alien things imposed upon the malleable, manipulable desires and interest" of the community, but rather as ways to facilitate the agency and moral imagination of this same community (Jennings, 1991, p. 448).

Better Stories, Better Assumptions, Better Process

The key value of change leadership emerges as finding a balance between appropriate ways to shorthand and the avoidance of "short change". To explain the need for this balance, I draw on the work of highly creative and progressive policy thinker John Forester. Forester (1993) argues that stories, just as policy and leadership, cannot concern only idealisation or imposition because both fail. People are not convinced by stories that over-idealise, Forester argues, as such stories do not sound believable. Nor are people drawn to stories that over-guide, because they do not activate agency. In these terms, music education leadership that presents strategies and grand visions, and that dissociates dialogue from actualisation, does not sound believable and thus fails. Further, leadership based on figures, facts and tactics alone does not incite participative understanding: it portrays a story with information and players, but without a plot it lacks a reason for being. These stories generate disengagement and they, too, fail.

Linking this to stories – stories as meaningful ways to understand practice – Forester (1993) argues that individuals function within two tensions: the need to use shorthand and the avoidance of short change. Shorthand is a metonymic way of understanding the need for context while being able to communicate without a constant and repetitive return to description and explanation. Social theory as a form of shorthand helps to cut through the background, while providing a framework for sense-making and decision-making. Experimental methods within research are also shorthand, as are planning strategies and tactics. The risk is the over-playing of shorthand – over-codifying and thus diminishing understanding or oversimplifying and thus reducing impact – which often leads to short change. The problem is that this is easier said than done.

Forester (1993) suggests that leaders facilitate a balance between the two by asking "What's the story?" and not "What's the problem?". I propose that leaders can learn from stories by carefully focusing attention to the intersection between needs, vision and individuals. Figure 4.1 presents a schematic representation of this idea, where leadership is represented as a centrifugal force that propels vision, moderates intersubjective relations with individual participants, and is aware of community, organisational and structural needs.

At the same time, leadership plays an argumentative role by serving as a facilitator for the practice stories that emerge from each of the three areas. This leadership, both at the centre and at the periphery, helps interaction at all three levels by facilitating the questions and actions that follow such areas. The areas

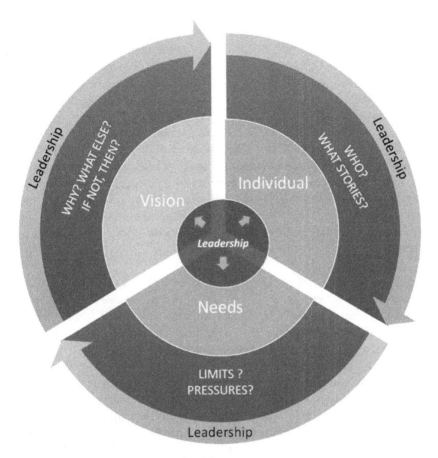

Figure 4.1 Leadership as a centrifugal force

are a representation of the territory idea discussed earlier, helping to generate motion, interaction, discovery, listening and learning by fomenting points of action that come from within individuals, needs and visions: fostering an inside-outward motion while facilitating a sharing of questions that emerge from each three segments.

The process acknowledges that leaders and leadership must find a balance between the space and time to plan and engage in decision-making, becoming apt at "learning in the thick of things, in the face of conflict" (Forester, 1993, p. 197). Leaders have to "find out not only how things are working but what is working well or poorly" and, as importantly, "they must learn not only about what someone has said but about what that means, why that is significant – all in the light of the inevitably ambiguous mandates they serve and the many, also ambiguous, hopes and needs" of members of their community of practice (Forester, 1993, p. 197).

In some ways and "whether they like it or not, leaders, as those engaged in policy thinking and action, are practical ethicists" (Forester, 1993, p. 198) in that they have to pick targets, set priorities and make judgements about what matters and why. But that does not mean that decision-making is absolved by these realities and thus can act unilaterally. On the contrary, compelling leadership requires a commitment to a complex system such as the one articulated at Figure 4.1. This is necessary if a balance between finding a frame – and thus a shorthand to difficult decision-making – and avoiding carelessly or ideologically short-changing individuals and community, is to be achieved. This is why Forester is interested in the role that stories of practice can have in changing the way we see policy and leadership. If leaders listen closely, not to the portrayals of fact in stories but to their claims of value and significance, Forester (1993, p. 199) claims:

> we discover an infrastructure of ethics, an ethical substructure of practice, a finely woven tapestry of value being woven sentence by sentence; each sentence not simply adding, description by description to a picture of the world, but adding, care by care, to a sensitivity to the practical world, to a rich prudent appreciation of that world.

This is the intersection of art and craft that Wildavsky (1988) advocated, and this is the potential in educating current and future and leaders into a framing capacity. Higher education in music faces enormous challenges, from labour to equity, artistic risk to curricular needs. And while many initiatives are promising, their integration into the formation of new assumptions and thus new systemic and innovative decision-making is far from obvious. In the next and final section, I present cases from North America and invite readers to consider whether, how and to what extend the ideas and frameworks might be made present in their own contexts.

Stories of Practice: Current Action and Food for Future Thought

The challenge of the undergraduate degree in music is multifaceted. It encompasses issues such as the diversity of the students in schools of music, the nature and impact of coursework, the new realities of employability and the nature of creative and artistic work today. The last two are particularly sensitive because traditional employers such as orchestras have experienced significant challenges over the past decade. Numerous articles have described the crisis of relevance and thus also the economic crisis that has engulfed Western music, particularly in North America, but much effort has been made in terms of generating innovation and change (see also how two articles in the *New York Times* exemplify this claim, https://nyti.ms/2rn6m1E; https://nyti.ms/2rndgnQ). Leadership as framing capacity has been at the centre of it all.

Story 1

In preparation for a 2015 mini-conference at the New World Symphony, the Houston Symphony (HS) compiled a case study of their path to restructuring the orchestra. Their aim was stated in simple terms, but the challenge was significant: "In 2025, the Houston Symphony will be America's most relevant and accessible top-ten orchestra." Director Mark Hanson was present at the conference and outlined the vision that led to this statement. To achieve its goal, HS re-engaged with both the community and musicians. The leadership spent time understanding the needs of the orchestra – its limitations and pressures – and attempted to develop a framing disposition that would increase the number of players, commit to repertoire or seats in the house, and define to a distinct view and direction. Their story was framed this way.

> Relevant and accessible are two words that aren't typically used to describe our country's top orchestras. How did this storied 100+-year-old institution come to embrace these values, and more importantly, how will they accomplish this aspirational goal? The story of what lead the Houston Symphony to articulating this vision and setting a bold, new direction is one of recognizing the sweeping demographic shifts that are taking place all across our nation, and especially in Houston, one of the most diverse cities in the U.S. But it's also about recognizing that the culture of the organization needed to be in alignment with these core values to enable real systemic change to occur.
>
> (Houston Symphony, 2015)

In 2015, the HS had 87 full-time orchestral musicians with 13 Asian musicians, one African-American and one Hispanic musician. But the issue was not simply internal, given that "of the Symphony's 143 Members of Board of Trustees, there [were] currently one African-American, seven Hispanics and six Asians". Consequently, a significant goal had to be a shift in the ways in which needs, vision and individuals interacted. For HS, this took the form of a Community Leadership Council Initiative. As Steve Wenig of the leadership team at HS says:

> Externally, we knew we had to get out and start talking to people in the community, so we formed the three leadership councils. Our approach

was to ask a lot of questions and listen. We thought that the best way we could begin engaging these groups was to start from a position of not assuming we knew the answers.

The HS seemed to want to hear new stories and produce new ones as well. In order to achieve this, internal initiatives departed from the recognition that the musician is at the centre of the entity where a critical constituency is to have a voice, while being themselves willing to change, if the organisation was to redesign its cultural planning in lasting and impactful ways. In this way, HS decided not simply to expand or redraw the map, but to change the territory. Recognising other programmes such as the New World Symphony's highly innovative initiatives reshaping the profile of the orchestral musician, HS decided to hire four new full-time musicians with a distinct mandate (and a distinct framing disposition). These are called *Community Embedded Musicians*, and 80 per cent of their contracted time is dedicated to help HS reframe its interaction with the community. This new *territory* for musical and cultural leadership will facilitate internal policy adaptation and external impact. It is generating a new *story* of who orchestral musicians are and what they can do.

Story 2

In 2013, the College Music Society (CMS) established its *Task Force on the Undergraduate Music Major* (TFUMM). With almost 600 Music degree programmes accredited by the National Association of Schools of Music (NASM) in the US alone and a remarkable homogeneity of content, structure and design, significant change in this environ is perhaps the most pressing and challenging issue for higher education in music. Stasis or innovation in this area defines and defies leadership.

The CMS task force aims were delineated by an important question which set up the policy/leadership process in a constructive way: "What does it mean to be an educated musician in the twenty-first century?" The challenge, as Myers (2016, p. 295) argues, is that while the institutionalised framing of the working musician/educator has not changed, as evident in programme design and curricular development, the sector has seen:

> over the past two decades a growing stream of graduates whose careers are marked by initiative, flexibility, and artistry beyond the usual parameters of studio teaching, opera and orchestral performance, and university teaching. Artists are engaging audiences as co-creators, managing their own careers, collaborating with other artists, and crossing roles among creators, performers, and producers of music. Musicians'

work is becoming increasingly rich in stylistic crossovers, incorporation of diverse cultures, and acoustic-technological expressions.

More to the point, "this new breed of musicians frequently reports that their collegiate programs failed to prepare them for the careers they have devised independently" (Myers, 2016, p. 296). While this is not the place for a detailed exposition on the TFUMM (the task force report can be found at www.mtosmt.org/issues/mto.16.22.1/manifesto.pdf), it is a pertinent example as the task force report has raised fundamental issues about music education's framing disposition. Rather than attempting to "solve the problem" (which would be rather naïve considering the complexity of the environment) and to detail generalised but detailed curricular replacements, the task force represented an attempt to tell a new story, to focus on facilitating a new framing capacity. Without knowing it, they followed Forester's advice on a better balance between shorthand and short change and Manski's concerns with unchecked assumptions. In Myers' (2016, p. 295) words:

> The task force determined that its work would not be limited to potential modifications of the present system. Rather, TFUMM charged itself with rigorous analysis of assumptions underlying the current system and how those assumptions might be recast, or perhaps eliminated, and alternative assumptions articulated. TFUMM chose not to provide formulas for changes … [but to] encourage rich discourse around the preparation of career musicians in the twenty-first century.

To Myers (2016, p. 297), the process was framed with the intent "to help attenuate tendencies to polarise between innovation and convention in change discourse". For him, the challenge was to provide a way to move *towards* and not *against* something so that "higher education analyses may confront the extent to which legacy assumptions are adequate for a changing world and, concurrently, consider new assumptions that both embody transcendent values and reflect era-specific needs of society" (Myers, 2016, p. 296).

The two stories are concrete exemplifications of the conceptual framing presented in this chapter. They are manifestations of the three dispositions articulated earlier, showing the ability to: 1) generate interaction; 2) shift conversations; and 3) take risks that are critical for change. This is where policy and leadership meet: that is, in the difficult work of challenging and divesting assumptions while developing new stories and new dispositions to acknowledge and embrace change in how we think and act. In both stories, individuals, vision and needs were carefully and creatively developed while attending to the balance between shorthand and short change. What we see is a multiple approach that, as Wildavsky would suggest, involves *art* and *craft*.

Final Thoughts

The stories and the argument made in this chapter point to the fact that, central to leadership in music and in higher music education is what Bachrach and Baratz (1970) have called the mobilisation of bias. This notion can be defined as the understanding of the deeply political manner in which decisions are often made, as well as the capacity to think about leading as a process of building discourse coalitions and aggregating actors who might agree or disagree with specific points but who, most significantly, share social constructs. There is no doubt that leadership in the arts is a complex enterprise and that creative and adaptable thinking is indispensable, but leadership in higher music education needs to disrupt the tendency towards simply moving from one outcome to the next and from one practice to the next, without taking the time to consider how to become more willing to develop our own adaptable framing dispositions.

An adaptable framing disposition is worth our careful examination given that higher music education, just as many other complex social environments, is a nested context. This means that it contends with multiple and various contexts including the diversity of challenges in terms of employability, academic publications, performing opportunities, music in schools and communities, governmental agencies and private grant environs. Leaders might also think of a nested context in terms of a single programme, for instance:

Level one: a programme's own internal context.
Level two: the proximate context within which a programme operates: the university, region and certification environment.
Level three: the macro context – organisations that might employ graduates, the labour market in general, innovation spaces.
Level four: global shifts regarding, for instance, funding for orchestras; global shifts to high accountability in music education; or the manner in which virtual and online environments have changed and challenged access to art and culture.

Beyond the recognition that higher music education operates within a very complex environment, the point of this chapter is that as features of the nested contexts change, and they do regularly, "participants may discover that the repetition of a successful formula no longer works" (Rein & Schön, 1993, p. 154). This is where music in higher education finds itself today and has done so for the better part of the past 20 years. Consequently, in order for different and better outcomes to come about, there is a critical need for better framing, better process and better stories. According to Healey (1993, p. 234):

the modern idea of planning ... is centrally linked to concepts of democracy and progress. It centers on the challenges of finding ways in which citizens acting together can manage their collective concerns with respect to the sharing of space and time.

The over presence of leadership and policy as *craft*, as articulated by Wildavsky, has overshadowed the *artistic* – that is, the adaptable, intersubjective and dialogical – framings that are nevertheless available.

By approximating leadership to policy, I hope to have provided an opening on how to rethink both leadership and policy and, in the process, to help the higher music education community to find ways to develop their own framing capacity, their agency, and their own sense of how to become active contributors in their own unique environments.

References

Ball, S. J. (1993). What is policy? Texts, trajectories and toolboxes. *Discourse, 13*, 10–17.
Ball, S. J. (2005). *Education policy and social class: The selected works of Stephen J. Ball.* London: Routledge.
Bachrach, P., & Baratz, M. S. (1970). *Power and poverty: Theory and practice.* New York: Oxford University Press.
Boisot, M. (1995). Preparing for turbulence. In B. Garratt (Ed.), *Developing strategic thought* (pp. 29–63). London: McGraw-Hill.
Davies, B., & Ellison, L. (1999). *Strategic direction and development of the school.* London and New York: Routledge.
Dryzek, J. (1990). *Discursive democracy: Politics, policy and political science.* Cambridge: Cambridge University Press.
Dryzek, J. (1993). Policy analysis and planning: From science to argument. In F. Fischer & J. Forester (Eds.), *The argumentative turn in policy analysis and planning* (pp. 213–232). Durham and London: Duke University Press.
Dunn, W. N. (1981). *Public policy analysis: An introduction.* Englewood Cliffs, NJ: Prentice-Hall.
Fischer, F. & Forester, J. (Eds.) (1993). *The argumentative turn in policy analysis and planning.* Durham and London: Duke University Press.
Forester, J. (1993). Learning from practice stories: The priority of practical judgement. In F. Fischer & J. Forester (Eds.), *The argumentative turn in policy analysis and planning* (pp. 186–212). Durham and London: Duke University Press.
Grace, G. (1995). *School leadership: Beyond educational management: An essay in policy scholarship.* London: Falmer Press.
Gutmann, A. & Thompson, D. (1996). *Democracy and disagreement.* Cambridge, MA: Belknap Press of Harvard University Press.
Gutmann, A. & Thompson, D. (2004). *Why deliberative democracy?* Princeton: Princeton University Press.
Hamel, G., & Prahalad, C. K. (2010). *Strategic intent.* Boston, MA: Harvard Business Press.
Haussman, J., & Wise, D. (Eds.) (1985). *Social experimentation.* Chicago: University of Chicago Press.
Healey, P. (1993). Planning through debate: The communicative turn in planning theory. In F. Fischer & J. Forester (Eds.), *The argumentative turn in policy analysis and planning* (pp. 233–253). Durham and London: Duke University Press.

Herold, D. M., Fedor, D. B., Caldwell, S., & Liu, Y. (2008). The effects of transformational and change leadership on employees' commitment to a change: A multilevel study. *Journal of Applied Psychology, 93*(2), 346–357. doi: 10.1037/0021-9010.93.2.346.

Houston Symphony (May, 2015). Houston Symphony Diversity and Inclusion Case Study. *Pathways to a Reflective Orchestra Conference*, proceedings. Miami: New World Symphony.

Jennings, B. (1991). Possibilities of consensus: Toward democratic moral discourse. *Journal of Medicine and Philosophy, 16*(4), 447–463. doi: 10.1093/jmp/16.4.447.

Jenkins, H., Purushotma, R., Weigel, M., Clinton, K., & Robison, A. J. (2009). *Confronting the challenges of participatory culture: Media education for the 21st century*. Massachusetts: MIT Press.

Jones, P. (2017). Policy and higher education. In P. Schmidt & R. Colwell (Eds.), *Policy and the political life of music education* (pp. 242–251). New York: Oxford University Press.

Latham, G., & Ewing, R. (2018). Conversation around 21st century teachers' mindsets and roles. In G. Latham & R. Ewing (Eds.), *Generative conversations for creative learning* (pp. 115–129). London: Palgrave Macmillan.

Lees-Marshment, J. (2016). Deliberative political leaders: The role of policy input in political leadership. *Politics and Governance, 4*(2), 25–35. doi: 10.17645/pag.v4i2.560.

Majone, G. (1989). *Evidence, argument and persuasion in the policy process*. New Haven: Yale University Press.

Manski, C. (2007). *Identification for prediction and decision*. Cambridge, MA: Harvard University Press.

Manski, C. (2013). *Public policy in an uncertain world: Analysis and decisions*. Cambridge, MA: Harvard University Press.

Mintzberg, H., Ghoshal, J., & Quinn, S. (1995). *The strategy process*. Englewood Hills, NJ: Prentice Hall.

Moldavanova, A., & Goerdel, H. T. (2018). Understanding the puzzle of organizational sustainability: Toward a conceptual framework of organizational social connectedness and sustainability. *Public Management Review, 20*(1), 55–81. doi: 10.1080/14719037.2017.1293141.

Myers, D. (2016). Creativity, diversity and integration: Radical change in the bachelor of music degree. *Arts & Humanities in Higher Education, 15*(3–4), 293–307. doi: 10.1177/1474022216647378.

Myers D., Campbell P., Sarath E., Chattah, J., Higgins, L., Levine, V., Rudge, D., & Rice, T. (2014). Transforming music study from its foundations: A manifesto for progressive change in the undergraduate preparation of music majors. *Report of the Task Force on the Undergraduate Music Major*. Missoula, MT: College Music Society.

Nagel, A. (2010). Comparing education policy networks. In K. Martens, A. Nagel, M. Windzio, & A. Weymann (Eds.), *Transformation of education policy* (pp. 199–226). New York: Palgrave Macmillan.

National Endowment for the Arts. (2015). *When going gets tough: Barriers and motivations affecting arts attendance*. Report, National Endowment for the Arts.

Nettl, B. (1995). *Heartland excursions: Ethnomusicological reflections on schools of music*. Urbana: University of Illinois Press.

Rein, M., & Schön, D. (1993). Reframing policy discourse. In F. Fischer & J. Forester (Eds.), *The argumentative turn in policy analysis and planning* (pp. 145–166). Durham and London: Duke University Press.

Sabatier, P. (2007). *Theories of the policy process*. Boulder, CO: Westview Press.

Schmidt, P. (2013). Creativity as a complex practice: Developing a framing capacity in higher music education. In P. Burnard (Ed.), *Developing creativities in higher music education: International perspectives and practices*. New York: Oxford University Press.

Schmidt, P. (2017). Why policy matters: Developing a policy vocabulary in Music Education. In P. Schmidt and R. Colwell (Eds.), *Policy and the political life of music: Standpoints for understanding and action* (pp. 23–36). London: Routledge.

Stone, D. (2011). *Policy paradox: The art of political decision making.* New York: W.W. Norton & Company.
Torgerson, D. (2008). Contextual orientation in policy analysis: The contribution of Harold D. Lasswell. *Policy Sciences, 18*(3), 241–261. doi: 10.1007/BF00138911.
Wildavsky, A. (1988). *Speaking truth to power: The art and craft of policy analysis.* New York: Routledge.

V
Educating Professional Musicians: Gender Equality, Career Creativities and Strategies for Change in Institutional Leadership

PAMELA BURNARD

When you ask professional musicians, "How do you think your gender affected your chances and choices for a successful career in music?" there is significant variance in response. Some see their gender as always and inevitably relevant in every situation and others see it as important but less relevant. Gendering of students, gendering of academic and support roles, the lack of female role models and masculine creative practices are key themes evidenced in empirical literature on higher music education practices. Issues of inequity in institutional practices in higher music education are mirrored in the gendered work of music industries. In this chapter, Pierre Bourdieu's tools of habitus, capital and field provide rich conceptual tools for making sense of empirical and anecdotal evidence, circulating among professional musicians, of gendered practices in higher music education institutions and industry workplaces. I argue that new institutional leadership strategies are required to enable more equitable opportunity structures for women. I ask what such developments bode for future relations between educating professional musicians, gender equality and women trying to make their mark in higher music education degree programmes.

Higher Music Education and Gender

Higher education institutions such as music conservatoires and music departments in universities evolve academic hierarchies of knowledge and learning cultures in which institutional leadership models the making of decisions about people, programmes, practices, performance specialism and professionalism at a high level of complexity and under great pressure to demonstrate world-class excellence (Perkins, 2013). Yet studies of work in the music industries have revealed the perpetuation of gender inequalities (Scharff, 2015). So, why is music in higher education still performing gender bias, still amplifying and reinforcing ideologies of gender inequalities, still gender stereotyping, and privileging certain sexual orientations over others (Born & Devine, 2015)?

In a time of too many graduates for too few positions and in a context where applicants have similar levels of educational capital, gender is one of the factors that influence graduate career trajectories. Yet, as one of several reports on the role of gender diversity in higher music education concludes, too little space is given to diverse voices that counter entrenched gender and class biases in academia or that challenge academic conventions (Bogdanovic, 2015).

Despite the proliferation of interest in gender and career creativities research in higher education, the problem of what constitutes equitable participation in and gendering of particular musical creativities in conservatoire education – the complex ways gendered formations and gender politics play out in relation to career creativities, and the implications for institutional leadership – remains unresolved.

A diversity of discourses and practices constitutes creativities that generate successful career trajectories in improvisational creativity, compositional creativity and performance creativity; however, the dominant romantic values of Western art music favour the dominant cultural myth of the "artist as male hero" (Bain, 2004, p. 172). As Taylor and Littleton (2012, p. 181) argue, "this probably derives from the celebrated named figures of European art, especially in the 19th century, the vast majority of whom were men". Following from this, aspiring professional musicians often see the individualistic, competitive dimension whereas popular music favours the social dimensions of collaborative creativity, and jazz music favours collective creativity. Perspectives on *who* is professionally successful in creating and innovating music production, *where* it is being made, and for *whom*, and the processes of exclusion/inclusion in relation to gendered formations and other intersecting differences in higher music education are as significant as the underrepresentation of gender diversity.

Career preparation for and representation of gender diversity in practices such as sound producing, sampling, resampling, mixing, mashing, coding, DJing, sonic art and song-writing are as important as composing, arranging, improvising and performing. What kinds of collaborative, intercultural and interdisciplinary venturing underpin any analysis of the gendered work of professional musicians at the beginning of the third millennium?

The Challenge of Gender Bias

We have few institutional models of leadership discourses other than those that preserve the typical conservatoire tradition of music training/education, self-perpetuating and feeding into systems that create themselves in their own image, with dominant constructions of gender that are rational from one viewpoint, but that prove exploitative from another. How do institutional leaders critique and monitor, pay attention to and improve the relationship between gendered inequalities that are reproduced through institutional structures and pedagogies in the context of current political struggles and divisions?

Reporting on masculine domination in private-sector popular music performance education in England, Dylan Smith (2015) argues for more critique and scholarship, consciousness-raising and politically directed action, in taking account of all of the effects of gender inequalities and gendered practices, structures and assumptions in higher music education. In short, and as argued by Bennett (2013) and Bjorck (2010), we are less creative and less distinctive and "less fundamentally imaginative in the arts and the sciences (including the social sciences) than we were in the nineteenth century" (Murphy, 2015, p. 84). We need higher music education institutions who are preparing graduates for employment in the music and creative industries to critically engage with the role that gender (and social class) as well as career creativities and related capitals have on both the aspirations and expectations of newly graduated music professionals.

According to the United Kingdom Department of Culture, Media and Sport (DCMS), women hold 36.7 per cent of jobs in the creative industries and 47.1 per cent in the UK economy as a whole. According to the 2012 employment census of the UK's creative media industries, women's representation in the creative media industries has increased. However, black, Asian and minority ethnic (BAME) representation has declined since 2009. These data suggest a creative industries workforce that is overwhelmingly white and mostly male, a finding duplicated in Born and Devine (2015). Studies that report on new modes of creative work (that is to say, diverse creativities), ingenious technologies in sound art and music, aesthetics and building blocks of new generations of gender constructions, gender diversity role models, career trajectories and diverse musical creativities are an imperative (see Burnard, 2012; Connell & Pearse, 2015).

The argument advanced here in response to the challenge of gender bias concerns human capital career creativities, from its outmoded, individual and singular phenomena to the perpetuation of gender-related values that bias life as a professional musician in favour of one sex or sexual orientation over another. In higher music education and the music industry, the management of gender biases continues to plague in ways over which academic institutions exercise influence and power (Berry & Loke, 2011). To be successful, creative workers need to maximise their potential by drawing on institutional specialisation and employing a potent mix of human capitals as professional musicians. So, how do they accrue more capitals and use them to play "the games of society" differently (Moore, 2008, p. 104)?

Gender Messaging, Career Creativities and the Insidious Human Capitals Divide

Classical music is a field strongly defined by role models and mentor relationships with few broadly visible women and LGTBQ communities represented at the top. The issue of gender messaging – in academia, the media and culture more widely – seriously influences the landscape in which young female and LGTBQ musicians grow their careers and career creativities. The social and cultural sites and activity systems in which diverse creativities manifest in the creative workforce (Conor, Gill, & Taylor, 2015), the music business (Bennett, 2015), higher music education (Bogdanovic, 2015) and, for popular music, early career professional musicians (Dylan Smith, 2015), are increasingly complex.

The gender inequalities that characterise how and where music is being created and consumed (Born & Devine, 2015), how and where gender inequalities in music careers are stereotypically identified and reinforced in education (Bull, 2015; Armstrong, 2011) and how and where networks as social capital in career creativities are valued (Bennett & Burnard, 2016) are widely acknowledged. Yet, to date, there has been far too little consideration of the significance of existing gender inequalities and the lack of gender diversity and role models in the training of professional musicians, as Bull's (2015) research on contemporary youth music education demonstrates.

In the world (or habitus) of the internet, e-learning and virtual realities, we also have virtual fields, the fields of the media and *globally networked* or *spatialised internet fields* in which to make digital and mobile music. The gendered messaging and dynamics of self-promotion sees female musicians disadvantaged and often unable or unwilling to pursue self-promotion in these fields. Drawing on 64 in-depth interviews with female, classically trained musicians in London and Berlin, Scharff (2015, p. 99) reported that "reflecting the entrepreneurial ethos of the cultural industries, many musicians described themselves as products that had to be sold. At the same time, they disliked the practice". Female musicians engage in a range of discursive strategies to negotiate and secure their identities as female artists. In the context of powerful gender norms which feature prominently in contemporary classical and popular music, self-marketing and the economisation of the self is registered, negotiated and lived out at a psychosocial gendered level.

The common ground among *social perspectives* (on collaborative and communal, collective and digital creativities) is that they are based on the conviction that forms of authorship and the practice of diverse creativities is vital to all societies, to all fields, domains and cultures. But who do we/you/others typically see as role models in the music professions we aspire to be successful in? Where are all the women? Where are all the female music producers, conductors and composers?

Scharff (2015) asks how female, classically trained musicians in London and Berlin find employment. Key findings include associations with "pushy behaviour that conflicts with normative expectations that women are modest" (Scharff, 2015, p. 97) and the description of self-promotion as a commercial activity and regarded as unartistic. The other key issue is the sexualisation of female musicians.

Social, cultural and psychological perspectives on higher music education are not, as some have suggested, just political; they should represent the lived meanings of diverse and new forms of musical, economic and social capital. If the cultural capital in music bestowed by higher music education institutions is too narrow and concentrates on one group over another, or indeed lacks sufficient representation of women, how can institutions inspire, embody and accelerate change in stereotypically gendered views, such as whether women can be great composers, conductors, producers and creators of music?

Women's careers in music and their human capital career creativities are, arguably, and often, dependent on male support and sponsorship. Unsurprisingly, the discourses that interrogate the white, male, middle-class hegemony are largely absent from higher music education. We need to understand where inequalities are perpetuated by structures, networks and gendered positioning in and across fields that do not allow women access or offer role models.

What might gendered work be in the human capital career creativities of professional musicians? What constitutes gendered work? How do professional musicians draw on institutional specialisations and what they learn as the human capitals of artists, authors, composers, entrepreneurs, managers, designers, cultural producers, culture bearers, academics and teachers? What are the official discourses from governments at both local and national levels that create the linear and meritocratic relationship between higher music education institutions and graduate employment? What data do we need to address gender politics and gender equity in the training of professional musicians?

Taken together, these differing human capitals for creating music form an integral part of generative social and musical practices in the lived-in world: generative in that they describe acts of creation or co-creation; social in that they each occur within social groups or partnerships; and highly gendered in the ways they privilege men and disadvantage women; the lived-in world connotes real practices and settings that manifestly broaden the remit of the term "musical" creativity and its invariable use in the singular and gendered sense. These diverse creativities involve capital conversion strategies and volumes of capital – hence those with limited asset structures entering into the music industries (along with the education sectors) need to be able to maintain or advance their position in the field by converting career creativities in terms of what musicians can and do create, reproduce and transform. The costs of privilege are high (Burke, 2016).

Green's seminal 1977 book *Music, Gender, Education* presents a theory of gendered musical meaning as it is manifested through women's historical musical practices and the gendered discourses surrounding them. Yet, more than 40 years on, a visionary new way to think about ideas on the gender politics of music still remains to be found. The imperative for the employability of new graduates is to have strategies that ensure graduate success equally for men and women. What follows in the next section outlines a range of music career creativities developed by successful professional musicians working in harshly competitive music industries.

Gender, Professional Capital, Career Creativities and Institutional Change Matters

At a time of too many graduates for too few jobs and in a context where applicants have similar levels of educational and professional capital, experiences of gendered cultures in workplaces are a significant factor that influences graduate career trajectories. When asked how they think their gender affected their working lives, professional musicians more often see their gender as always and inevitably relevant. Women remain severely underrepresented in many mainstream music industries. Gendered expectations, having fewer opportunities to experience internships and lacking respect and confidence can lead newly graduated musicians to begin to doubt that they will fit into a professional culture. What music graduates need is recognition of the importance of professional capital and career creativities as the driving force for preparing them for, and sustaining them in, the gendered cultures they must navigate. This is largely unrecognised (Bennett & Burnard, 2016).

Gendered workplace cultures cause threats to the professional status of both men and women. Aspiring music professionals enter the academy having already been exposed to messages about their gender and sexuality from their parents, their schooling and society. The transition from one stage of education to the other is an important but also risky point in a student's life. This risk is only increased by learning to tolerate stereotypically masculine cultures and the marginalisation of stereotypically feminine interests, which can be both inhibiting and undermining.

When considering ways to enhance the professional training of tomorrow's industry-savvy musicians about human capital career creativities and gender politics, we must first recognise what it is that the contemporary, real-world practices of professional musicians reveal. We know there is a multiplicity of musical creativities that empower and characterise successful musicians for whom, for example, entrepreneurial creativity can act as a catalyst for an innovative and often experimental set of practices (Burnard & Haddon, 2015). Equally, career-positioning creativity involves judging how and where to position oneself within and across industries (Haddon & Burnard, 2017; Burnard & Haddon, 2016). This type of industry awareness and knowing how the industry sector works emerges as an important capital is critical. Whether their ambition is to develop specific creativities, such as improvisational and song-writing creativities, or enterprise and entrepreneurial creativities, successful musicians must experience and navigate a diversity of human capital career creativities to define successful career paths (Bennett, 2008; Bennett & Burnard, 2016).

The Research Study

The data in this chapter come from a study of 19 musicians aged between 22 and 62 years, part of a sample drawn from a larger multidimensional study involving 47 participants, all of whom are visible members of musical communities recognised by wider society. Drawn from diverse sites and settings, these professional musicians agreed to be interviewed about their creative practices, career paths, institutional and industry experiences and human capital career creativities.

In conducting an inquiry that seeks to advance sociological views and understand accounts of practices, I work with Bourdieu's concept of habitus, which recognises that individuals, just as with institutions, constitute a complex amalgam of agency and structure (Bourdieu, 1993). The impact a cultural group or social class has on an individual's behaviour is mediated through an institution (Reay, David, & Ball, 2001). Field is understood as designated bundles of relations; a particular social setting where class and gender dynamics take place, for example, a classroom or a workplace, or the field of higher music education, as sites of practice. One's habitus interacts with the field of action, which is "endowed with a specific gravity which imposes on all the objects and agents which enter in it" (Bourdieu & Wacquant, 1992, p. 16). Capital can be thought of as the resources and rewards available in these fields of action and social space. These resources are accrued purposively by people and are operationalised. For Bourdieu, capital is not readily available to everyone on the same basis.

The idea of a narrative of practice involved three to six interviews over 12 months, during which time bringing together sociological and phenomenological readings beginning with analytic induction to enhance data by examining similarities and differences and then pattern analysis with multiple readings of each case using Bourdieu's tools. His impact on the sociology of music taste, in particular, has been profound, his ideas directly informing our understanding of how musical preferences reflect and reproduce inequalities between social classes, ethnic groups and diverse genders (see Burnard, Hofvander-Trulsson, & Soderman, 2015).

In order to put to use Bourdieu's trilogy of thinking tools – habitus, capital and field – as understood through the practices constituted by the social and cultural actions of the participants, I employed two distinct phases of data collection. The first explored human creative capitals in detail. To understand how these capitals might play out in broader terms, the second phase explored their creative work and detailed mappings of their creativities in practice.

Several early career music professionals and their educational trajectories were featured in this study (see Burnard, 2012). The following quote by a young singer-songwriter, Roshi, articulates the significance at entrance to higher education and the institutional habitus and the role of gender.

> It was when I went to music college that I think gender started playing a role in my decision-making. I started having lessons from a world-class pianist. It was here that I learned that things are not the same for men and women in the music business. It was at music college that I was made to have a rethink about myself when my teacher told me that "You're not bad. Look, you're even musical, and you got into in the college, OK because you're musically creative, but you don't really have much technique, and, as a woman in this profession, if you really want to make it as a pianist you need to do more than just practise for six hours a day, and do your scales. You need to do this and more." OK, so I wasn't a child prodigy who'd played a piece I'd composed myself at six years old with hands like Liszt! … I'd missed getting the kind of rigorous training which people need to have if they're going to become successful women classical players and go on to be a world-class women concert pianist. So, I changed to composition in my second year, because I thought that would be more creative, more inclusive. But in a way that too had its own dogma.

For Bourdieu, the family is the key player in habitus formation, placing parents as key actors in forming their children's attitudes towards education and choice of profession. Aspirations to create new works in Western art music is stereotypically associated with an inspired individual – usually considered to be a genius male composer – sitting at the piano in his study painstakingly moulding or divinely pouring musical ideas into a masterwork; or an instrumentalist/singer who requires instrumental/vocal virtuosity to make it as a performer rather than, or including, being also a sound engineer in producing their own recordings. These are specific manifestations of myths in music, myths about music, and gendered myths about music's creativities and production.

The extent to which parents – particularly working-class families – know or understand how to play the game and the school's role in habitus formation is key along with the role played by institutions, which impacts directly on students' aspirations and expectations as they move from secondary (high school) to higher education destinations. The serious lack of career advice, and development of career creativities which can counter the stereotyping of female artists in society, perpetuates greater and unregulated inequality (Bennett & Burnard, 2016).

In the discussion and labelling of women's music and female composers (never seen, however, is the equivalent "male" composers) we see continued use of gender stereotypes by critics' telling use of vocabulary, such as described by Pasler (2008) in the "ironies of gender" and voiced by this female composer, Liza:

> There are some major effects of socialization and gender stereotyping from which you get so many negative and disruptive messages; you can easily lose contact with and confidence in your own visions and voice … there's even more pressure now with new media and technologies which is about moving away from the highly individual, with an overriding message about conforming to a utilitarian, economically and gender driven view of things … society is a very big teacher.
> (Burnard, 2012, p. 139)

While it is unwise to generalise, even within this small sample, these narratives resonate strongly with previous literature, which suggest that the strategies undertaken by graduates, illustrated by the direct influence of aspirations and expectations coupled with the influence of both family and the educational system, enables aspiring professional musicians to negotiate the graduate employment field in light of the gendered character of particular professions. Institutions need to be contemporary environments in which diverse creativities are embedded, cultivated, modelled and resourced, creating career capital to successfully navigate and negotiate the graduate employment field.

A critical feature of successful institutions is the ingredient of leadership. Music institutions, typically, feature academic hierarchies of knowledge, a context in which leaders make decisions about the forms of capital (economic, cultural, social, and symbolic) that feature across graduate employment practices of professional musicians. We see gender politics play out in higher music education institutional programmes, practices, performance specialism and professionalism at a high level of complexity. We see higher music educational institutions under great pressure to demonstrate world-class excellence and global reach. Additionally, we recognise that there is little space given to transcend or counter entrenched gender (and class) biases and social reproduction in academia. The challenge is that people do not take kindly to being told that structural barriers greater than themselves can prevent or influence their life histories and trajectories (Bennett & Burnard, 2016).

Recognising gender as an axis of power imbalance and inequality has been reported in studies illustrate the gendered representations of creative work (Burnard, 2012, 2013; Taylor & Littleton, 2012). In a report commissioned by the National Association of Music in Higher Education in the United Kingdom, gender issues were examined in higher music education departments, schools and institutions (Bogdanovic, 2015).

In line with several other reports on internships and freelancing in the creative industries, including the film and television industries, the gendering of roles, gender division of labour and gendered workplace practices and behaviours play a big part of creative labour, resulting in the persistent underrepresentation of women in many areas, particularly at senior management and policy-making levels (Conor et al., 2015). For example, gender inequalities and gender inequalities including gendered forms of discrimination are perpetuated in the boardrooms of higher music education.

The number of women working at executive committee levels in the music professions or large corporates remains a bottleneck for senior female executives. Men and women do not just experience gendered motivations for participating in music industries, pre-existing gender-based narratives also influence the division of labour and responsibilities in the ways they are recruited, access power or are promoted (Bogdanovic, 2015). In most industries, perceived gender biases in the evaluation of creativity negatively affect women's work experiences and their chances of success (Proudfoot, Kay, & Koval, 2015).

The underrepresentation and subordination of women in the music profession is linked to an interrelated set of gendered forms of power relations and social practices (Connell, 2005). We see how gendered power relations and stereotypical gender identity play out in the recollections of institutional gendered experiences and trajectories.

> Pippa: I was always seen as "the classical musician" who had got lost … my experiences of doing music at university are peppered with painful scenarios … I was always put together in tricky ensembles … I had to work with a drummer who was second study, so he wasn't fantastic on drums and yet he insisted on what we should and shouldn't play. Then there was a guy on guitar who just wanted to play soul and R&B and another guy, who insisted we play metal. I felt like I was caught in the middle of a genre war … They'd come in to rehearsals with different dress styling saying "this is the sound of me" … I wanted to prove to them that I could sing anything and that I could play anything and most of all, that I could stick up for myself, but in a nice way, without destroying their egos

> ... I learned a lot about how you define yourself as a female musician in the music business. But it was hard.
>
> (Burnard, 2012, p. 80)

How can music institutions address stereotypically gendered views, such as the representation of gender diversity rather than structural inequalities that characterise occupations seen to belong to a previous and outdated gendered model? There has been far too little consideration of the significance of gender inequalities for burgeoning, precariously employed music graduates and a new vision of gender equity performed in the higher music education sector. We need a new vision of leadership that is driven by a belief that teaching is about enabling learning communities to understand where gender inequalities are perpetuated by structures, networks and gendered positioning in and across institutional structures and industry fields that do not enable gender diversity or offer role models. Where is peddling of power exercised in the various forms of capital that perpetuate gender dynamics, driving patterns of work segregation according to sexual orientation? How does gender contribute to and/or restrict music undergraduates' and graduates' musical actions and interactions? What are the gender-related issues that impact on authorial practices in, and principles of, diverse creativities? What needs to change? How do we go about collapsing the uncertainty of institutional habits and perpetuating mindsets, so as facilitate change agendas?

Leadership and Institutional Change

The influence of leadership and the gender relations that come into being are dimensions that facilitate or impede the creativities of faculty staff and students. A structure of relations, along with gendered dynamics and gendered modes of behaviour, define possibilities for action and their consequences. The centrality of gender models and the empowering potential of diverse creativities to sustain an institution's competitive edge and adapt to the changing landscape, need to be themes woven through all levels of strategic decision-making and professional judgment in music institutions. The scope and dimension of creativities as a field of leadership inquiry and action is evidenced in the growing recognition that effective *leadership* needs to combat the unremitting perpetuation of the gender politics of music through education.

Widening the net of engaged colleagues that recognise gender inequality strengthens the likelihood and extent of potential collegial engagement in decision-making and institutional change. Our ability to imagine, and then invent, institutional change is one of our greatest assets. To be successful, we need to recognise and harness our ability to influence gendered musical practices and gendered creativities, both within our experiences of music and in our constructions of ourselves, our colleagues and our students; we need to continually adapt and invent creativities for accomplishing institutional change, leading to equitable gender practices in an ever-changing and increasingly complex world. What, then, are the questions we need to be asking within our institutions? How do the social construction of gender and the regimes of power that intersect with gender, race and class manifest in your institution and how much does this reflect the music industry?

Professional musicians work within and beyond the music industries. New industries overlap the music and creative industries. However, what constitutes the music industry is rapidly changing (Hesmondhalgh & Baker, 2011). The music industries are part of a generic entertainment industry wherein major corporations position themselves according to their expected market shares. A nearly 20-year-old model of the music industry is given in Zelinksy, Leyshon, Matless and Revill (1999). This features distinctive, yet overlapping, musical networks, one of which is the network of creativity within which music is created, performed and recorded. This network includes an army of stakeholders and brokers working in the record industry with producers, sound engineers, recording companies, managers, lawyers and so on. But this model is a patriarchal one and, like the vast majority of music that surrounds us, is produced by men. It is one of a multiplicity of musical networks in which women musicians must operate, although there are of course exceptions.

It is, therefore, critical that committing to gender equality means building understanding, respect and stronger relationships between colleagues, irrespective of gender orientations, rendering diverse musical career creativities in higher music education and in institutional leadership. The multiple human capital career creativities inscribed in the practices of successful professional musicians working in the music industry (and across creative industries), that graduates need to develop, include: social network and community building, career positioning and position taking and space-claiming across fields, along with self-monitoring and seeking out mentorship and role models (see Bennett & Burnard, 2016). The effect of these facilitative skills and practices has the potential to fuel and sustain the challenges and changes that characterise multiple, concurrent roles within portfolio careers through to the kinds of work that transcends fields, thus enabling access, movement and progress across the creative and music industries.

As shown in Figure 5.1, the field-to-field interactions of music are enacted and driven by the logic of the fields of music and the interrelationships between and within fields are themselves bounded. Figure 5.1 offers a static representation of a dynamic and ever-changing process. Composers who work with contemporary ensembles and depend on collaborative projects between musicians and media sponsors also move within the fields of industries, commerce, music, cultural production and technology. Audio sound designers working in the gaming industry often come up with products that give consumers what they want, thereby driving revenues within the fields of commerce, technology and industry. DJs and originals bands are field participants in the field of popular music, as well as in the field of music technology, all of which are male-dominated.

We know that professional musicians' professional capital career creativities arise within and depend upon the legitimising frameworks of public opinion, conventions and gatekeepers. By its very embodiment in the plurality of fields of action (see Figure 5.1) as sites of endless change, "where agents and institutions constantly struggle according to the regularities and the rules constitutive of this space of play" (Bourdieu & Wacquant, 1992, p. 102), professional musicians are constantly repositioning themselves across multiple fields.

We know there is a very low level of female representation in the gaming industry (6 per cent), compared to the music industry, which sees a figure of 32 per cent women and 68 per cent men (Hesmondhalgh & Baker, 2015). Whether working as a DJ, music producer, classical musician and/or in the rap industry, all of which involves working in male-dominated spaces, the common ground among social perspectives is that the rules of fields represent the lived meanings (remits, trends, dominant logics and locations of work across different industries) in the gender-specific issues that mark the music industry. There is, however, at the present time, little interaction or overlap between educational institutional systems and the "real-world", insidious gender divide in being a professional musician working in the music industries.

The reality for graduates, then, is that in order to prepare for work in diverse professional settings they need diverse strategic practices and ways to reflexively name, pin down or even evaluate the characterising or defining features of their own diverse creativities. Why reflexivity? Because it seeks to know, and at the same time situate, ways of thinking about who we are and what we do as creative workers, and how we make meaning from being a professional musician. Thus, we might say that *individual creativity* allies itself as a *form of authorship* which comprises *self-contained individualism* and assumes the high-art model where mediating modalities form the impetus and endeavour of the individual grounded in *"self-responsibility"*.

It is commonly believed, especially with classical contemporary composers, who often narrate *practice principles* filled with the dualism of individual-inward and socially constituted-outward practices that individual creativity is defined by the intent of composing. An example is the Australian composer Liza Lim, who frequently works with ELISION, a contemporary music chamber ensemble that specialises in contemporary classical music, concentrating on the creation and presentation of new works that create opportunities for experimentation (see www.elision.org.au). Liza values "individual creativity" and offers this description of her form of authorship:

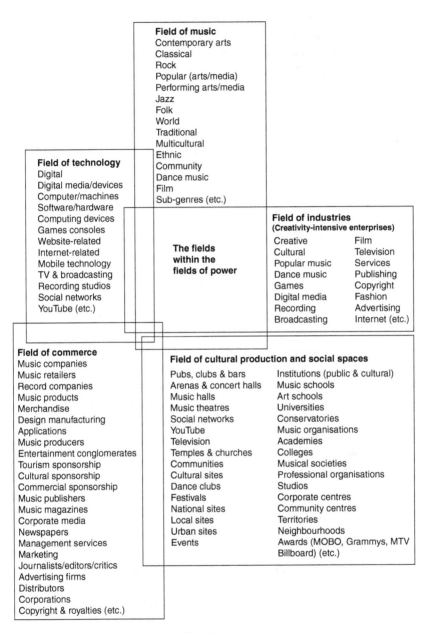

Figure 5.1 The fields within the fields of power

> Working with ELISION offers me all types of opportunities for just plunging in and trialling and testing ideas ... that's why I said that the contact with performers was absolutely critical, because for me this type of creative laboratory is crucial for finding out what works and what doesn't work, in a very concrete sense ... And it's not just the technical, but it's the interpersonal level as well that's really important here... I don't lose contact with my own specific individual creativity ... there's even more pressure now with new media and technologies which is about moving away from the highly individual ... I think that individual expression in all areas of composition even if it only holds a very tiny place in the bigger picture has value.
>
> (Burnard, 2012, pp. 138–139)

In contrast, *collaborative (or group) creativity* is more often grounded in a *form of authorship*, which involves a *shared-responsibility* where actual practices arise from, or in, joint creative endeavours. Practice principles are generated from joint thinking and from sustained, shared struggles to achieve shared musical outcomes and ownership. Mediating modalities depend on a shared system of creative conventions; no one can create music without first internalising the rules and conventions of the domain – a kind of codified practice with emphasis placed on the *significance of relationships*, on synergy in relationships, partnerships and on valuing the other, which characterises the work of originals bands (Burnard, 2012).

Similarly, *communal creativity* involves a form of authorship grounded in a *socially distributed, relationship-oriented* view, often the characteristic practice of community musicians. The mediating modalities are determined and play into the meaning of one's self and self-development *in relation to others* rather than being individualised; the practice principles are developed through *mutuality, interaction* and *exchange* between actors within wider circles of community and creativity and are seen as an ongoing accomplishment of that process (Burnard, 2012; Lapidaki, de Groot, & Stagkos, 2012).

It is here that the framework for understanding professional capital career creativities provides opportunities to reflexively situate this knowing and bridge the divide between academia and the public sphere and gendered practices. It encourages us to examine how manifold forms of creativities are observable and are located and applied in practice. Understanding the gendered nature of the music industries and becoming a successful creative worker are shaped by individual experience. This is where personal biography and gendered practices constitute considerable barriers and become problematic. There is often a gendered nature to the more entrepreneurial elements of the strongly gendered discourse, with talk of aggressive, strong-willed characters, hustling and fighting battles – which often forms a subtext to descriptions of the "particular type of person" that is being sought (Bennett, 2015, p. 48).

The demands of moving across multiple fields for professional musicians means that they engage multiple forms of capital and do not operate in isolation. Rather, each field operates in relation to other fields as an arena of struggle and success, in the appropriation and negotiation of less gendered perceptions, pathways and practices that are more inclusive. Professional and strategic practices through which musicians learn to develop contemporary identities and engage in creative work are interconnected and complex. Higher music education institutions need to recognise how professional musicians position themselves and understand the dynamics of career trajectories in order to navigate careers, to exercise professional capitals and understand the importance of human capital career creativities within these fields of action. All of this may well depend upon how higher music education institutions recognise and practise gender equity.

Developing Passionate Leadership for the 21st Century

In a deeply pluralistic world, where gender domination is seen as morally reprehensible, gender stereotyping and inequalities are ongoing injustices that undergraduates and professional musicians experience. Revised institutional leadership strategies are essential to attending to and doing more than merely disrupting the pervasive and deeply entrenched imbalance of power in the social relations between men and women as professional musicians working in the music, creative, digital and/or cultural industries (Comunian & Gilmore, 2016).

To accomplish this end, gender diversity, epistemological and hierarchical assumptions need to be challenged in an ethical approach to passionate leadership in higher music institutions based on democratic educational relationships. Leadership that is passionate about caring emphasises visions that listen to and act on a variety of voices: an articulation that addresses the kinds of questions about orientations and how bodies and objects become oriented through their interrelations; that links political and social questions about gender, sexuality and race, for example, as ways of asking what our orientations towards diverse gender should look like and how and where will we find support for which Ahmed (2006, p. 178) argues "a politics of disorientation puts other objects within reach, those that might, at first glance, seem awry".

Higher music education executives and senior leadership teams need to step up and invoke positive change. Actions for leaders include gender equity training that is foundational to the learning culture of the institution and sending clear signals in a gender-inclusive way, by rewarding and supporting inclusive behaviour and interventions facilitated and authorised by a clear stance on the culture of the institution; this needs to be carried through into systems, structures, curriculum and teaching.

Teaching diverse creativities has intrinsic value in preparing women for careers in the profession of music and for the demands of the 21st century and ensuring that they are appropriately supported in rising to this challenge. There is also the development of the new skills and strategic capacities of bestowed gift-giving creativity. This is a type of entrepreneurial capital that involves engaging in a range of discursive strategies to negotiate and secure support for launching, supporting and enhancing careers. It is given away in forms as such mentorship and *pro bono* work.

Community-building creativity represents new practices of enhancing professional networks, repertoires and building new communities of practices. Then, again, there is the all-important rigour of establishing and sustaining a creative career and professional capital creativities called *inspiration-forming creativity*, which includes role models, inspirational figures and supporters. These can be significant others who have played a role in creative and business choices and who have the ability to adapt to financial pressures and fragmented careers and narrate their work, articulating a sense of agency with who I am and who I wish to become, and connect, showing biographical/personal continuity in a labour market in which work-histories are often erratic and discontinuous.

This chapter contributes to the drive to see consideration of the significance of gender and gendered practices as anchored in the real world and increasingly featured in educational settings. It also calls for radical institutional change, rooted not in mystified consciousness that only need to be enlightened but in dispositions that are aware of the structure of the domination of which they are the product. The education of professional musicians requires us to reposition our institutions to effect lasting societal change, starting with the raising of consciousness concerning all the actions and effects of gendering that are embedded in institutionalised cultures, and the specifics of gender injustice, systemic sexism, and gendered formations, in specific institutional and industry settings.

Fixing these issues alone will not be enough to support the careers of ambitious women. The culture in music institutions and the workplace needs to change. That needs the collaboration of men. We need to develop specific programmes, review the way we teach, and develop their confidence to face the challenges they can expect to meet in the workplace. As educators of professional musicians, we need to take political action against all the effects of gendering and commence a never-ending campaign of consciousness-raising for the progressive withering away of gender injustices.

References

Ahmed, S. (2006). *Queer phenomenology: Orientations, objects, others*. London: Duke University Press.
Armstrong, A. (2011). *Technology and the gendering of music education*. Farnham: Ashgate.
Bain, A. (2004). Female artistic identity in place: the studio. *Social and Cultural Geography, 5*(2), 171–193.
Bennett, D. (2008). *Understanding the classical music profession: The past, the present and strategies for the future*. Aldershot: Ashgate.
Bennett, D. (2013). The role of career creativities in developing identity and becoming expert selves. In P. Burnard (Ed.), *Developing creativities in higher music education: International perspectives and practices* (pp. 224–244). London: Routledge.
Bennett, D., & Burnard, P. (2016). Human capital career creativities for creative industries work: Lessons underpinned by Bourdieu's tools for thinking. In R. Communion & A. Gilmore (Eds.), *Higher education and the creative economy* (pp. 123–142). London: Routledge.
Bennett, T. (2015). *Music business: Evaluating the "vocational turn" in music education*. London: UK Music.
Berry, J., & Loke, G. (2011). Improving the degree attainment of black and ethnic students. *Equality and Inclusion Unit, Higher Education Academy*. Retrieved from www.ecu.ac.uk/wp-content/uploads/external/improving-degree-attainment- bme.pdf.
Bjorck, C. (2010). *Claiming space: Discourses on gender, popular music and social change*. Gothenburg: University of Gothenburg.
Bogdanovic, D. (2015). *Gender and equality in music higher education: A report commissioned and funded by the National Association for Music in Higher Education*. Retrieved from www.namhe.ac.uk/publications/reports/gender_and_equality_2015.pdf.
Born, G., & Devine, K. (2015). Music technology, gender and class: Digitization, educational and social change in Britain. *Twentieth-Century Music, 12*(2), 135–172. doi: 10.1017/S1478572215000018.
Bourdieu, P. (1993). *The field of cultural production*. Cambridge: Polity.
Bourdieu, P., & Wacquant, L. (1992). *An invitation to reflexive sociology*. Chicago: University of Chicago Press.
Bull, A. (2015) *The musical body: How gender and class are reproduced among young people playing classical music in England*. Unpublished PhD thesis. London: Goldsmiths, University of London.
Burke, C. (2016). *Culture, capitals and graduate futures*. London: Routledge.
Burnard, P. (2012). *Music creativities in practice*. Oxford: Oxford University Press.
Burnard, P. (Ed.). (2013). *Developing creativities in higher education: International perspectives and practices*. London: Routledge.
Burnard, P., & Haddon, L. (Eds.). (2015). *Activating diverse musical creativities: Teaching and learning in higher music education*. London: Bloomsbury.
Burnard, P., Hofvander Trulsson, Y., & Soderman, J. (2015). *Bourdieu and the sociology of music*. Farnham, Surrey: Ashgate.
Comunian, R., & Gilmore, A. (Eds.). (2016). *Higher education and the creative economy: Beyond the campus*. London: Routledge.
Connell, R. (2005). *Masculinities USA*. Berkeley, CA: University of California Press.
Connell, R., & Pearse, R. (2015). *Gender in world perspective*. Cambridge: Polity Press.
Conor, B., Gill, R., & Taylor, S. (2015). *Gender and creative labour*. London: Wiley.
Duggan, L. (2003). *The twilight of equality: Neoliberalism, cultural politics and the attack on democracy*. Boston: Beacon.
Dylan Smith, G. (2015). Masculine domination in private-sector popular music performance education in England. In P. Burnard, Y. Hofvander Turlsson, & J. Soderman (Eds.) *Bourdieu and the sociology of music education* (pp. 61–78). Surrey, England: Ashgate.

Green, L. (1977). *Music, gender, education*. Cambridge: Cambridge University Press.
Haddon, E., & Burnard, P. (Eds.). (2017). *Creative teaching for creative learning in higher music education*. Abingdon, Oxon: Routledge.
Hesmondhalgh, D., & Baker, S. (2011). *Creative labour: Media work in three cultural industries*. London: Routledge.
Hesmondhalgh, D., & Baker, S. (2015). Sex, gender and work segregation in the cultural industries. In B. Conor, R. Gill & S. Taylor (Eds.) *Gender and creative labour* (pp. 23–26). London: Wiley, Blackwell.
Hussain, M. (2016). Why is my curriculum so white? Retrieved from www.nus.org.uk/en/news/why-is-my-curriculum-white/.
Lapidaki, E., de Groot, R., & Stagkos, P. (2012). Communal creativity as socio-musical practice. In G. MacPherson & G. Welch (Eds.). *Oxford handbook of music education* (pp. 371–388). Oxford: Oxford University Press.
Moore, R. (2008). Capital. In M. Grenfell (Ed.), *Pierre Bourdieu: Key concepts* (pp. 101–117). Stocksfield: Acumen.
Murphy, P. (2015). *Universities and innovation economies: The creative wasteland of post-industrial society*. Farnham, Surrey: Ashgate Publishing.
Pasler, J. (2008). *Writing through music: Essay on music, culture and politics*. Oxford: Oxford University Press.
Perkins, R. (2013). Hierarchies and learning in conservatoire: Exploring what students learn through the lens of Bourdieu. *Research Studies in Music Education*, 35(2), 197–212. doi: 10.1177/1321103X13508060.
Proudfoot, D., Kay, A., & Koval, C. (2015). A gender bias in the attribution of creativity. *Psychological Science*, 26(11), 1751–1761. doi: 10.1177/0956797615598739.
Reay, D., David, M., & Ball, S. (2001). Making a difference? Institutional habituses and higher education choice. *Sociological Research Online*, 5(4). Retrieved from www.socresonline.org.uk/5/4/reay.html.
Scharff, C. (2015). Blowing your own trumpet: Exploring the gendered dynamics of self-promotion in the classical music profession. In B. Conor, R. Gill, & S. Taylor (Eds.), *Gender and creative labour* (pp. 97–112). Oxford: Wiley Blackwell/The Sociological Review.
Tanaka, A., Tokui, N., & Momeni, A. (2005). *Facilitating collective musical creativity*. Paris: Sony Computer Science Laboratory.
Taylor, S., & Littleton, K. (2012). *Contemporary identities of creativity and creative work*. Farnham, England: Ashgate.
West, C., & Zimmerman, D. H. (1987). Doing gender. *Gender and Society*, 1(2), 125–151.
Zelinksy, W., Leyshon, A., Matless, D., & Revill, G. (1999). The place of music. *Economic Geography*, 75(4).

VI

Student Commentary: Institutional Leadership from the Point of View of a Latin American Student; Being Aware of the Wall

EURIDIANA SILVA SOUZA

The chapters in the first section of this volume remind me of the metaphor of the wall, included by cultural theorist Raymond Williams in his 1989 text "Communications and Community". In analysing protest movements in relation to communication failures throughout our society, the author suggests that those movements reach a very solid wall and that "its stones essentially are power" (Williams, 1989, p. 19). We must be attentive to this wall, because attention allows us "to get under the wall, to realize its height, to be reminded quite sharply of your own size and where you are" (Williams, 1989, p. 20). Here then I draw attention to this metaphor because of *who I am*: a Music Education PhD student in Latin America, studying different views on the development of institutional leadership in music from the North axis: a broad conception of developing countries from North America, Europe, Japan and Australia. Although the aim of this chapter is not to discuss those differences, they must not be overlooked, because the structural and conjunctural differences that constitute societies and economies directly influence the construction and experience of leadership concepts in its various areas of application, such as policy and administrative governance of public and private education matters.

The Context

To be aware of the wall in Latin America is to understand that the "stones" of economic capital and social inequality are the foundation that also exerts direct pressure on education and political relations. Ianni (1988, p. 2) rightly points out that "we" speak from a region where "the State is strong, democracy is episodic, and dictatorships are recurrent", a place where "the deliberative elites – military, civil, oligarchic, business, technocratic – are those who know and can do anything". On one hand, the State, as a bureaucratic institution, is strong. On the other hand, as a policy project of a nation, the State is fragile and can easily succumb to temporary government policies that change structures and practices for the benefit of "deliberative elites", which in this sense allows education to exist in a space of power disputes for the advancement of political projects. This becomes clearer somewhat through the changes in the funding processes of education institutions.

The leadership of higher education institutions (teachers, researchers, administrators) and, consequently, all those connected to them (students, employees, local communities) are often placed in extreme or precarious situations in relation to low budgets. Many examples of research, infrastructure works and scholarships, among others, are interrupted or cut with regularity, often at the whim of political aims and interests, thus compromising the running of the higher education system. As a student, this impacts me not just on diminished research budgets, but specifically, because I see myself as an academic leader in training. The academic leadership discussion of power in this training (postgraduate course) puts in evidence the instability of academic environments faced with political decisions. These decisions, in the great majority, are dictated by people outside the higher music education area, evidenced by games between different capitals in the field of power.

Although each author of this section has chosen a particular theme under the umbrella of institutional leadership, each text emphasises politics, power and the global economy in different ways. In geo-economic theory, the term "North axis" is a broad conception of developed countries from North America, Europe, Japan and Australia (Kummu & Varis, 2011). As someone who lives and works in South America, I can understand and indeed I share the authors' views because the academic landscapes in the North and South axis are similar (despite the deep social and economic implications that this statement may entail). The current historical moment of the global economy, based on market capitalism, privileges models of institutional management developed in the North axis, which are imported to the South. In this way, both sides feel the impact of standardisation and accountability processes, focused on increasing expectations of productivity in educational systems. These impacts seem to be based on the clash between the persistence of a traditional or conservative bureaucratic model in institutional practices and the renewal and innovative needs of these practices, under the motto "innovate or die".

Innovation efforts appear to highlight the commodification of education. They can be observed in the processes related to the production and cost of educational systems or related to the adoption of new and better techniques, in a co-evolutionary approach between development of technologies and organisations. The views presented consider past and present, practice and theory. From an innovative and renewal approach on institutional leadership, some key concepts deserve attention.

Policy, Curriculum and Community

The political theme addressed by Schmidt (Chapter IV) emphasises the need to teach and understand politics as art. This approach, in my view, brings the dimension of governance to the spheres of microeconomics and micro-society. In other words, it brings it down to the sphere of interpersonal relations in an educational institution – that is, the classroom (either in person or in virtual spaces) – through the relationship of transmission and construction of knowledge.

As Paulo Freire reminds us (1996, 2015), the classroom is the first space for teachers to act and intervene as authority, hence as a leader. Bringing the teacher–student relationship to the classroom space is to develop institutional structure in practice. Practices imbued with organisational processes, values and principles do not always match the individual worldviews of teachers and students. This is where the curriculum is made, co-created and updated in the relationship between teachers and students as agents in this process, with its explicit and hidden dimensions. In these practices one witnesses the *curriculum in action*.

Curriculum also shows itself as a seminal challenge for higher music education. As a prescriptive document, a kind of map, the curriculum for music schools needs to consider the administrative and managerial aspects of academic systems. However, music as a field of knowledge as well as a wide and diversified social and professional activity is a kind of "territory" (*MUSIC, Music, music*, as proposed by Elliot, 1995; or *Musicking*, as proposed by Small, 1998). Maps cannot contain territories (Schmidt, Chapter IV) because maps are prescriptive and static while territories are in the realm of performance and movement. However, over time, maps are revised with the aim to present more accurate and effective information.

Carruthers (Chapter II), using the notion of cyclical revision, stresses that the curriculum is at the core of education restructuring. He highlights the need for flexibility, broader curricular constitution, diversity of content with a special emphasis on community music, and spaces for experiential learning, all leading to a partnership of sorts established between academic space, community and labour market. These findings are crucial because they provide elements of real life – of *praxis*, for restructuring institutionalised curricula that are more coherent with their time and cultural/social context.

Carruthers' findings were quickly discussed within professional music organisations in Latin America (for example, the 2017 Latin American Regional Meeting of ISME, see http://abemeducacaomusical.com.br/anais_

isme/index.asp; the Federal University of Minas Gerais Music Education Seminary in 2017 (Feichas & Souza, in press)). These discussions revealed that career development learning, including that undertaken in partnership with the broader labour market, typically takes the form of isolated teacher-driven projects rather than wide institutional leadership practice. In other words, the discussions revealed a gap between organisational proposals and discussions, and the reality presented in the classroom.

It is possible to suggest why this happens based on my experience as a student and representative in the administration of the university of which I am a member. One reason relates to bureaucratic processes of the academic system, which make it difficult to insert changes in curricular documents. It is quite common to see processes of modification in governmental policies every presidential term, overlapping with long discussions and actions for changing curriculum. These challenge administrative processes, teacher performances and students' paths into the institutions. Faced with the bureaucratic processes, it seems easier to meet the real needs of stakeholders by establishing new, individualised practices. However, the centrality of individual practices seems to be an inherited issue from education in general and can be an important point in seeking to understand universities' political and economic crisis.

According to Santos (2013), the university sector has since the end of the 20th century been experiencing a crisis that operates according to three central elements: hegemony, legitimacy and institutional autonomy. Hegemony is perceived, since the university is not the only institution in higher education and research. Specialised knowledge produced by universities is also no longer the only legitimate knowledge in the face of market demands (particularly in higher music education). In addition, the university has been losing its character of an autonomous institution, under pressure generated by effectiveness and productivity parameters imported from business administration and market capitalism. In the last political instance of crisis, since the beginning of 21st century, higher education has been shown as a "service that has access, not through citizenship but through consumption" and developed through an ideology "centered on the individual and individual autonomy" (Santos, 2004, p. 16).

Here, one perceives how individualistic logic permeates the whole educational system, creating the institution not as a collective construction but as a "choir of soloists". However, the development of *policy frame capacity* can be a path to circumvent these individualistic realities.

> The aim of a policy framing capacity is then to insert in individuals – but also in institutions, organisations, and community – a process-based understanding of leadership, where central values are grounded by three

capacities: 1) to generate interaction; 2) to shift conversations; and 3) to take risks.

(Schmidt, Chapter IV)

A policy framing capacity positioned as *creative disposition* and *strategic intent* brings to institutional leadership, in its individual and collective scope, the responsibility to reproduce or change institutional systems. Burnard (Chapter V) argues that changes should be based on strategies that consider intersections among higher education, vocational training, entrepreneurial capital and the labour market. These strategies may raise awareness of the processes of injustice against minorities and may strengthen *community building creativity*, which has been noted as the possible alternative to deal with the politics and economic issues that affect higher education.

In this section of the book, the authors stress, using different approaches, the needs of developing mutual responsibility and engagement: responsibility that searches for the effective democratisation of the curriculum as a space of action and engagement between institutional leadership as collective instance and individual assumption.

Final Words

I end by returning to the metaphor of the wall and inviting the reader to consider that democratisation is not limited to expanding access to the curriculum or, ultimately, access to higher education itself. Democratising is related to values of politics as art and to look straight to the other. It is related to the vivid meaning of the neighbouring term typical of communities (Williams, 1989). Although the wall lies ahead and the field of power, especially of economic power, dictates the rules of the game, it is important to remember that the game "played in fields has no ultimate winner, it is an unending game, and this implies the potential for change at any time" (Thomson, 2010, p. 79).

There is a pressing need for change in what we have experienced in terms of higher musical education in multiple countries and contexts. We know, however, that no one changes anyone; people change in relationship with others (Freire, 1996). After all, systems are made by people. Change is the responsibility of each one of us, not as an individual but as part of a conscious collectivity.

References

Elliot, D. (1995). *Music matters: A new philosophy of music education*. Oxford: Oxford University Press.

Feichas, H., & Souza, E. (Eds.). (In press). *Por diferentes caminhos: Novas propostas de aprendizagem em música*. Proceedings of the *Seminário de Educação Musical 2017*. Brazil: Federal University of Minas Gerais, July.

Freire, P. (1996). *Pedagogia da autonomia: Saberes necessários à prática educativa* (23rd edn). Rio de Janeiro: Paz e Terra.

Freire, P. (2015). *Pedagogia do oprimido* (51st edn). Rio de Janeiro: Paz e Terra.

Ianni, O. (1988). A questão nacional na América Latina. *Estudos avançados*, *2*(1), 5–40. doi: 10.1590/S0103-40141988000100003.

Kummu, M., & Varis, O. (2011). The world by latitudes: A global analysis of human population, development level and environment across the north–south axis over the past half century. *Applied Geography*, *31*(2), 495–507.

Santos, B. S. (2004). *A universidade no século XXI*. São Paulo: Cortez Editora.

Santos, B. S. (2013). *Pela mão de Alice: O social e o político na pós-modernidade* (9th edn). Coimbra: Edições Almedina.

Small, C. (1998). *Musicking: The meanings of performing and listening*. Hanover: Wesleyan University Press.

Thomson, P. (2010). Field. In Grenfell, M. (ed.), *Pierre Bourdieu: Key concepts* (3rd edn, pp. 67–83). Durham: Acumen.

Williams, R. (1989). Communication and community. In R. Williams, *Resources of hope: Culture, democracy, socialism* (pp. 19–31). London and New York: Verso. [Taken from the F. Harvey memorial lecture, 1961].

VII
Developing Leadership Capacities with Generation Z Students in Higher Music Education

SUSAN A. O'NEILL

Higher music education institutions play a crucial role in shaping the musicians and music educators of today and tomorrow. Many institutions already employ innovative programmes aimed at broadening students' horizons; however, few of these programmes are implemented in music-related areas. With a focus on Generation Z – "digital natives" born between 1995 and 2010 – this chapter considers some of the key challenges and constraints on efforts to engage the most recent generation of students in developing and strengthening their leadership capacities in higher music education. Specifically, this chapter focuses on the profile of Generation Z undergraduates based on recent research, the affordances and constraints of Generation Z's engagement in leadership development, and the development of leadership capacities with Generation Z using an ally or "critical friend" approach. It is argued that through the development of leadership capacities, Generation Z learners gain a sense of direction and the resiliency necessary for negotiating key transitions and transformations associated with today's fluid, fast-paced and changeable world.

Generational Issues in Higher Music Education

The majority of today's educators in higher music education are "baby boomers" and from Generation X (born after World War II and before 1980), who teach undergraduate students mostly from Generation Y (Millennials born between 1981 and 1994) and Generation Z (digital natives born between 1995 and 2010). Although the dates applied to each so-called generation can be fairly arbitrary, there is growing consensus among scholars about key differences that characterise Generation Y and Generation Z students. As rapid changes in technology continue to alter the context of young people's lives, there are fewer years spanning Generation Y and Generation Z than previous generations (Hope, 2016).

This growing trend among recent generations, which is rooted in discourses associated with technological change, the knowledge economy and enterprise education has propelled today's young people to understand themselves and their aspirations anew (Loveless & Williamson, 2013) and to "find a new relationship with the world" (Barnett, 2012, p. 9). This new relationship with the world is made up of social networks and participatory learning cultures which emphasise connectedness through *affinity spaces* (Gee, 2004): a sense of equity and distributed expertise across networked communities with interest-driven affiliations of people, tools and resources (see also Warschauer & Matuchniak, 2010). Further, there is increased emphasis on *lifewide* learning (Jackson, 2012): learning that takes place in multiple spaces inhabited simultaneously across physical and virtual worlds.

In the higher education arena, Generation Z students demand a voice in the decisions that affect their lives. And yet, in higher education "the concept of student voice can be passive and disempowered, governed and operated by the institution rather than by students themselves" (Kay, Dunne & Hutchinson, 2010, p. 1). Kay and colleagues argue that this passive notion of student voice has reinforced the idea of students as customers or consumers. However, with the growing presence of Generation Z students in higher education, this focus has started to shift rapidly and a new understanding of students as change agents has taken root. Increasingly, higher education institutions in Australia, Canada, Europe, United Kingdom and the United States have been working on how they might engage students actively through innovative programmes aimed at broadening students' horizons, such as "individual learning through enquiry and challenge" (Kay et al., 2010, p. 7). The authors suggest that "the very meaning of being a student needs to be reconsidered, and how it can fit with the new rhetoric of community, collaboration and co-creation rather than that of customer" (Kay et al., 2010, p. 7). They continue by emphasising that a focus on students as change agents instead of customers requires institutions to be "more relaxed about the ownership of expertise" (p. 7) and to create meaningful opportunities for students to develop leadership capacities.

Being an effective educator with Generation Z students in higher music education involves a significant investment in effort on the part of instructors to relate to, understand and support these students as change agents and to help bridge divides between the generations. This chapter takes as a starting point the idea that this investment on the part of educators can stimulate creative opportunities for engaging Generation Z students in developing leadership capacities. Indeed, developing leadership capacities has been high on the agenda of Generation Z students since they first started to appear on campuses in 2012 and 2013 (Hope, 2016).

Drawing on two recent publications, *Generation Z Goes to College* (Seemiller & Grace, 2016) and *Understanding Generation Z Students to Promote a*

Contemporary Learning Environment (Mohr & Mohr, 2017), which profile the characteristics, motivations and perspectives of Generation Z students, this chapter aims to provide a better understanding of the needs of the youngest students in higher education. I believe this knowledge can assist music educators in thinking about what the newest generation of students is thinking, what concerns them, and what they care about. Later in the chapter, I draw on my own experience and research on young people's music engagement to shed light on how to best engage Generation Z students in their music-related interests, while developing their leadership capacities using an ally or "critical friend" pedagogical approach.

Who are Generation Z?

According to Seemiller and Grace (2016), Generation Z are the most diverse of any previous generation in higher education. Their labels include "digital natives" and "information curators", due to their seemingly instinctive reflex to engage with digital technology and to use the internet to interpret the world. In Seemiller and Grace's (2016) study of over 1,000 undergraduates in the United States, Generation Z students described themselves in an online survey as loyal, thoughtful, compassionate, open-minded and responsible. Although Seemiller and Grace do not claim that their study provides a definitive picture of Generation Z, it does offer a useful snapshot from which educators can compare their experiences; these include experiences with students from different countries and cultures.

Seemiller and Grace (2016) find that Generation Z undergraduates are much more complex and multidimensional than they are often perceived to be. They are also more "we-centric" than Generation Y people, who are considered more "me-centric". Generation Z students are more collaborative in their view of relationships and in their approach to working with authority figures than are Generation Y. Generation Z students tend to view a career as being focused on solving problems, whereas Generation Y students tend to view a career as a place to serve. Also different is Generation Z students' view of technology as something you "live" rather than something you "employ" (Generation Y). Their view of the future has moved beyond Generation Y's optimism to embrace the idea of being actively engaged in solving problems for the future: "equipped with the power of knowledge, concern for the world around them, and technological resources unimaginable to previous generations, Generation Z is speculated to be ambitious and motivated" (Seemiller & Grace, 2016, p. 15).

Hope (2016) provides a useful summary of Seemiller and Grace's (2016) findings, which identified the following key characteristics of Generation Z students:

- **Information.** These students expect any information they need to be at their fingertips. They don't have to hope the journal is on the shelf. And if it's online they think it must be true.
- **Connection.** Gen Z is constantly connected. They suffer from FOMO: "fear of missing out".
- **Creative entrepreneurship.** Gen Z students believe that sharing can be revenue generating. They want to be their own bosses. They observe examples such as Uber, the world's largest taxi company, which owns no vehicles; and Airbnb, the world's largest accommodations provider, which owns no real estate.
- **Leadership.** Students see more women and people of colour in leadership roles, but they know that those are still the minority. They believe in reaching for their dreams while being realistic.
- **Social justice.** Social movements on equity and equality matter to Gen Z students.
- **Finances.** Budget cuts are a reality for these students. Knowing that getting stable work might not be easy, they are financially conservative.

If you dig deeper into Seemiller and Grace's (2016) findings, you discover that Generation Z students prefer particular types of learning. Of interest, their learning preferences are well-aligned with what are considered necessary learning processes for mastering music-related activities. These include "learning that is practice based, facilitative learning, independent work, solo work that leads to group work, setting their own pace, and self-reflection" (Hope, 2016, p. 4). However, there is a twist here that needs to be considered, particularly for Generation Z students from the United States and Canada.

While growing up, many Generation Z students experienced declining arts and music programmes in their primary and secondary (high school) years. Seemiller and Grace (2016) speculate that this might contribute to their lack of preference (when asked) for creative or imaginative processes: their tendency to be more solutions-oriented. Further, Generation Z students' expectations for music learning within a classroom context may vary significantly from their music learning activities in everyday life outside the classroom (O'Neill, 2012). They might not be aware of connections between school-based and outside school music activities (O'Neill, 2017a). This suggests a need for higher music education instructors to help students realise the potential for their creative activities outside their programmes to be relevant to their studies and capable of contributing to their learning in the higher music education environment.

Despite their affable self-description, Seemiller and Grace (2016) note that Generation Z students appear to be rather conflicted: although they want to show compassion, they admit to being critical of their peers; and although they identify with being entrepreneurial, they do not see themselves as creative.

They also report being excited, but fearful, about the future. Further, despite their collaborative "we-centric" view of relationships and wanting to work collaboratively with those in authority positions, they show less preference for working with their peers.

Hope (2016, p. 4) summarises this point: "They want to be around others but not work with them." They also report suffering from FOMO anxiety (Strong, 2016, in Mohr & Mohr, 2017, p. 87). According to Mohr and Mohr (2017, p. 87), "such paradoxical insights might foster a review of how instructors use class time and assign projects". For example, Generation Z students may need more guidance and options when asked to communicate effectively in groups. It is, however, encouraging that Generation Z students want to be around people who are "passionate about the same things they are" (Hope, 2016, p. 4).

Generation Z students who transition into opportunities for teacher education will continue to pose challenges for educators who seek effective ways to develop and strengthen their leadership capacities. In the OECD report *Preparing Teachers and the Development of School Leaders for the 21st Century* (Schleicher, 2012), the implications of changes in educational systems are made especially salient through a shift in educational policy from educational provision to outcomes, user-generated knowledge rather than teacher-delivered knowledge, and an expectation of differentiated pedagogical practices that embrace diversity and personalised learning experiences.

According to Schleicher (2012, p. 11), "the kind of teaching needed today requires teachers to be high-level knowledge workers who constantly advance their own professional knowledge as well as that of their profession". Schleicher's report calls for "education systems to transform the leadership" of schools and to embrace a changing profile of school leadership that includes fostering high-quality professional development, not only for existing teachers and school leaders, but for future teachers. Teachers are encouraged to develop a network for sharing and engaging in collaborative leadership where they take the lead in their own learning and use innovative approaches to develop student engagement in learning and leadership and in making connections with the wider community (Schleicher, 2012). For this to happen, it is essential for students to become engaged in a process of leadership development. This process requires them to step out of their comfort zones, explore their values and perspectives, and engage in activities that develop social entrepreneurship and innovation competencies so that they begin to see themselves as change agents.

Being a Change Agent

What does it mean to be a change agent in today's world and how might this impact on teaching and learning in higher music education? Generation Z students seek to be change agents and they believe in making a difference (Mohr

& Mohr, 2017; Seemiller & Grace, 2016). According to Seemiller and Grace (2016, p. 15), "they are motivated by not wanting to let others down, advocating for something they believe in, making a difference for someone else, having the opportunity for advancement, and earning credit toward something". They would rather have the opportunity for advancement or to earn credit for their achievements than to receive a prize or a gift. They also understand the importance of having credentials which bolster their future career options more than they value prizes or awards. Generation Z students are "interested in lifestyle-change challenges and appreciate standards. They want to know what competencies are expected in their aspired professions" (Mohr & Mohr, 2017, p. 88).

To illustrate what being a change agent means to young musicians, I draw on an example first published in O'Neill (2017a). Here, I referred to an account of Jen Long, a young woman from England who was introduced prior to her speech at a Youth Music conference as a youth music entrepreneur and a young, fresh music talent from outside the normal channels (Long, 2013). Jen was in the first wave of Generation Z students to graduate. By the age of 22, she had already presented her first radio show for the BBC and was writing about, promoting, recording and managing new bands – mostly young, unsigned, undiscovered and under-the-radar musicians.

In her speech, titled "Music Careers in the 21st Century," Jen reiterated some common assumptions: "music is important in the lives of young people, it shapes their identities, and for many it is a 'passion'". She went on to describe how she wanted to play in a band but didn't think it was something "you could learn"; rather, she thought it needed to happen "organically and through practice". In her speech, Jen advocated a "do it yourself" ethos to *making* a career in music and suggested that music education should provide more young people with opportunities to develop skills in music technologies and "hands-on" experience through music apprenticeships and internships. She also advocated for more to be done to encourage girls, observing that music is "a very male dominated industry".

Through Jen's description of her musical life, it is possible to recognise how she both shapes (through agentic, individual distinctiveness and autonomy) and is shaped by (through structural, culturally bounded but fluid networks of people who come to share the meaning of specific ideas, material objects and practices through interaction) her engagement in music-related opportunities. Jen sees herself as someone who is able to learn within specific musical contexts and she seeks out and engages in life experiences that are sustained and nurtured through relationships within those contexts. Her musical identity has developed within particular learning ecologies consisting of social structures and power relations that address, represent and act upon her as a certain kind of learner who is able to access and create her own opportunities "to become involved in music in many different ways". Her identity is infused with modern notions of independent authority and autonomous expertise that "reshape" the way her actions are interpreted and understood as emerging from her own initiative to discover, create, record, write about and share music.

Jen learns and works independently within her peer group and youth culture, both in-person and online. She engages in self-directed and collaborative music activities using technological advances, information sharing and social media, which tend to promote the experiential expertise of many different "lay experts" who mediate the expertise of professional musicians in ways that may or may not reflect accurately their experiences. Jen's engagement in music-related leadership activities permeates deeply into her everyday life but also mediates her sense of connectedness in particular ways. She believes, for example, in taking action to advocate for women and other marginalised groups to gain an equal place in the music profession. These complex social processes and relationships contribute to Jen's notion of "making" her own musical career, which is infused with leadership capacity-building and indicative of an imaginative act that is woven into the textures of her everyday life, personal aspirations and sense of self.

Jen's experience as a change agent is indicative of growing recognition within higher education institutions of the need to create opportunities for students to learn how to work as change agents. According to van der Heijden, Geldens, Beijaard and Popeijus (2015), change agents in educational contexts can learn and be reflective, give guidance and be accessible, positive, committed, trustful and self-assured, be innovative and responsible, and be collaborative. Fostering change agents requires educators to take on the role themselves; and yet being a change agent within higher education is difficult to achieve in practice. Harris (2015, n.p.) describes her own experience as an educator and argues that "those who dare to step out of their prescribed roles in the classroom to reach for something more for their students or colleagues are often looked upon [by other students or colleagues] with suspicion or fear" (para 2). She goes on to say that change agents "must be willing to admit that we 'don't know what we don't know', and approach opportunity with vulnerability and compassion" (para 2). There is also a need for systemic change focused on building a culture of change agents as necessary to higher education practice.

In reviewing the literature and through my own research (for example, O'Neill, 2017a, 2017b, forthcoming), I recognise three main characteristics associated with Generation Z students and their engagement as change agents. These three characteristics are important for higher music educators to identify and cultivate with their Generation Z students if they are to have the best chance of engaging these students in developing the leadership capacities that are both needed and acceptable to today's young people. The three main characteristics are as follows.

Sense of Connectedness

Students' music learning takes place in contact zones across physical and virtual life spaces and the places of home, school, local and online communities, and (mostly through the internet) the wider world. Their connected lives have helped them to shape and develop their sense of music as far more interconnected than previous generations. Music educators can help students to make connections and feel a sense of connectedness within and between the places and spaces where their diverse music activities take place. Music educators can help to cultivate students' sense of being global citizens who share different worldviews, languages and aesthetic music and cultural experiences, and yet who interact within a dynamic media cultural matrix that is both local and global ("glocal"), homogenising and diversifying (Smith & Hull, 2012).

Social Innovation

Students are enmeshed within agentive music learning ecologies where they tend to demonstrate a sense of empowerment and connectedness that aligns, in a reciprocal relationship with their musical selves, to a sense of responsibility and social engagement with the world around them. Students are compassionate and want to engage in creative activities to develop solutions that are capable of improving the well-being of people and society. Higher education is "well placed … to stimulate discussions about social innovation" and to provide "opportunities for exploring ideas, strategies and success stories about higher education's involvement in social innovation" (Egron-Polak, 2015, p. 1). Music educators can create opportunities for inquiry-based projects where students can engage in music-related activities that might benefit others, such as music education advocacy or the development or enhancement of campus and/or community-based activities.

Leadership for a Sustainable Future

Students recognise that they need to take a lead in helping to build a sustainable future for themselves and others. Their sense of leadership is deeply intertwined with their sense of social justice and their hope for creating a more equitable and sustainable world. Music educators can create opportunities for students to develop leadership capacities through individual self-reflection, informal small-group dialogue (in person and online) and inquiry-based projects focused on constructing meaning and knowledge about issues that matter to students – see also Berger (Chapter IX), Pike (Chapter X) and Weller (Chapter XII), this volume). This requires music educators to create opportunities for students to co-construct the curriculum and to be involved in decision-making and in the planning strategies for implementing new initiatives. Following this line of thought, Dean and Stanley (2015) adapted recommendations from Dunne and Zandstra (2011) to put forward four dimensions that need to be taken into account when framing opportunities to develop student leadership.

- Student leaders as evaluators includes those processes through which the institution and external bodies listen to the student voice in order to drive change.
- Student leaders as institutional decision-makers emphasises institutional commitment to greater student involvement and leadership in institution-wide improvements to teaching and learning and curriculum development. This particularly speaks to the role of student leaders in governance.
- Student leaders as experts and partners emphasises active student engagement as co-creators of knowledge at the very heart of curriculum development and its improvement.
- Student leaders as drivers of change requiring a move from institution-driven to student-driven agendas and activities.

Affordances and Constraints to Developing Leadership Capacities with Generation Z

Until relatively recently, leadership programmes in higher education were not taken very seriously by the academic community, who did not tend to regard leadership studies as a serious discipline (Greenwald, 2010). Part of the problem, which still remains, is that books on leadership include self-help books alongside books by politicians, motivational speakers and chief executives who offer their strategies and "tips" for becoming a successful leader (Greenwald, 2010). Add to this the common-sense belief that leaders are born and not made and that not everyone can become a leader, and there may be those who conclude that leadership programmes offer students "a false promise" (Greenwald, 2010, p. 1). Arminio (2011, p. 137) adds that leadership education programmes are more successful "at institutions where student engagement is encouraged or expected in and outside the classroom" compared to those "institutions where students are expected to simply sit, absorb and replicate class and workshop content".

Seemiller and Grace (2016) argue that although there has been an increase in the United States in college-level leadership programmes, there are significant barriers to engagement in these programmes for Generation Z students, including cost, time and students' perspectives on leadership. The authors argue that even if cost and time barriers are overcome, Generation Z students may not view the "formal, positional leadership" (p. 5) training offered by higher education institutions to be relevant to their needs (see also Schmidt, Chapter IV, this volume). Seemiller and Grace (2016, p. 5) offer the example that many Generation Z students "believe that politicians are dishonest, selfish, and argumentative", which makes them reluctant to engage in positional leadership opportunities such as student governments or councils.

Another interesting finding reported by Seemiller and Grace (2016, p. 5) is that Generation Z students have "a potentially inflated sense of their own leadership ability". The authors cite a 2014 survey of more than 150,000 Generation Z students, in which many students rated their leadership ability as either above average or in the top 2 per cent. Seemiller and Grace (2016, p. 5) remark that "in one sense, they see leadership as negative when practiced by many positional leaders, yet in another, they see themselves as being extremely proficient in it". Despite the potential challenges and barriers, an increasing number of leadership programmes are being offered or proposed at both the undergraduate and postgraduate levels. Although many institutions struggle to define student leadership in meaningful ways, there are increasing efforts to engage students in development leadership capacities within the undergraduate curriculum (see Demenoff et al., 2013).

One way of conceptualising the development of student leadership is to consider the gap between a student's existing leadership stance and experience and the pathway to the destination in which leadership might be enacted. Gaps provide opportunities for questioning and becoming suddenly struck by something we never noticed before (Bolton, 2010). It is during these times, in particular, when new understanding or possibilities emerge, that it is possible to see important transformations in learners' interest and engagement. Indeed, the most immediate and recognisable outcome of introducing leadership capacities as a form of learner-centred activity into classrooms is a positive change in learners' engagement as their curiosity and interest become newly sparked, renewed or deepened (Dinwoodie, Pasmore, Quinn, & Rabin, 2015).

In thinking about student leadership development, Komives, Dugan, Owen, Slack, Wagner and Associates (2011, p. 34) remind us that the "complexities of developing leadership in college students are supported by understanding the intersections of leadership development with other aspects of student development and with pedagogical practices grounded in learning theory". For example, the Social Change Model of Leadership Development, which asserts that leadership is a relational, transformative, process-oriented, learned and change-directed phenomenon (see Rost, 1991) provides a useful starting point for considering young people's engagement in leadership as "a purposeful, collaborative, values-based process that results in positive change" (Ginwright & James, 2002, p. 9).

Finally, Arminio (2011) argues for the need to connect leadership development programmes to institutional missions and to remove barriers and constraints to creating and sustaining an effective leadership development programme. Many leadership scholars agree that the development of allies is a crucial step in helping institutions to engage in authentic leadership "that aids individuals in understanding their interdependence with others" (Munin & Dugan, 2011, p. 157). Komives and her colleagues (2011, p. 164) discuss the crucial role that allies play in the development of students' leadership capacities. They argue: "Allies know that they do not have all the answers and continually seek the advice, input and collaboration of others."

Allies in Generation Z Leadership Development: Towards a Pedagogical Practice

In the context of this discussion, allies – often referred to as adult allies in youth development research (for example, Khanna & McCart, 2007) or critical friends in educational research and related fields (for example, Bullen, Chatterton, & Hartley, 2011) – are higher education instructors who are engaged in helping Generation Z students make their voice heard. Allies are specifically associated with advocating for a Generation Z leadership and empowerment agenda in higher education that will impact positively on decisions that affect young people's lives. Students and allies work collaboratively, in partnership, through a mutually interdependent relationship aimed at purposeful and meaningful engagement in building leadership capacities. These partnerships focus on "teaching each other, learning from each other, and making decisions and acting together" (Bullen et al., 2011, p. 2).

In addition, allies can be powerful catalysts for encouraging self-reflection among Generation Z students about issues that matter to them. By encouraging Generation Z students to engage in critical reflection and inquiry projects into issues that are related to both their lives and their higher music education programme activities, it is possible to encourage more meaningful connections and engagement that, in turn, will assist students in developing their leadership capacities. Research indicates that a key reason for young people, including Generation Z students, not to become involved in leadership activities is that they are not asked (see Hall, McKeown, & Roberts, 2004). Allies play a vital role in pointing students towards leadership opportunities, particularly for students who have never been introduced to or encouraged to engage in these sorts of activities.

Higher music education institutions are often not structured to support an allies approach to working with students (Ast & Fowler, 2004; Knowles, 2007). Because of this, an allies approach requires a concerted effort on the part of educators and senior administrators to create opportunities and spaces for

Generation Z students to become more engaged in developing their leadership capacities and for educators to become more effective allies. Khanna and McCart (2007) considered both the opportunities and challenges and present a list of ideas for encouraging this process.

- Arrange the classroom in a circle to diffuse the power base from the front of the room.
- Create opportunities for students to share decision-making in the classroom, where appropriate (for example, ground rules, deadlines, assignments and so on).
- Recognise that students can both learn and educate (for example, peer education).
- Encourage students to become engaged in their learning (for example, recognise that it is just as important to foster a positive concept of learning as it is to deliver content).
- Support, rather than direct (for example, ask questions rather than provide answers).
- Focus on making lessons interesting, fun and exciting for both teachers and their students to be engaged.

Allies take on numerous roles as they work in partnership with students to develop leadership capacities (Camino & Zeldin, 2002; Larson, Walker, & Pearce, 2005; Zeldin, McDaniel, Topitzes, & Calvert, 2000). They do this by:

- facilitating opportunities for students to contribute meaningfully;
- linking students experiencing personal difficulties with appropriate support services;
- posing guiding questions so that students can work through problems themselves rather than providing answers;
- providing immediate structures to break down tasks to be manageable;
- checking in with students;
- giving personalised feedback and providing an effective balance between informal support and critical analysis;
- cultivating a culture of fairness and opportunity;
- providing boundaries and structure;
- playing multiple roles simultaneously;
- ensuring safety for students to take risks;
- navigating expected and unexpected challenges within student–ally relationships;
- sharing personal motivations for being involved;
- focusing on both student and ally development;

- providing experience and expertise to contribute to the collective partnership; and
- thinking creatively and encouraging students to do the same.

Allies are often found in the accounts of people involved in social justice education, such as those who work with students from marginalised backgrounds or who strive to reflect on the dynamics of privilege and oppression in the classroom (Davis, Mirick, & McQueen, 2015). The roles of an ally differ from traditional teacher-directed roles. Although there is no absolute right or wrong way for students and adults to collaborate, allies can work with students "to actively reduce the barriers that negatively affect their engagement" (Khanna & McCart, 2007, p. 9). The concept of reciprocity is key to student–ally partnerships. In this way, student–ally partnerships resemble a form of creative collaboration through which process a topic may shift and evolve. Also, of fundamental significance is that participants need to attend to each other through episodes of what Noddings (2002, p. 17) refers to as "interpersonal reasoning", where a participant "may pause to remind the other of her strengths, to reminisce, to explore, to express concern, to have a good laugh, or otherwise connect with the other as cared-for". As such, student–ally partnerships imply a seeking to understand the "other" by reaching "across the ideological gap to connect with each other" (Noddings, 2002, p. 17).

Conclusion

Generation Z students are distinct from previous generations. This chapter has considered the role that higher music education institutions play in shaping the music education leaders of today and tomorrow by engaging Generation Z students in the development of leadership capacities. Although an increasing number of institutions are employing innovative programmes aimed at broadening Generation Z students' horizons, there remain key challenges and constraints on efforts to engage them in developing and strengthening their leadership capacities. Current challenges include aspects of accessibility, funding, relationship disconnect and segregated educational approaches. The chapter suggests using an ally approach to engage Generation Z students in developing leadership capacities while focusing on activities related to being a change agent. The aim is to create opportunities for Generation Z students to develop leadership capacities in higher music education while maintaining a sense of direction, negotiating key transitions, and deepening their sense of local and global community involvement.

Generation Z students are not only capable of adapting to change, they want to be equipped to make their own opportunities and to *lead change* as they position and reposition themselves in a fast-changing world. Increasingly, higher education is being tasked with the job of ensuring that students are equipped with the skills, knowledge and qualities that leadership programmes cultivate: "self-reliance, social and cultural capital, appreciation for lifelong learning, creativity, conflict-resolution and team-building skills, ethics, understanding of economics, and more" (Greenwald, 2010, para 9). These qualities resonate well with Generation Z students who are, in turn, transforming higher education institutions and making them more accountable (Ginwright & James, 2002).

According to Kay et al. (2010, p. 2), students as change agents requires the creation of opportunities for them to be "actively engaged with the processes of change, often taking a leadership role. They are engaged deeply with the institution and their subject areas, and the focus and direction is, to a far greater extent, decided by students." Understanding the needs of Generation Z students challenges educators in higher music education to focus on creating leadership development opportunities to help students gain a sense of direction and the resilience necessary for negotiating the key transitions and transformations associated with today's fluid, fast-paced and changeable world.

References

Arminio, J. (2011). Establishing and advancing a leadership program. In S. R. Komives, J. P. Dugan, J. E. Owen, C. Slack, W. Wagner, & Associates (Eds.), *The handbook of student leadership development* (2nd edn, pp. 137–157). San Francisco, CA: Jossey-Bass.

Ast, R., & Fowler, P. (2004). *Towards SchoolPLUS: Empowering high schools as communities of learning and support*. Community Education Unit, Children's Services and Programs Branch. Saskatchewan: Saskatchewan Learning.

Barnett, R. (2012). The coming of the ecological learner. In P. Tynjälä, M-L. Stenström, & M. Saarnivaara (Eds.), *Transitions and transformations in learning and education* (pp. 9–20). New York: Springer. doi: 10.1007/978-94-007-2312-2_2.

Bolton, G. (2010). *Reflective practice: Writing and professional development* (3rd edn). London: Sage.

Bullen, P., Chatterton, P., & Hartley, P. (2011). Critical friends: A valuable role in educational innovation? *Higher Education Academy Annual Conference*, July 2011. Retrieved from www.heacademy.ac.uk/knowledge-hub/critical-friends-valuable-role-educational-innovation.

Camino, L., & Zeldin, S. (2002). From periphery to center: Pathways for youth civic engagement in the day-to-day life of communities. *Applied Developmental Science*, 6(4), 213–220. doi: 10.1207/S1532480XADS0604_8.

Davis, A., Mirick, R., & McQueen, B. (2015). Teaching from privilege: Reflections from white female instructors. *Affilia: Journal of Women and Social Work*, 30(3), 302–313. doi: 10.1177/0886109914560742.

Dean, D., & Stanley, K. (2015). The student leadership in curriculum development and reform project. Retrieved from www.uws.edu.au/__data/assets/pdf_file/0011/910379/Student_Leadership_HERDSA_23_Aug_.pdf.

Demenoff, S., Pascal, G-R., Labbé, J., Bourgault, R., Lewis, J., et al. (2013). Blind curves or open roads? Student leaders speak on the future of Canadian post-secondary education. *Collected Essays on Learning and Teaching*, 6, 142–146. doi: 10.22329/celt.v6i0.3722.

Dinwoodie, D., Pasmore, W., Quinn, L., & Rabin, R. (2015). *Navigating change: A leader's role*. White paper by the Centre for Creative Leadership. Retrieved from https://media.ccl.org/wp-content/uploads/2016/09/navigating-change-a-leaders-role-center-for-creative-leadership.pdf.

Dunne, E., & Zandstra, R. (2011). *Students as change agents – new ways of engaging with learning and teaching in higher education*. Bristol: University of Exeter/ESCalate/Higher Education Academy. Retrieved from http://escalate.ac.uk/8064.

Egron-Polak, E. (2015). *Social innovation: Challenges and perspective for higher education*. Welcome message to the Sixth Global Meeting of Association of Universities and other Higher Education Institutions (GMA). Retrieved from www.eiseverywhere.com/ehome/iaugma6/home/.

Gee, J. P. (2004). *Situated language and learning: A critique of traditional schooling*. London: Routledge.

Ginwright, S., & James, T. (2002). From assets to agents of change: Social justice, organizing, and youth development. *New Directions for Youth Development*, 96, 27–46. doi: 10.1002/yd.25.

Greenwald, R. (2010). Commentary: Today's students need leadership training like never before. *The Chronical of Higher Education*. Retrieved from www.chronicle.com/article/Todays-Students-Need/125604.

Hall, M., McKeown, L., & Roberts, K. (2004). *Caring Canadians, involved Canadians: Highlights from the 2000 national survey of giving, volunteering and participating*. Ottawa, Canada: Statistics Canada. Retrieved from www.givingandvolunteering.ca.

Harris, C. (2015). *It is not easy to be a change agent in education*. The Educator's Room. Retrieved from http://theeducatorsroom.com/2015/07/it-is-not-easy-to-be-a-change-agent-in-education/.

Hope, J. (2016). Get your campus ready for Generation Z. *The Successful Registrar*, 16, 1–7. doi: 10.1002/tsr.30216.

Jackson, N. J. (2012). Lifewide learning: History of an idea. In N. J. Jackson (Ed.): *The lifewide learning, education and personal development e-book*. Retrieved from http://lifewideeducation.co.uk/sites/default/files/chapter_a1_jackson.pdf.

Kay, J., Dunne, E., & Hutchinson, J. (2010). *Rethinking the values of higher education – students as change agents?* Quality Assurance Agency (QAA) for Higher Education. Retrieved from www.qaa.ac.uk/en/Publications/Documents/Rethinking-the-values-of-higher-education-students-as-change-agents.pdf.

Khanna, N., & McCart, S. (2007). *Adult allies in action*. Toronto, ON: Centre for Excellence in Youth Engagement. Retrieved from www.abcee.org/cms/wp-content/uploads/2011/11/adults-as-allies.pdf.

Knowles, L. (2007). *Youth engagement: Effective classroom practice*. Centre of Excellence for Youth Engagement. Retrieved from www.engagementcrntre.ca/files/YEInEducation.pdf.

Komives, S. R., Dugan, J. P., Owen, J. E., Slack, C., Wagner, W., & Associates. (2011). *The handbook of student leadership development* (2nd edn). San Francisco, CA: Jossey-Bass.

Larson, R., Walker, K., & Pearce, N. (2005). A comparison of youth-driven and adult-driven youth programs: Balancing inputs from youth and adults. *Journal of Community Psychology*, 33(1), 54–74. doi: 10.1002/jcop.20035.

Long, J. (2013). *Fresh thinking for music education*. Presentation to Youth Music UK. Retrieved from www.youtube.com/watch?v=FZA1Inn9gVI.

Loveless, A., & Williamson, B. (2013). *Learning identities in a digital age: Rethinking creativity, education and technology*. London: Routledge.

Mohr, K. A. J., & Mohr, E. S. (2017). Understanding Generation Z students to promote a contemporary learning environment. *Journal on Empowering Teaching Excellence*, 1(1), Article 9. doi: 10.15142/T3M05T.

Munin, A., & Dugan, J. P. (2011). Inclusive design. In S. R. Komives, J. P. Dugan, J. E. Owen, C. Slack, W. Wagner, & Associates (Eds.), *The handbook of student leadership development* (2nd edn, pp. 157–177). San Francisco, CA: Jossey-Bass.

Noddings, N. (2002). *Educating moral people: A caring alternative to character education*. New York: Teachers College Press.

O'Neill, S. A. (2012). Becoming a music learner: Towards a theory of transformative music engagement. In G. E. McPherson & G. Welch (Eds.), *The Oxford handbook of music education* (Vol. 1, pp. 163–186). New York: Oxford University Press.

O'Neill, S. A. (2017a). Young people's musical lives: Learning ecologies, identities and connectedness. In R. A. R. MacDonald, D. J. Hargreaves, & D. Meill (Eds.), *Oxford handbook of musical identities* (pp. 79–104). New York: Oxford University Press.

O'Neill, S. A. (2017b). Music and social cognition in adolescence. In R. Ashley & R. Timmers (Eds.), *The Routledge companion to music cognition* (pp. 441–452). New York and London: Routledge.

O'Neill, S. A. (forthcoming). New materiality and musical learning lives: Young people's connectedness across physical and virtual life spaces. In J. Waldron, S. Horsley, & K. Veblen (Eds.), *The Oxford handbook of social media and music learning*. Oxford and New York: Oxford University Press.

Rost, J. C. (1991). *Leadership for the twenty-first century*. Westport, CT: Greenword Publishing.

Seemiller, C., & Grace, M. (2016). *Generation Z goes to college*. San Francisco, CA: Jossey-Bass.

Schleicher, A. (Ed.) (2012). *Preparing teachers and developing school leaders for the 21st century: Lessons from around the World*. Paris, France: OECD Publishing. doi: 10.1787/9789264xxxxxx-en.

Smith, A., & Hull, G. (2012). Critical literacies and social media: Fostering ethical engagement with global youth. In J. Ávila & J. Zacher Pandya (Eds.), *Critical digital literacies as social praxis: Intersections and challenges* (pp. 63–84). New York, NY: Peter Lang.

Strong, R. (2016). Social media, FOMO and the perfect storm for the Quarter-Life Crisis. Retrieved from www.huffingtonpost.com/rebecca-strong/social-media-fomo-and-the_b_9880170.html.

van der Heijden, H. R. M. A., Geldens, J. J. M., Beijaard, D., & Popeijus, H. L. (2015). Characteristics of teachers as change agents. *Teachers and Teaching*, *21*(6), 681–699. doi:10.1080/13540602.2015.1044328.

Warschauer, M., & Matuchniak, T. (2010). New technology and digital worlds: Analyzing evidence of equity in access, use, and outcomes. *Review of Research in Education*, *34*(1), 179–225. doi: 10.3102%2F0091732X09349791.

Zeldin, S., McDaniel, A. K., Topitzes, D., & Calvert, M. (2000). *Youth in decision-making: A study on the impacts of youth on adults and organizations*. National 4-H Council: University of Wisconsin-Madison.

VIII
Leadership as an Essential Graduate Attribute for Musicians

ANNA REID, DAWN BENNETT AND JENNIFER ROWLEY

Leadership development and musician identity are complex ideas that may be understood from theoretical and practical perspectives. Higher music education students are actively involved in developing their musician identities, comprising their sense of self or being. However, formal studies rarely lead to a deep understanding of potential professional worlds, or to the leadership that is required of musicians in professional settings. This chapter reports on an internship programme established to provide music students with authentic workplace experiences. We explore how leadership and musician identity are understood from the perspective of complexity theory. Following this discussion, we bring to light how leadership is played out in the experience of students who have undertaken internship programmes. In the internship context, students reimagine what their musical world means and how their own capabilities and creativity can be utilised as leaders. The chapter reveals how students experience the liminal space between formal music study and internship work experiences and how, in turn, they transform their thinking from situation to situation.

Creative innovation and musician identity are graduate qualities that music educators assume students will encounter and develop throughout their studies. These qualities – creative innovation and identity – are also essential characteristics of leadership in general. Although the qualities have been explored in empirical terms, there is very little research that shows how students come to acquire or engage with creative innovation and identity during their studies. A complexity is that these qualities are not tied to specific curriculum; they are encountered through formal studies and through students' activities outside the academy (see also O'Neill's, Chapter VII, this volume). Musicians' leadership development and identity work, then, evolve out of a lifetime of study and experience. To understand the manner in which they are developed in practice, against the rhetoric that surrounds them, in this chapter we use the lens of complexity theory to expose the thinking of students engaged in an internship programme.

When student musicians perform or work it is possible to consider them as part of different communities of practice. As student musicians, they belong to a learning community and they are expert in that domain by the time they complete their studies. But they are also a part of multiple worksites where they can interact with peers, who are students like themselves, or with long-time professionals. In the latter case, they are also part of the professional community of practice, but still as novices in that context. These and other communities enable them to consider their leadership roles and musician identities in different ways (Reid, Abrandt Dahlgren, Petocz, & Dahlgren, 2011).

The idea of a community of practice (Wenger, 1998) has been long established in business contexts as a community that comprises people who share a particular passion and, through that passion, engage with others in specific ways. The work of systems theorists such as Senge (1994) suggests that internal and external situations strongly influence individuals' leadership styles and activities. Unsurprisingly the musician's community is uniquely complex (Hennekam & Bennett, 2016) and often transient (Bennett, 2013).

For many workers, a single or dominant organisation provides the main external influence which, in many commercial situations, is saturated with complex ideas and relationships. However, student and graduate musicians may be part of multiple related and competing workplaces, as is increasingly the case across the labour market (World Economic Forum, 2016). Each of those sites affords students different opportunities to learn about their musicianship, musician identity, leadership capability, communication styles and so on. Each different worksite provides remuneration for different aspects of their musicianship and this, in turn, plays an important role in their development of musician identity. To confuse issues further, much of the research literature related to leadership development is situated in the field of business, which brings to it the assumption of a logical outcome such as a profit.

From the perspective of complexity theory, "almost anything can effect anything else" (Bolman & Deal, 1997, p. 22). According to Marion (1999, p. xii):

> Leadership begins when the behaviour of one system stimulates certain behaviours in another system, that in turn stimulates another, and another; eventually the chain of stimulation returns to motivate, or catalyse, the original system and the cycle is reinforced. Order … [therefore emerges] not because someone or something expends energy to create it; [but] rather order emerges from the natural, and free, consequences of interaction.

This complex view of stimulating interactions is problematic in the music industries as many of the activities undertaken by musicians do not make money; nor are they located in clearly established organisations. Rather, leadership is dispersed throughout a musical activity and the development of leadership skills comes within a liminal space.

Within the pre-liminal space, musicians have multiple socially and culturally defined identities endorsed through musical encounters, role models and aspirations. Musicians' work-related identity or identities often incorporate an intrinsic "calling" (Randle & Culkin, 2009) that represents the whole self and is expressed in such a way that nothing else can be imagined. Moreover, the musician identity encapsulates "the importance of shared understandings and practices in musical, social and cultural terms" (Hargreaves, MacDonald, & Miell, 2009, p. 465), highlighting the networked community context of musicians' practice and identity.

In music, the strong focus on performance and creation is reinforced long before students enter higher music education (Freer & Bennett, 2012). At odds with this is the complexity of musicians' practice, which most often involves multiple and changing roles within and beyond music. As such, the liminal space is crucial because it "enables the student to try out, perhaps to 'try on', a variety of new perspectives, mindsets and identities" (Griess, 2014, p. 39). This speculative and adventurous affective tension (Dewey, 1910/2008) requires the reconciliation of multiple, often changing professional selves into one, multimember, fluid nexus (Wenger, 1998).

Solomonides and Reid (2009) observe that simultaneously singular and multiple identities are seen in both practising (professional) and aspiring musicians. Thus, a student's *sense of being* and *sense of transformation* forms the ontological core of identity and engagement. Around this are epistemological spokes such as professional knowledge, discipline knowledge and engagement. From their core identity, different experiences provide the situations in which these spokes become active. Different performance works or arts management activities help consolidate musicians' ontological core and also serve to prompt change to that core.

Given the multiplicity of experiences that lead student musicians to develop their musician identity and leadership, exploring this multiplicity through the lens of complexity theory is likely to give us some more nuanced insight into their experience. As an approach to research, *complexity theory* is concerned with studying complex systems and problems that are dynamic, unpredictable and multidimensional, consisting of a collection of interconnected relationships and parts (Byrne, 2001). Mason (2008, p. 35) summarises the process as follows:

> Given a significant degree of complexity in a particular environment … new properties and behaviours, which are not necessarily contained in the essence of the constituent elements or able to be predicted from a knowledge of initial conditions, will emerge.

Curlee and Gordon (2011, p. 1) acknowledge the distributed nature of leadership and creativity inherent in complex worksites. Commenting on specific situations, the authors write that project managers "realise that creativity occurs on the fringes of complexity or chaos. Those teams that appear to be in total chaos may be doing the best work". Curiously, this sort of view supports the idea that, in some instances, totally "off-the-wall" situations prompt results that can be more positive.

From the perspective of students who engage in industry projects, this account goes a long way to explaining how students can move through sometimes novel, chaotic experiences and yet experience the positive development of their leadership skills and musician identity. Students do not necessarily have rigidity or certainty when at the early stage of their professional work because they are still in the process of integrating and forming their musician identity (Rowley & Munday, 2014); indeed, we would argue that identity is a process of becoming – of change – throughout the career lifecycle, albeit particularly tenuous in the early stages of career transition. This led us to query the extent to which engaging in an internship might influence students' sense of self.

Approach and Context

The Sydney Conservatorium of Music (SCM) has worked as a traditional preparation for professional musicians for a long time. It has focused on developing the musical skills and performance practices that can be adapted to professional contexts later in life. However, this traditional perspective is of little utility in a modern world where students need the advantage of work-related preparation. More recently, the institution adopted a different model, which sees students engage with a wide variety of professional experiences during their studies. These experiences may be formally developed and they may award students with credit towards their degree; they may also be totally informal in their orientation.

The formal internship programme at SCM aims to develop awareness and knowledge of the arts sector, combined with knowledge and understanding of workplace practices. The internship works as an exchange of services for experience between student and employer. Students use an internship to determine if they have an interest in a particular career, to create a network of contacts and/or to gain credit towards their degree. Students are introduced to collaborative skills and techniques for working in a team setting using knowledge and skills learned in their university programme. From this comes an understanding of effective professional capacities and knowledge of leadership and management techniques essential for developing professional practice: for example, autonomy, intrinsic motivation and self-efficacy.

Musicians construct their identities taking into account their musical, social, cultural and psychological theories, which help to explain the behavioural aspects of musician identity (Hargreaves et al., 2009). The internship unit of study operationalises this thinking by allowing students to apply their musical knowledge to the broader arts community as they engage in specifically designed internship programmes for professional practice. Students choose a project that involves working with an organisation in the arts sector. The internship is a system of on-the-job training, and the structured unit of study seeks and selects the most appropriate places for students according to students' interests and expertise and the availability of suitable host employers.

To investigate the assumptions that we had made regarding the efficacy of the internship programmes to develop leadership and musician identity, we initiated a research project that involved some of the public outcomes of students' experience. A total of 75 students completed their internship unit in 2013–2015 and 61 students who enrolled for academic credit submitted their written reflections as part of the internship's assessment task. The analysis undertaken by the research team identified comments of interest, which led to seeking written permission from those whose comments are reported in this chapter. Student reflection tools did not ask any questions about leadership; rather, we analysed to see whether students raised these themes as a natural component of their reflective practice.

The team employed deductive analysis to analyse the reflections, searching for keywords such as "leadership" and for leadership themes as described in the following section. The qualitative responses were firstly read without predetermined codes being applied. Next, we discussed leadership themes that seemed apparent in the data. Other prominent ideas were also coded through this process using newly identified keywords. Subsequently, the coding was reviewed, with the data providing meaning and context to the final three leadership themes: bridging the gap between theory and practice; flexibility; and reorienting learning as career relevance is realised.

Results and Discussion

It is important to expose the experiences of students as they develop their leadership and musician identity through the internship programme. Consequently, we present quotations from the students' reflections as a representative sample of their collective voice. We use their words to show that the internship experience has assisted students to develop a professional ability, take on new roles and responsibilities, and adapt to and work with new knowledge (Rowley, 2012). We focus on the three interrelated leadership domains. In the following text, the letters after each quotation are identifying initials. The last identifying letter is an indication of the student's gender, which participating students identified as either male (M) or female (F).

Bridging the Gap Between Theory and Practice

The complexity of musicians' work heightens the need for a "growth" mindset: identity development as a process of integration and formation not bound within the constraints of discipline, sector or traditional ways of working (see Dweck, 2006, and in the music context, Rowley & Munday, 2014). In reality, then, musician identity develops alongside a sense of self that can be disrupted and reinforced, feared and ideal, liminal, troublesome and transformative. This disruption needs to occur during higher education studies, by supporting student musicians in the development of their musician identities through "a dynamic interplay between the two notions of who the person is becoming and what they are coming to know" (Reid et al., 2011, p. 15). Central to this are experiences, such as those reported here, which link theory and practice through exploration of music and self within the context of community.

> *Reorientation:* "As an operatic artist, I am always learning and evolving … this internship has provided a platform for some fundamental skills that I can build on and expand … and I definitely need to keep on improving vocally and continue to work on my stagecraft skills in order to succeed in this highly competitive industry."
>
> (Student TRF)

TR's experience (above) demonstrates a reorientation perspective as her existing capacities are evaluated in the light of a "competitive" industry. The industry experience has shown her how to refocus in the student domain. This student is now able to see the relevance of professional work to her current study, and to see current study as a preparation for a newly appreciated work situation.

The professional experience of an internship programme can operationalise a reversal of what is traditionally experienced in formal studies by leading the student towards a deeper understanding of potential professional worlds. In this instance, the student encountered an authentic learning experience within a workplace context. Such contexts can prompt students to reimagine what their musical world might look like. In this case, the liminal space provided by the professional experience exposed the power of the student's individual capabilities and creative leadership.

Flexibility

Taken from a reflective component of the unit assessment, the student below demonstrates a sophisticated view of leadership. As in the other cases, this student dances in the liminal spaces between experiences and is able to focus on the things required of each situation as the situation demands.

> *Bridging:* "critical thinking, communication, collaboration and creativity … all of these things I experienced allowed for a shift in my practice being realised."
>
> (Student CDM)

By acknowledging the emergent skills required for a successful transition to graduate life, students such as this one can begin to probe their sense of self or being. Such realisations of personal musical identity show maturity and leadership, including identity work in which new facets of professional musicians' practice are acknowledged.

As seen below, some students reported new flexibility in their career thinking as a result of undertaking the internship programme.

> *Career relevance:* "my everlasting passion lies in music, however, I recently discovered a more profound passion, that is, teaching music."
>
> (Student LMF)

For this student, experiencing the liminal space between formal music study and what the internship programme provided as an experience, created an opportunity for a transformation of career thinking. The student utilised the authentic learning experience to develop a new self-view that contributes to a personalised – rather than externally defined – professional identity as a musician.

Reorienting Learning as Career Relevance is Realised

The previous quote from student LM showed how prior experiences are considered differently in the light of the internship experience. LM now sees herself strongly as part of the community of musicians and also of the subset of musician teachers. The language she uses strongly demonstrates her transforming identity.

In the quotation that follows, there is a somewhat reverse orientation. DS is already embedded in music education as his primary degree focus, but the internship experience has enabled him to articulate other personal attributes. The situation in the internship programme enabled him to change the emphasis of his knowledge to suit the new situation. In that sense, he was able to make a bridge between one community and another.

> *Bridging:* "music education now as a lifelong career choice, maybe not always teaching as I have developed a range of skills that include being able to clearly articulate the skills I have now."
>
> (Student DSM)

The organisation hosting this student was a strong influence in developing his ideas about the future. In a sense, this quote extrapolates the concept of complexity theory by showing how student musicians' experiences form part of a related but competing view of musicians' work.

Another aspect of reorientation concerned the realisation that music work is most often undertaken within networks, which are an essential component of communities of practice. In fact, this is the essence of creative leadership within communities of practice: recognising the ability to build on team passion and skills.

> *Creative leadership:* "Through the internship program I realised that music programs are created through hard work and pushed to a high standard by those who care. Someday I wish to be in a musical setting that sets up music and musicians for the next generation."
>
> (Student LCM)

Here, we see LC acknowledging that the musical world of work can be much more than the music-making for which he has been trained through his post-secondary studies. It is apparent that LC is thinking reflectively about his future by viewing his musical identity through a lens of future professional practice. Also exposed through this quote is how the internship has provided a learning situation whereby students can envisage being part of those leading the next generation of musicians.

> *Creative leadership:* "pulling together a network of like-minded individuals and pooling resources to make things happen was the core lesson in this internship."
>
> (Student VNM)

In their study of leadership students, Hawkins and Edwards (2015) describe students' doubts and anxiety about the learning process as "symbolic liminal 'monsters'". Indeed, they contend that "the experience of doubt is a central thread through the processes of *learning about* and *doing* leadership … laced with power relationships and transformative potential" (2015, p. 27, emphasis in the original). For Hawkins and Edwards, as for us, these monsters emerged as "moments in and out of time" (Delanty, 2010, p. 31).

In a sense, we deliberately released the monsters by challenging students to engage in experiences outside their areas of comfort. We were attempting to bridge the gap between theory and practice; however, we acknowledged that releasing the monsters would be insufficient in and of itself. As Lewin (1947, p. 35) suggests, the "emotional stir-up" within the liminal space creates a state of disequilibrium, affective tension, frustration and conflict. And yet liminal monsters are rarely shared with teachers and supervisors unless students are given the time and an environment of trust in which to critically reflect on their experiences: "the time to step out of the doing into a space of thinking about the doing might be understood as the creation of an internal liminal space" (Cook-Sather & Alter, 2011, p. 65).

The metacognitive aspect of students' experiences is crucial here because liminality and learning begins when a trigger event such as an internship moves a learner's state of mind from stable and pre-liminal (Wright & Gilmore, 2012) to unstable, liminal and, eventually, to a "different cognitive state" (Griess, 2014, p. 188). If, as Weick (2001) suggests, leadership practice is "the legitimation of doubt", liminality is at its core. Our experience suggests that Locke's (2008) three strategic principles for leadership educators hold true for any educators who facilitate students' liminal experiences: for students to a) embrace not knowing; b) nurture hunches; and c) disrupt order.

Complexity theory suggests that across multiple domains there are usually around three elements that enable the diverse situations to cohere (Manson, 2001). In this study, our student musicians moved through multiple domains during the internship programme. The short student statements provided evidence of the three different leadership domains; however, these statements formed part of longer narratives that contributed to the overall pool of meaning in the study. As Curlee and Gordon (2011) indicate, chaos is analogous to the liminal space – a space of uncertainty – through which the students move. Perhaps this space is a positive one.

Concluding Comments

This chapter illustrated how higher music education students experience the liminal space between their formal music study and internship work experiences and the impact of these dual experiences on their thinking about self and career. Through an exploration of leadership, we discussed musician identity from the perspective of complexity theory. The discussion of how leadership is evidenced in the experience of students who have undertaken internship programmes within the music industries was supported by selected student comments. These afforded insights into the impact of professional musician identity development on the efficiency of leadership, supporting Lührmann and Eberl's (2007) claim that identity theory provides a useful theoretical basis from which to gain deeper insights into leadership processes. At the conclusion of the SCM internship programme, students were able to demonstrate an ability to apply relevant theories, skills and knowledge to the workplace; they also demonstrated development of leadership qualities.

The student musicians' experiences enabled them to bridge the gap between theory and practice, to notice the need for flexibility in the workplace and in their own thinking about self, and to develop the creative skill of reorienting learning as career relevance is realised. Thus, the inclusion of experiential learning in the education of professional musicians can be seen to enable student musicians to develop essential, transferable skills such as leadership, communication, teamwork, workplace negotiation and problem-solving.

This chapter revealed how students experience the liminal space and how they transform their thinking from situation to situation. The capacities identified by students are the same qualities identified by employers as being vital to successful transition to a career, and the same qualities identified by practising musicians as being vital to leading complex careers within and beyond the music sector, often from the point of graduation.

The ability of students to reimagine what their musical world might mean and how their own capabilities and creativity might be utilised as leaders, is evidenced in their reflections on important professional experiences such as aspects of their internship reported here in selected comments. However, the question remains as to why higher music educators would release these liminal monsters. Surely, if students have come to higher music education with a lifelong commitment to music, particularly to a narrow specialism such as performance or composition, our task is to foster their growth *within* this speciality.

The most obvious argument against a monster-free approach is that almost every music graduate will need to engage in and manage a broad and changeable range of roles in order to meet their career-oriented and personal needs. We could add to this the economic data that people average four different careers and 17 different jobs across their careers (McCrindle Research, 2014). As we have contended, only by challenging students to engage in experiences outside their comfort zone or zone of proximity can we create the state of disequilibrium from which they learn these strategies.

Less discussed in the literature and at the core of our argument is that across their lifetime people transform experiences into "knowledge, skills, attitudes, values, emotions, beliefs, and the senses" (Jarvis, 2002, p. 37). This exploration and transformation lies at the core of continuous identity renewal prompted, in turn, by the circumstances that create new experiences and challenges from which we learn and evolve. This liminal space is one with which learners need to become familiar and for which they need to understand the metacognitive strategies of learning for the longer term.

References

Bennett, D. (2013). Creativity beyond the notes: Exploring future lives in music to develop self-concept and salient identity. In P. Burnard (Ed.), *Developing creativities in higher music education* (pp. 234–244). London: Routledge.

Bolman, L., & Deal, T. (1997). *Reframing organisations*. San Francisco: Jossey-Bass.

Byrne, D. (2001). *Complexity theory and the social sciences: An introduction*. London: Routledge.

Cook-Sather, A., & Alter, Z. (2011). What is and what can be: How a liminal position can change learning and teaching in higher education. *Anthropology & Education Quarterly, 42*(1), 37–53. doi: 10.1111/j.1548-1492.2010.01109.x.

Curlee, W., & Gordon, R. L. (2011). *Complexity theory and project management*. Hoboken, NJ: John Wiley & Sons.

Delanty, G. (2010). *Community* (2nd edn). Abingdon: Routledge.

Dewey, J. (2008). *How we think*. Champaign, IL: Book Jungle. (Original work published 1910.)

Dweck, C. S. (2006). *Mindset: The new psychology of success*. New York: Random House.

Freer, P., & Bennett, D. (2012). Developing musical and educational identities in university music students. *Music Education Research, 14*(3), 265–284. doi: 10.1080/14613808.2012.712507.

Griess, K. (2014). *Leadership liminality: How catalytic experiences develop leaders*. Unpublished doctoral thesis. Minneapolis: Capella University.

Hargreaves, D. J. MacDonald, R. A. R., & Miell, D. E. (2009). Musical identities. In S. Hallam, I. Cross, & M. Thaut (Eds.), *The Oxford handbook of music psychology* (pp. 462–469). Oxford: Oxford University Press.

Hawkins, B., & Edwards, G. (2015). Managing the monsters of doubt: Liminality, threshold concepts and leadership learning. *Management learning, 46*(1), 24–43. doi: 10.1177/1350507613501736.

Hennekam, S., & Bennett, D. (2016). (Self)managing complexity: Managing work in the Netherlands creative industries. *International Journal of Arts Management, 19*(1), 31–41. Retrieved from www.gestiondesarts.com/en/self-management-of-work-in-the-creative-industries-in-the-netherlands#.V9u7xJN94W9.

Jarvis, P. (2002). Lifelong learning: Which way forward for higher education? In D. Colardyn (Ed.), *Lifelong learning: Which ways forward?* (pp. 34–45). Utrecht: Lemma.

Lewin, K. (1947). Frontiers in group dynamics: Concept, method and reality in social science; Social equilibria and social change. *Human Relations, 1*, 5–41. doi: 10.1177/001872674700100103.

Locke, E. A. (2008). How can we make organizations more ethical? In D. Barry & H. Hansen (Eds.), *Sage handbook of new approaches in management and organization*. Los Angeles: Sage.

Lührmann, T., & Eberl, P. (2007). Leadership and identity construction: Reframing the leader-follower interaction from an identity theory perspective. *Leadership, 3*(1), 115–127. doi: 10.1177/1742715007073070.

Manson, S. (2001). Simplifying complexity: a review of complexity theory. *Geoforum, 32*(3), 405–414. doi: 10.1016/S0016-7185(00)00035-X.

Marion, R. (1999). *The edge of organization*. Thousand Oaks, CA: Sage Publishers.

Mason, M. (2008). What is complexity theory and what are its implications for educational change? *Educational Philosophy and Theory, 40*(1), 35–49. doi: 10.1111/j.1469-5812.2007.00413.x.

McCrindle Research. (2014). Job mobility in Australia using HILDA and Department of Employment data. Available at: http://mccrindle.com.au/the-mccrindle-blog/jobmobility-in-australia.

Randle, K., & Culkin, N. (2009). Getting in and getting on in Hollywood: Freelance careers in an uncertain industry. In A. McKinlay & C. Smith (Eds.), *Creative labour* (pp. 93–115). London: Palgrave.

Reid, A., Abrandt Dahlgren, M., Petocz, P., & Dahlgren, L. O. (2011). *From expert student to novice professional*. Dordrecht: Springer.

Rowley, J. (2012). Final year music students' identities: Music student or music teacher? *Victorian Journal of Music Education, 2012*(1), 22–33.

Rowley, J., & Munday, J. (2014). A Sense of self through reflective thinking in ePortfolios. *International Journal of Humanities Social Sciences and Education 1*(7), 78–85. Retrieved from www.arcjournals.org/pdfs/ijhsse/v1-i7/9.pdf.

Senge, P. (1994). *The leader's new work: Building learning organisations*. In C. Mabey & P. Iles (Eds.), *Managing learning* (pp. 5–21). Oxford: The Open University and Thompson Business Press. Retrieved from https://sloanreview.mit.edu/article/the-leaders-new-work-building-learning-organizations/.

Solomonides, I., & Reid, A. (2009). Variation in student engagement: A design model. *Pedagogical Research Maximising Education, 3*(2), 115–128. Retrieved from https://core.ac.uk/download/pdf/5465.pdf#page=117.

Weick, K. E. (2001). Leadership as the legitimation of doubt. In W. Bennis, G. M. Spreitzer & T. G. Cummings (Eds.), *The future of leadership* (pp. 91–102). San Francisco, CA: Jossey-Bass.

Wenger, E. (1998). *Communities of practice: Learning, meaning and identity*. Cambridge: Cambridge University Press.

World Economic Forum (2016). *The future of jobs*. Retrieved from www3.weforum.org/docs/WEF_Future_of_Jobs.pdf.

Wright A. L., & Gilmore, A. (2012). Threshold concepts and conceptions: Student learning in introductory management courses. *Journal of Management Education, 36*, 614–635. doi: 10.1177/1052562911429446.

IX
Educing Leadership and Evoking Sound: Choral Conductors as Agents of Change

MARTIN BERGER

Choral singing is one of the most popular and widespread modes of music-making. In higher music education, the training of choral conductors has for a long time tended to focus exclusively on the development of artistic excellence. In contrast, conductors today are more than ever expected to be "agents of change", who contribute towards society in a variety of ways. The development of leadership skills and identity for choral conducting students is thus a complex enterprise, and yet few universities adopt a transdisciplinary approach that might offer choral conducting students the requisite skills and experience with which to fulfil such a leadership role. In this chapter, I first summarise findings of previous research concerning the relationship between choral conducting as a university subject and leadership theory. Utilising approaches of comparative music education, I then explore choral conducting pedagogy of the past and its possible progression into the future. I also raise the question of how the training of choral conductors at universities might contribute to the pioneering process of music-making in a multicultural society by combining musical excellence, creativity and social justice. In this chapter, my aim thus is to provoke a critical evaluation of existing choral programmes, philosophies and methodologies in line with the multifaceted societal role of choral conductors.

Choral Conducting in Context

Choral music exists in all civilisations and the distinctive need to express oneself through singing seems to be innate in human beings (Blacking, 1976; Durrant, 2005). Since each musical interaction is based on action and reaction, question and answer, or call and response, music-making that involves more than one person also involves a leadership role. Given the need to bring together talent, personality, devotion and the voices of others, leadership emerges as a core requisite for conductors.

The activity of beating time for a group of singers can be traced back to the ancient Sumerians, Egyptian, Greeks and Christians (Durrant, 2005), and yet choral conducting as an autonomous university discipline gained a foothold only during the 20th century and has largely focused on the development of artistic excellence. Although the pedagogical approaches may differ, there is wide agreement on the definition of artistic excellence in choral music. This can be seen in Van der Sandt's (2013) review of 37 choral conducting syllabi from universities in 17 different countries. Van der Sandt goes on to report that choral conducting is mainly taught as a means of communicating artistic intentions; students learn to execute preparations and beats, how to set tempo and control the pacing of the music, how to listen critically and unify singers, how to determine style and its possible interpretation, and, in particular, how to evoke sound.

Universities have established comprehensive systems of instruction for choral conducting within a range of undergraduate and graduate programmes. Aspiring conductors are given a wide-ranging education in music history and music theory, including an analytical understanding of the main style periods of classical music. Most universities request appropriate keyboard and vocal skills, which are intended to develop the student's ability to analyse music up to the level of oratorios and to consider their interpretations even before they have actual access to an orchestra or choir.

Many choral conductors are former members of choirs or orchestras, which gives them an understanding of how orchestras and choirs are conducted and rehearsed. However, the role of a conductor as leader has significantly changed, and universities have failed to adapt their curricula accordingly. Conductors in the 21st century are more than ever expected to be "agents of change", contributing towards society in a variety of ways. These might include positively influencing individuals by equipping them to think critically and motivating them to be collaborative citizens. It might also involve developing tools to shape cultural identity and a more just society.

Although many suggestions have been put forward as to how to build a model for the effective training for choral conductors, most of these repeat old answers without answering the new questions. This is despite recent studies which have addressed issues such as effectiveness (e.g., Con, 2015), score preparation (e.g., Battisti, 2007), the effective use of verbal language (e.g., Skadsem, 1997), the effect of seating arrangement on choral sound (e.g., Ekholm, 2000) and perceptions of conductor and ensemble expressivity (e.g., Silvey, 2015). Such studies have the potential to provide future choral conductors with an array of technical and scholarly knowledge never seen before. The question of how to lead and what kind of generic leadership skills are required at the intersection of professional education and societal impact is seldom discussed, either in the literature or in the classroom. Very few universities address the leadership dimension of conducting, either in teaching or in their scholarly work. Leadership is mostly seen as an accompanying outcome of other preparation, a process of natural selectivity or a type of talent with which some students are gifted.

Arguably, no other field of *musicking* (to use Small's (2011) famous gerund) requires leadership skills as much as conducting. Choral conducting students study under a paradox: professionally trained at high standards, most of them will never enter the professional market since the great majority of choral singing takes place in schools, churches and communities, with requirements that are far below those for which they have been trained. In other words, despite their professional training, few student conductors are prepared for the work they are likely to do as graduates. Freer (2011, p. 170) elucidates the challenges that can result.

This paradox is experienced when choral music teachers seek to balance the competing goals of performance and pedagogy. Instead of balance and harmony, the paradox creates tensions affecting curriculum, instructional techniques, repertoire selection, assessment techniques, classroom environment, and performance expectations. Without a clear set of guiding principles, we are often reluctant to make choices and/or changes in response to these tensions. We instead acquiesce to traditional and conservative standards for choral performance in education, riding the prevailing winds of the profession regardless of how they agree or disagree with our personal philosophies.

Present-day students' career trajectories will be different from those of the previous generations and are likely to become more complex in the future. Our understanding of the world and our being human cannot but have an impact on how we educate students, if we want them to become successful future colleagues. Jorgensen (2003) remarks that we live in a time of rapid and profound change and that this change will automatically lead to changes in the way we educate the next student generation. However, in the case of choral conducting tuition at music institutions there appears to be no such change. There is also no evidence that change will happen automatically. In the 21st century, students born in the 20th and 21st century are still educated with strategies from the 19th century. The definition of a choral conductor as a leader and a multiplier must thus be stretched far beyond performance skills and the focus on artistic excellence. Rather, it should recognise the different aspects of identity shaping for which a career in choral conducting calls.

Leadership Theory

During the last decades, "leadership" has become an enormously popular buzzword. Being or becoming a leader is attractive and it satisfies the human desire to make a difference and to give meaning to life. However, the understanding of leadership and leadership effectiveness has changed considerably. In the first three decades of the 20th century, definitions of leadership focused on centralisation of power, control, strength and hierarchical structures. Leaders, often described as a single and transfigured person at the top of an organisation, were thought to be in control. They were also pictured as white, male and born to lead: "The scientific study of leadership began at the turn of the 20th century with the 'great man [sic]' ... which saw the shaping of history through the lens of exceptional individuals" (Day & Antonakis, 2012, p. 7). This point of view changed during the 1930s, when leadership was increasingly viewed in terms of influence, rather than domination. Day and Antonakis (2012, p. 7) explain that leadership traits became the focus of scholarly research, with the assumption that the characteristics of good leadership might be analysed and reproduced.

> This school of thought suggested that certain dispositional characteristics (i.e., stable personality attributes or traits) differentiated leaders from non-leaders. Thus, leadership researchers focused on identifying robust individual differences in personality traits that were thought to be associated with effective leadership.

According to Northouse (2013), research undertaken during the 1940s described leadership as the behaviour of an individual when directing group activities. This opened the perspective that leadership skills can be taught effectively. Day and Antonakis (2012, p. 8) describe "consideration (supportive, person-oriented leadership)" and "initiating structure (directive, task-oriented leadership)" as the two overarching leadership factors from this time.

During the 1950s, scholars continued to examine the behaviour of leaders by considering "leadership and efficiency" and "leadership as relationship with a group in order to develop shared goals". Leadership was now seen as a reciprocal process of mobilising effective leadership, which "occurred when one or more persons engage with others in such a way that leaders and followers raise one another to higher levels of motivation and morality" (Burns, 1978, p. 20). Put another way, good leadership depends on transformational skills. As Day and Antonakis explain (2012, p. 8), the lack of consistency in these findings led to further angst as:

> leadership research found itself again in crisis because of contradictory findings relating behavioral "styles" of leadership to relevant outcomes. That is, there was no consistent evidence of a universally preferred leadership style across tasks or situations. From these inconsistent findings, it was proposed that success of the leader's behavioral style must be contingent on the situation.

An important observation during the 1980s was the emerging scepticism of previous evaluation methods. According to Day and Antonakis (2012, p. 10), scholars "argued that leader evaluations were based on the attributions followers make in their quest to understand and assign causes to organizational outcomes". Leadership was therefore often a "way of explaining observed results, even if those results were due to factors outside of the leader's control".

The increasing popularity of publications about leadership since the 1990s blurs the line between valid academic research and superficial guides. However, Northouse (2013, p. 3) suggests that a consensus has emerged on at least four characteristics of leadership: namely that:

1. leadership is a process;
2. leadership involves influence;
3. leadership occurs in groups; and
4. leadership involves a common goal.

Having summarised the trajectory of previous research on effective leadership, the following section uncovers parallels with the changing image of (choral) conductors. It further aims to evidence that leadership skills are culturally dependent and that they need to be shaped.

Leadership and Choral Conducting

In line with the idea of leadership as a centralisation of power, strength and hierarchical structures at the beginning of the 20th century, Boult (1936), Wood (1945) and Finn (1946) nourished the impression of the conductor as a charismatic leader with an "adorable" personality. Publications from this time tend to glorify the role of a conductor, often using military language, emphasising domination and creating a strong sense of hierarchy. Wood (1945) mentions the need for the conductor to be an educator for children (from the podium, of course) and devotes a chapter to women in the orchestra. Thomas (1935) was the first to draft a comprehensive syllabus for choral conducting as a teachable (university) subject. By approaching all main technical aspects of choral conducting systematically, this contributed decisively to the professionalism of the discipline.

The new awareness that conducting skills might be formally taught led to subsequent publications at a much higher level, and scholars such as Kruger (1958), Ehret (1959) and Stanton (1971) offered comprehensive textbooks. Accordingly, choral conducting as a developing university subject was now seen as an attractive, but complex, field of training. Thomas, Mann and Reese's (1971) English translation of Thomas (1935) is still recognised as one of the standard references for the discipline. Since the 1970s, nearly all publications have communicated the opinion that leadership can be successfully modelled. The focus shifts towards a broader view of the discipline, identifying pedagogical approaches and social literacy as key criteria of efficient leadership (Behrman, 1984; Cox, 1989; Garretson, 1981; Lamb, 1979).

By the end of the 1980s, the importance of choral music as a subject for general music education was fully understood within universities. This changed the perspective of leadership skills immensely. Numerous publications conveyed the function of the choral conductor as an educator and facilitator, and working with children and youth choirs emerged as a new specialised field (Rao, Dolloff, & Prodans, 1993).

Modern conducting involves shared responsibility and goal-orientated principles of operation, rather than hierarchical authority or power (Brinson, 1996; Cox, 1989; Durrant, 2000). Research from the beginning of the 21st century focuses increasingly on the potential impact of choral conducting on social interaction, social justice and equality (Allsup & Shieh, 2012: Con, 2015; Durrant, 2003, 2005; Freer, 2011; Garnett, 2009; Wis, 2007). Leadership is thus seen as an agency for change, with a focus on society and not only on art. There remain, however, three aspects of leadership that remain underexplored.

The first of these is that definitions of leadership refer to the societal context in which they occur. Westerners tend to understand the 20th century, particularly since World War II, as a constant enhancement of democratic principles and of progress towards social justice and equality. Each important societal discussion during the last decades (gender, equality, race, social justice, environmental awareness, to name but a few) has contributed to the embrace of a certain perception of leadership. The idea that leadership and social influence are interlinked is therefore deeply rooted in our understanding of society and democracy. If music educators are to be leaders, they are to be agents of change towards the principles of dialogue and democracy (Schmidt, 2012; Woodford, 1996, 2005).

The second underexplored aspect of leadership is that the dominant leadership discussion takes a solely Western point of view. This is as exclusive and narrow a view, which often ignores the different concepts of leadership to be found in other cultures. This also indicates that the interaction between leader and followers might be ideologically determined, since other systems have different perceptions. Very few sources refer to other views of leadership as valuable alternatives. If the way we live, including our beliefs, values and relationships with others, is influenced by global factors, our idea of leadership needs to be broadened, too. Eastern philosophies, for example, tend to emphasise the awareness of unity and the interrelatedness of everything, and as inseparable parts of the whole. While Western scholars (and artists) often strive to find and prove a specific "truth", many Eastern societies accept the truth as given and are more interested in finding "balance". The prevailing dichotomous distinction between Western and Eastern cultures is misleading and often subconscious: principles of leadership in Indian and Chinese philosophies, for example, are as far away from each other as they are from our Western point of view. The lack of debate about these differentiations is a shortcoming in contemporary debates about leadership.

The final underexamined aspect of leadership is the exclusive division between Western and Eastern viewpoints, which ignores an important part of the world: the South. Agawu (2003a, 2003b) argues that the concept of the autonomous individual as we know it from a Western point of view is unknown in most African cultures. Looking at sub-Saharan Africa, the relationship between an individual (or a leader) and a group can be understood with the connotations of the word *ubuntu*. Gade (2011) explains the different understanding and impact of *ubuntu* in a very comprehensive way: coming from the Nguni languages and roughly translated with humanness or human kindness, *ubuntu* describes a person as individual only because of a specific relationship to other individuals: "*Ubuntu ngumntu ngabanye abantu* is roughly translated as *a person is (can only be) a person through other persons*" (Albion, 2008, p. 85, in Gade, 2011, p. 318). While written sources about *ubuntu* prior to 1950 mainly define the word as a human quality, the term developed more towards an understanding of an "African humanism, a philosophy, an ethic, and as a worldview" (Gade, 2011, p. 303).

The idea of *ubuntu* is deeply entrenched in a search towards African identity, and this has an inevitable effect on how African conductors think and act, as well as on their perception of leadership. African leadership perception therefore differs in many ways from a Western understanding. *Ubuntu* "involves aid-giving, sympathy, care, sensitivity to the needs of others, respect, consideration, patience, and kindness" (Prinsloo, 1998, p. 42, in Gade, 2011, p. 317). *Ubuntu* therefore has a strong moral quality, and recipients are obliged to give back to the community and to share, especially in relation to sharing knowledge. New curricula for the education of choral conducting students will need to explore these questions.

Towards the Education of Choral Conducting Students

In the preceding sections, I summarised findings of previous research concerning the relationship between leadership theory and choral conducting as a university subject. The development of leadership skills and identity for choral conducting students emerged as a complex notion, since choral conductors are more than ever expected to be change agents who contribute towards society in a variety of ways. Yet, few universities adopt a transdisciplinary approach that might offer choral conducting students the requisite skills and experience with which to fulfil such a leadership role. It also became apparent that Western definitions of leadership tend to be exclusive and often ignore divergent concepts of leadership to be found in other cultures. In this section, I discuss how the training of choral conductors at universities might be refined to contribute to the pioneering process of music-making in a multicultural society: specifically, by combining musical excellence, creativity and social justice.

Developing an identity as a musician is crucial for music students. Compared with their fellow music students, conductors are in a far more complex situation when it comes to achieving this goal: along with singers, they are the only kind of musician to create music without an external instrument. Conductors make use of other people's talent, personality and dedication to create and interpret sound. Identity is, therefore, a process of striving for constant change, and students need to be "actively involved in developing their concept of self as a musician while engaged in their formal musical studies" (Rowley, Bennett, & Reid, 2016, p. 47). The future training of conductors will become more interdisciplinary than in the past because students will have to learn how to achieve both artistic excellence and local relevance by working with people both creatively and compassionately. Choral music contributes to the welfare of a country by educating students to be critical thinkers and engaged citizens, through the development of intellectual capital and human potential. This might serve as a tool to shape cultural identity and a more just society. Universities will have to pioneer a process of music-making by combining musical excellence, creativity and social justice, taking them far beyond the considerations of practical training.

The key qualification to achieve this goal is awareness. Durrant (2005, p. 89) proposes "a series of interrelated attributes that contribute to the understanding of effective choral conducting" in the 21st century, which he lists as "philosophical underpinning, music-technical skills and interpersonal skills". I might suggest four additional areas that could contribute to a more multifaceted conductor education:

1. Expanding awareness;
2. Empowering leadership skills;
3. Educing transcultural skills; and
4. Encouraging creative skills.

I elaborate on these suggestions in the following paragraphs.

Expanding Awareness

Awareness is always based on information or experience. If we state that expanding awareness can contribute to a more multifaceted education of choral conductors, we need to specify what kind of awareness we expect our students to achieve and whether we want them to develop their leadership skills further. Taking the previous findings into consideration, three important aspects of awareness for choral conductors might be awareness of cultural identity, awareness of social justice and awareness of different perceptions.

Modern leadership will have to make a meaningful contribution to the further development of cultural identity. Being excellent and locally relevant is a key attribute for which students should aim, and cultural identity is the crucial factor within the process of globalisation. This formation of cultural identity has to include music: as Robertson (2004) argues, cultural identity is the sum of our communal beliefs, principles, traditions, behaviours and arts facts. At the very core of each culture is its poetry, its song, its folklore and its stories. Kohler (2008) states that the experience of one's own culture is always determined by a foreign culture, and that we need the aspect of a foreign culture as a second point of reference. For Dei (2000, p. 21, in Bradley, 2006, p. 13), multiculturalism in music education works "with the notion of our basic humanness and downplays inequities of difference by accentuating shared commonalities". Robertson (2004) calls these commonalities *experience* and defines cultural identity as awareness of a shared experience. I would add that a modern way of teaching choral conducting must interact with what is culturally relevant, without neglecting the pursuit for technical standards that have been agreed upon internationally.

The alignment of music and social justice has become an important point of discussion in recent years, and choirs are sites of this discussion. Providing a definition of what social justice means is difficult, since terminology often lacks rigour and leads to ambiguity. Allsup and Shieh (2012), Kertz-Welzel (2012) and Woodford (2005) point out that the aesthetic-creative potential of music education must be to provoke change in the context of a democratic society. Elliott (2007, pp. 84–85) argues that music teachers, and in our case choral conductors, must be empowered to offer artistic responses to contemporary social, moral and political questions.

> If we are serious about developing transformative and durable practices, we need to reconsider our most deeply ingrained assumptions. Are we purely teachers, musicians, academics, and/or public intellectuals? Or can we "move out into the social world", developing new ways of educating a critical mass of future music teachers who have the understandings (both theoretical and practical) and the dispositions to infuse their aims and pedagogies with goals of social justice and social activism? If the latter, we need to renounce counterproductive theories and practices and replace them with better ones.

In this interaction between music and the needs of society, choirs can serve as a platform to develop musical responses to societal questions. However, they can do so only if their members and leaders are empowered to create change. As Elliot (2007, p. 87) attests:

> we need to empower music students and music education majors as artistic and socially just musical citizens. What this means is that we need to enable our students to develop musical replies to the social/moral/political dilemmas of today and tomorrow by creating musical expressions of social problems.

Awareness of Different Perceptions

In a time of global change, we need to prepare students for multicultural approaches to their music-making. Most universities still focus on a core repertoire of Western classical music and do not take into account the different cultural perceptions of a choral sound. In many African cultures, for example, the "ideal" choral sound is more forced: this is seen as natural and strong. Another example of difference is that Western music interpretation often considers technical perfection and intonation to be the most important criteria on which to judge a performance. Numerous African cultures, however, consider intonation less of a priority. A different vowel formation leads to a "deeper" sound than in Western choirs, and vibrato is seen as positive and a quality criterion. Some languages, such as *Igbo* in Ghana, are tonal languages, and subtle variations in tone can change the meaning of words. The habit exists to capture the tonal patterns or flexions in the songs, which lead into a subconscious rise or lowering of pitch in the singing. From a Western perspective, this is often misunderstood as faulty intonation.

The intercultural environment in which many conductors work sees them interact with different cultural perceptions. The simple question of why people would join a choir will elicit different responses from different cultural groups; in many cases, music-making will be only one motivation alongside social dimensions and the enhancement of (musical) knowledge and proficiency. The "cultural space" to which conductors and singers belong influences their modes of perception and subsequent reflection of music. This environment interacts with different forms of aesthetics, and good leadership requires awareness of the problem: Are our categories of musical and aesthetical thinking universally fixed, or are they conditioned by our respective culture? What criteria do we use to reach value judgements? Are different aesthetic concepts of singing and choral music of equal value? Can terms such as "beautiful", "melodious" and "perfectly formed" claim transcultural validity? Kohler (2008) argues that an aesthetic relativism that denies the existence of absolute, culturally independent values will ultimately lead to aesthetic arbitrariness. The recent calls for a decolonisation of syllabi at African, specifically South African universities, proves the need for intense debate.

Empowering Leadership Skills
Empowering leadership skills is tantamount to developing a student's identity. This is next explored in relation to the development of identity and creativity, and educing transcultural skills.

Developing Musician Identity
Rowley et al. (2016, p. 2) assert that "Leadership and musician identity are graduate qualities that we expect music students to acquire during their time in higher music education". Identity is a process of striving for constant change, and conducting students need to be more actively involved in developing individual concepts of being a musician. The complicated situation for conducting students is that they are, along with singers, the only students who create music without an external instrument. Conductors (and singers) *are* the instrument: they have, in addition, to make use of other people's talents, gifts, personalities and dedication in order to create sound, interpretation and quality.

Developing Leadership Identity
Leadership skills need to be authentic and transformational. If leadership is the ability to influence the behaviour of others, choral conducting students need to learn how to inspire others to eagerly seek defined objectives. Good leaders develop future visions and motivate others to want to achieve these. An example of this is transformational leadership, which causes positive change in those who follow and creates a fruitful and enriching atmosphere. Transformational leadership is proactive, inspirational, intrinsic, interpersonal and collaborative, and therefore more effective than transactional leadership, which "motivates followers by appealing to their self-interest" (Yukl, 2002, p. 261). Shamir and Eilam (2005) emphasise that leadership also needs to be authentic: The students' goals must be motivated by true beliefs and values, passions and a self-expressive behaviour that is consistent with the group's values and identities.

Educing Transcultural Skills
An intercultural approach of training choral conductors implies that we must interact with different forms of aesthetics. The cultural space to which our students and singers belong influences their modes of perception and subsequent reflection of music. A close look at the repertoire choice might come to the conclusion that this is less diversified than we would wish it to be.

Developing Creativity
Bennett (2008) argues that the definition of what a musician is must be stretched far beyond merely being a performer, and that universities should better recognise the variety of roles and identities that a career in music asks for. Perkins and Williamon (2016) suggest more spaces for creativity and reflectivity at universities, seeing that "spaces for learning have sat uncomfortably with priorities on musical specialism and outdated measures of musical success" (Perkins & Williamon, 2016, p. 18). They add that learning and teaching in the 21st century must entail "multiple forms of leadership, multiple learning styles and, crucially, adaptive and responsive learning environments that enable learning to flourish".

Conclusions

The training of choral conductors in higher music education has for a long time focused exclusively on the development of artistic excellence, and this chapter aimed to provoke a critical re-evaluation of existing philosophies in line with the multifaceted societal role of choral conductors. The chapter has illustrated that conductors today are more than ever expected to be agents of change who contribute towards society in a variety of ways. Since the great majority of choral singing takes place in schools, churches and communities, the requirements for leadership are different from those for which these conductors have been trained. The development of leadership skills and identity for choral conducting students is a complex enterprise, and universities must adopt a transdisciplinary approach to offer choral conducting students the requisite assistance and experience with which to fulfil such a leadership role.

Leaders lead people, conductors evoke sound: the future of choral conducting as a prospering university subject will, especially in a multicultural society, depend on role models of modern leadership. New repertoire, internationally competitive but locally relevant, might open new windows to the people's respective culture and bridge the gap between the artificial "ivory tower" in which universities can find themselves, and the places to which they belong.

Defining the role of a modern conductor can be compared with leadership as a process: it is rather a transformational event that occurs between the conductor and his/her choir than a trait or a characteristic that exists in the respective student. Choral conductors must be empowered to work concurrently towards two (possibly conflicting) goals: the artistic quality of the performance; and the quality of the education with which their singers are provided. Acknowledging the validity of both goals, choral conductors "need to increase awareness of how their goals affect decisions concerning policy, pedagogy, and musical practice" (Freer, 2011, p. 164).

This broadening of the discipline must retain the commitment to technical excellence, but not necessarily as an end in itself; good intonation may be impressive, and rhythm may be rousing, but only sound has the unique quality to touch people and to make a difference. Moreover, conductors will need to be aware that artistic excellence is culturally determined, as is the motivation to sing. Each piece of music provides us with the possibilities to deal with our respective culture and keeps us involved with the sounds of a society.

Conductors taking up this challenge will be contributing to the society in a much wider field than ever before. Being both artists and agents of change, they will be positioned to be effective music-makers: educing modern leadership and evoking the sounds of our times.

References

Agawu, V. K. (2003a). *Representing African music: Postcolonial notes, queries, positions.* New York: Routledge.

Agawu, V. K. (2003b). Contesting difference. A critique of Africanist ethnomusicology. In M. Clayton, T. Herbert & R. Middleton (Eds.), *The cultural study of music: A critical introduction* (pp. 227–237). New York: Routledge.

Allsup, R. E., & Shieh, E. (2012). Social justice and music education: The call for a public pedagogy. *Music Educators Journal*, 98(4), 47–51.

Battisti, F. (2007). *On becoming a conductor: Lessons and meditations on the art of conducting.* Galesville, MD: Meredith Music.

Behrmann, M. (1984). *Chorleitung.* Neunhausen-Stuttgart, Germany: Hänssler.

Bennett, D. (2008). *Understanding the classical music profession: The past, the present and strategies for the future.* Aldershot, UK: Ashgate.

Bennett, D. (2011). Rethinking success: Music in higher education. *International Journal of the Humanities*, 9(5), 181–187.

Blacking, J. (1976). *How musical is man?* London: Faber and Faber.

Boult, A. (1936). *A handbook on the technique of conducting.* Oxford, UK: Hall.

Bradley, D. G. (2006). Music education, multiculturalism, and anti-racism: Can we talk? *Action, Criticism, and Theory for Music Education*, 5(2), 1–30.

Brinson, B. A. (1996). *Choral music – methods and materials.* New York: Schirmer Books.

Burns, J. M. (1978). *Leadership.* New York: Harper & Row.

Con, A. (2015). Effective conducting in the choral classroom. *Choral Journal*, 55(9), 30–38.

Cox, J. (1989). Choral conducting: More than a wave of the hand. *Music Educators Journal*, 75(9), 26–30.

Day, D., & Antonakis, J. (2012). *The nature of leadership* (2nd edn). Thousand Oaks, CA.: Sage.

Durrant, C. (2000). Making choral rehearsing seductive: Implications for practice and choral education. *Research Studies in Music Education*, 15, 40–49.

Durrant, C. (2003). *Choral conducting: Philosophy and practice.* New York: Routledge.

Durrant, C. (2005). Shaping identity through choral activity: Singers' and conductors' perceptions. *Research Studies in Education*, 24, 88–98.

Ekholm, E. (2000). The effect of singing mode and seating arrangement on choral blend and overall choral sound. *Journal of Research in Music Education*, 48(2), 123.

Elliott, D. (2007). "Socializing" music education. *Action, criticism, and theory for music education*, 6(4), 60–95. Retrieved from http://act.maydaygroup.org/articles/Elliott6_4.pdf.

Ehret, W. (1959). *The choral conductor's handbook.* New York: E. B. Marks Music Corp.

Finn, W. J. (1946). *The conductor raises his baton: The mystery of music is in the upbeat.* London: Dennis Dobson Ltd.
Freer, P. (2011). The performance-pedagogy paradox in choral music teaching. *Philosophy of Music Education Review, 19*(2), 164–178.
Gade, C. B. N. (2011). The historical development of the written discourses on Ubuntu. *South African Journal of Philosophy, 30,* 303–329.
Garnett, L. (2009). *Choral conducting and the construction of meaning: Gesture, voice, identity.* Farnham, Surrey: Ashgate.
Garretson, R. L. (1981). *Conducting choral music.* Boston: Allyn and Bacon.
Jorgensen, E. R. (2003). *Transforming music education.* Bloomington: Indiana University Press.
Kertz-Welzel, A. (2012). Social justice. Oder: Der Traum von der gesellschaftlichen Relevanz des Musikunterrichts. In J. Vogt, F. Heß & C. Rolle (Eds.), *Musikpädagogik und Heterogenität. Wissenschaftliche Musikpädagogik* (pp. 55–73). Bd. 5. Münster: LIT-Verl. S.
Kohler, R. A. (2008). Das problem der werturteilsbildung in einer interkulturellen musikästhetik. In J. P. Hiekel (Ed.), *Musik-kulturen: Texte der 43. Internationalen Ferienkurse für Neue Musik 2006* (pp. 16–22). Saarbrücken: Pfau.
Kruger, K. (1958). *The way of the conductor.* New York: Charles Scribner's Sons.
Lamb, G. H. (1979). *Choral techniques.* Dubuque, IA: William C Brown.
Northouse, P. G. (2013). *Leadership: Theory and practice.* Thousand Oaks: Sage.
Neuen, D. (1988). Focus: Choral music: The sound of a great chorus. *Music Educators Journal, 75*(4), 42.
Perkins, R., & Williamon, A. (2016, July). *Musicians as researchers: The development and evaluation of a conservatoire-based MSc in Performance Science.* Paper presented at the 21st International Seminar of the ISME Commission on the Education of the professional musician. Retrieved from www.isme.org/sites/default/files/documents/ISME%20CEPROM%20Proceedings%202016_final.pdf.
Prinsloo, E. D. (1998). Ubuntu culture and participation management. In P. H. Coetzee & A. P. J. Roux (Eds.), *The African philosophy reader* (pp. 41–51). London: Routledge.
Rao, D., Dolloff, L.-A., & Prodans, S. (1993). *We will sing! Choral music experience for classroom choirs.* New York: Boosey & Hawkes.
Robertson, M. (2004). "Imagining ourselves": South African music as a vehicle for negotiating white South African identity. *Journal of the Musical Arts in Africa, 1*(1), 128–137.
Rowley, J., Bennett, D., & Reid, A. (2016). Leadership as a core creativity for musician identity. In E. K. M. Chong (Ed.), *Proceedings of the 21st International Seminar of the Commission on the Education of the Professional Musician (CEPROM)* (pp. 43–51). Saint Andrews, Fife. Retrieved from www.isme.org/sites/default/files/documents/ISME%20CEPROM%20Proceedings%202016_final.pdf.
Schmidt, P. (2012). What we hear is meaning too: Deconstruction, dialogue, and music. *Philosophy of Music Education Review, 20*(1), 3–24.
Shamir, B., & Eilam, G. (2005). "What's your story?": A life-stories approach to authentic leadership development. *The Leadership Quarterly, 16*(3), 395–417.
Silvey, B. A. (2015). Effects of conducting plane on band and choral musicians' perceptions of conductor and ensemble expressivity. *Journal of Research in Music Education, 63*(3), 369–384.
Skadsem, J. A. (1997). Effect of conductor verbalization, dynamic markings, conductor gesture, and choir dynamic level on singers' dynamic responses. *Journal of Research in Music Education, 45*(4), 509–520.
Small, C. (2011). *Musicking: The meanings of performing and listening.* Middletown, CO: Wesleyan University Press.
Stanton, R. (1971). *The dynamic choral conductor.* Delaware Water Gap, PA: Shawnee Press.
Thomas, K. (1935). *Lehrbuch der Chorleitung.* Wiesbaden: Breitkopf & Härtel.
Thomas, K., Mann, A., & Reese, W. H. (1971). *The choral conductor: The technique of choral conducting in theory and practice.* New York: Associated Music Publishers.

Van der Sandt, J. T. V. D. (2013). *Towards a curriculum for the training of undergraduate choral conducting students*. Doctor Musicae (Performing Arts) thesis, University of Pretoria. Retrieved from http://repository.up.ac.za/handle/2263/31574.

Wis, R. M. (2007). *The conductor as leader: Principles of leadership applied to life on the podium*. Chicago: GIA Publications.

Wood, H. J. (1945). *About conducting*. London: Sylvan Press.

Woodford, P. (1996). Developing critical thinkers in music: Fostering critical-thinking skills in students empowers them to control their own musical growth. *Music Educators Journal, 83*, 27–32.

Woodford, P. (2005). *Democracy and music education: liberalism, ethics, and the politics of practice*. Bloomington: Indiana University.

Yukl, G. (2002). *Leadership in organizations* (5th edn). Upper Saddle River, NJ: Prentice Hall.

X

The Tapestry of Leadership, Creativity and Advocacy: Weaving Musicians' Core Abilities into the Curriculum

PAMELA D. PIKE

Making music by generating novel solutions to musical problems, or creating innovative musical works by availing of domain-specific musical skills, imaginative problem-solving strategies and appropriate motivation tools, is inherently creative. However, research reveals that music students may not be graduating with the creative attributes they need to pursue and establish gratifying musical careers in the 21st century. Within the American cultural climate, as elsewhere, professional musicians are asked to quantify musical experiences for utilitarian purposes, suggesting a renewed need to advocate for the intrinsic value of music and creative experiences. Through the lens of leadership, creativity and advocacy, this chapter explores findings of an in-depth survey of professional musicians in one US state. The survey included Likert-type, short-answer and open-ended questions to identify how professional musicians earned their income, which skills they used regularly and which skills acquired during their degree programmes were beneficial. Data were analysed and comparisons were made between recent graduates and established teachers. Teaching and church positions were the primary income sources for the respondents. While many musicians engaged in collaborative performances, these provided little income. Domain-specific music skills employed regularly included technique, collaborative performance, efficient practising, and sight-reading. Important teaching skills included assigning appropriate technique and repertoire, teaching practice strategies, student performance preparation and business management. Business-related activities occupied much of the professionals' time. Musicians who regularly assumed leadership roles within various music organisations reported satisfaction with daily professional pursuits and their activities included high levels of creativity and advocacy.

Leadership, Creativity and Advocacy

> Leaders achieve their effectiveness chiefly through the stories they relate ... Leaders in the arts characteristically inspire others by the ways they use their chosen media of artistic expression, be they the phrases of a sonata or the gestures of a dance ... In addition to communicating stories, leaders *embody* those stories.
>
> (Gardner, 1995, p. 9)

In recent years, demonstrations of leadership, creativity and advocacy have been used as markers for acceptance into university, to gauge the future success of new employees, and to justify the need for various professions and their associated university programmes, including those in music (AACU, 2013; Adams, 2013; Benedictus, 2013; Vendler, 2012). Creativity is often cited as a by-product of music study (Bújez & Mohedo, 2014; O'Brien & Walton, 2011); easily recognisable examples of musical creativity are composition and improvisation (Myers & Sarath, 2014; Sawyer, 2006). Artistic performance, where one interprets and conveys a composer's notated intentions through live or recorded performance, is another commonly mentioned outcome of musical creativity (Running, 2008).

Although artistic performances are recognisable musical "products", there is little agreement on how to measure creativity in music (for example, Running, 2008). Furthermore, if a student simply follows interpretive instructions dictated by a teacher, how much musical creativity is really displayed? Forms of musical creativity beyond those listed above should be considered as well (Burnard, 2014). Creative thinking is a skill often cited by music educators as important in musical creativity (Webster, 1990). Creative thinking is generally recognisable by researchers and educators alike and can lead to creative outcomes (Amabile, 1996), but which creative thinking skills are required of practising professional musicians today, and are these being developed in traditional undergraduate music programmes so that future musicians can develop requisite creativity skills?

Demonstrating leadership skill has become increasingly important in the 21st century. Indeed, developing and exhibiting leadership skills starts early among aspiring professionals in the US, where Ivy League and private universities (and, increasingly, larger, state-funded schools) use a student's high-school leadership experience and success as an important measure when selecting students (Vendler, 2012). Hiring managers in various fields cite leadership skills as a factor in the hiring process among recent baccalaureate graduates, even if they are not applying for traditional managerial positions within companies or institutions (AACU, 2013). The belief that individuals need to exhibit leadership qualities is a common refrain in numerous First World cultures, where economic and business models have become dominant and have even replaced shared societal and cultural values and norms in education (Adams, 2013; Benedictus, 2013).

The shift towards more positivistic, measurable outcomes has manifested itself in American music education culture (CMS, 2015). Since the middle of the 20th century, music curriculum designers and standard bearers have embraced curricula that produce measurable outcomes among music students of all ages; however, some of these curricula have lost the relevance and connection between music and our broader culture (Myers, 2016). Moreover, the ability to advocate for music education and for music as a critical art form is increasingly important due to the lower standing that music occupies in secondary education, if it is present at all (Elpus, 2007; Libman, 2004). It is clear that new generations of professional musicians need to develop skills such as the ability to creatively lead and advocate for music; however, do recent graduates believe that such skills were developed during their tertiary music studies? If not, educators must consider how to devise assignments and activities that will enable students to develop and refine broad creative competencies.

In this chapter, I explore relevant research on leadership, creativity and advocacy in music education. Then, findings from a survey of essential skills reported by professional musicians will be explored through the lens of music teaching, advocacy, creativity and leadership. Since creativity is culturally contextual, the findings will be explored within the context of music education in the US. Through the subsequent discussion, I hope to elucidate ways to promote the development of such creative and leadership skills in tandem with traditional technical and musical abilities in undergraduate music curricula. Principles and ideas can be adapted by educators for their specific teaching contexts.

Transformational Leadership, Indirect Leadership and Following the Leader

Leadership is an influential subcategory in business, with entire courses of study and sections of bookshops devoted to the field. Despite the many courses and books on the subject, some suggest that there is a crisis in leadership early in the 21st century as people demonstrate less trust in conventional leaders, governments and large corporations. In the 21st century, the ability to demonstrate leadership has become increasingly important. No longer is leadership the sole purview of the stereotypical white male managing an enterprise from a corner office or boardroom. Today, youth are encouraged to develop leadership skills in high school and to demonstrate leadership prowess on university applications (Vendler, 2012). Too often, the kind of leadership that is prized favours the extrovert rather than the creative introvert. Skills associated with effective leadership include passion, discipline, knowledge of oneself, reflectiveness and the ability to get people to follow (Campbell, 2013).

McManus and Perruci (2015, p. 55) suggest that leadership is a process where "leaders, followers, goals, environmental context, and cultural context" are equally important. Recently, educators, too, are exploring the value of "followers", those members of the group who turn the vision of the leader into reality. Vendler (2012, p. 28) asks if universities "have room for the reflective student as well as for the future leader", implying that reflection and leadership are incompatible. Kelley (1988) notes that effective followers understand that they are integral to project completion and they exhibit independent thinking, problem-solving, energy, assertiveness and grit. These skills are remarkably similar to those demonstrated by creative thinkers and creative artists (Amabile, 1996; Balkin, 1990).

Effective followers also work well with peers and superiors, know how to develop individual credibility and maintain high ethical standards, and manage time effectively (Kelley, 1988). While music students learn to follow the maestro in large ensemble rehearsals, the benefits of small-group rehearsals are often overlooked. Negotiating musical tasks with peers in chamber ensembles is a promising way to develop both leadership and followership skills (Sawyer, 2006). The ability to think and act creatively, in tandem with others, is a critical piece of the leadership puzzle (Kouzes & Posner, 2002; Puccio, 2014; Ruggio, 2015). Indeed, these skills are similar to those exhibited by transformational leaders.

Transformational leaders are guided by long-term goals, values, emotions and ethics (Hall, 2008). Transformational leadership is often discussed with respect to music as there is an intersection of goals and emotion in both transformational leadership and musical practice. Gardner (1995, p. 36) references *indirect leadership* as typical among artists and musicians. Indirect leadership features a relationship between the leader and followers that is "ongoing, active and dynamic". In this democratic approach to leadership, the roles of leader and follower are fluid based on the stated problem or desired outcome. In music, this might be demonstrated during a chamber music rehearsal, where each member contributes to the technical and musical outcome. Members may take turns leading the rehearsal, sharing ideas, exploring musical possibilities and collaborating in ways that enable each musician to contribute, ensuring a rich musical outcome. Such democratic leadership is usually not possible in large-ensemble rehearsals. For new music graduates to lead throughout their careers, we should ensure that requisite skills are developed during undergraduate studies.

Creativity

Psychologist Howard Gardner (1995) makes a case for considering leadership and creativity together. Scholarship on leadership suggests that the ability to think and act creatively are critical to effective leadership (Kouzes & Posner, 2002; Puccio, 2014; Ruggio, 2015). However, definitions of creativity vary. Csikszentmihalyi (1996, p. 6) explores the broad category of creativity and the expert individuals who have wide influence upon their respective fields. He suggests that creativity occurs when three elements interact, "a culture that contains symbolic rules, a person who brings novelty into the symbolic domain, and a field of experts who recognize and validate the innovation". He contends that one must master the domain prior to being able to function in it creatively, and that new ideas are not automatically passed on to the next generation, but must be taught. While Csikszentmihalyi limited his study to creative individuals who innovated and ultimately changed their domain, the advancements put forth had to be accepted by experts and gatekeepers within each field. Similarly, children and young musicians must learn the accepted rules of their musical traditions. Surely teachers can encourage young musicians to be creative using their chosen instrument in tandem with skill development.

Csikszentmihalyi studies "big C" Creativity. Tertiary music educators should help students develop "small c" creativity, to lay the groundwork for more influential types of creativity once they begin working as professional musicians. Students in music history, theory and analysis classes might explore improvisatory styles, music and cultures that are more diverse and globally inclusive than those typically addressed in most 20th-century music curricula (for example, Burnard, 2014; Deliège & Wiggins, 2006). Students might further explore these ideas through improvisation and composition in individual lessons, small, student-led ensembles and performance opportunities outside the academy (Myers & Sarath, 2014; Sawyer, 2006). "Small c" creativity can further be developed when music students explore musical identities and negotiate shared musical practice by engaging with peers and community members through service-learning projects that bring students into contact with people who do not share similar musical or cultural backgrounds and experiences (see Kautsky, 2017; Pike, 2015, 2017; Reid, Bennett and Rowley's description of a work integrated learning internship experience, Chapter VIII of this volume).

Amabile, who studies how we measure creativity and evaluate artistic outcomes, suggests that for a work to be creative it must be novel, an appropriate response to the task, and heuristic (Amabile, 1996). This definition is frequently used as the psychological and educational definition of creativity. Amabile's framework of creativity has been widely adopted by educators who need to create classroom environments in which creative work can take place and who need to assess a student's creative output. In her model of creativity, three overlapping skill sets are necessary to undertake creative work; these are domain-specific skills, cognitively creative skills and task motivation (see Figure 10.1). The domain-relevant skills are those required for performance in any domain. In music, domain-relevant skills include motor skills and other specialised techniques; theory; or contextual understanding of musical elements. The skills required for domain-specific tasks are the most specialised of all skills used in creative pursuits. Creativity-relevant skills include one's ability to problem solve, apply divergent and convergent thinking that is appropriate to completing the task and the ability to self-regulate. These are the most general of the skills required, as different skills may be used by individuals; these may vary from one task to the next and they might be used across domains.

Amabile suggests that task motivation skills are the most important for any given creative activity. Individuals may fail to complete the task or produce a creative artefact, if not motivated in response to a specific goal within the domain. Likewise, completing increasingly challenging creative projects and persisting through the creative process over time are important components for creative development. Amabile contends that creative works produced using these skills can be evaluated for creativity by appropriate judges. Based on this model and subsequent studies by others, in order to engage in musical creativity, musicians need the requisite music skills, various creative skills and intrinsic motivation to solve the creative task. Creative skills include diverging

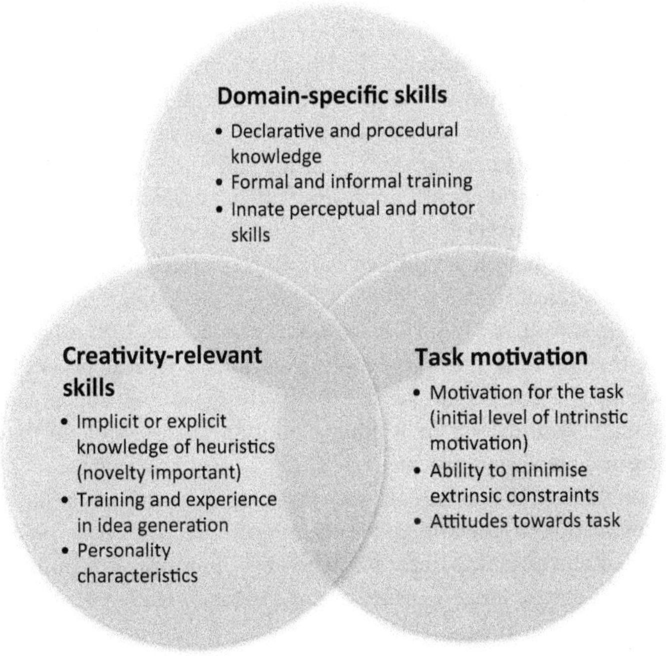

Domain-specific skills
- Declarative and procedural knowledge
- Formal and informal training
- Innate perceptual and motor skills

Creativity-relevant skills
- Implicit or explicit knowledge of heuristics (novelty important)
- Training and experience in idea generation
- Personality characteristics

Task motivation
- Motivation for the task (initial level of Intrinsic motivation)
- Ability to minimise extrinsic constraints
- Attitudes towards task

Figure 10.1 Three skill sets required to demonstrate creativity, based on Amabile (1996)

and converging abilities, generation and elaboration of ideas, flexibility and persistence.

The motivation to solve problems creatively and persist through challenges is enhanced when students encounter real-world problems in unfamiliar paradigms. In contrast, current music curricula may not be compelling students to grapple with culturally diverse and cross-disciplinary skills that can promote creative learning and understanding (Myers & Sarath, 2014). A possible solution can be seen in Soulé and Warrick's (2015) *patterns of innovation* model, which includes engaging the community while developing student creativity. Positive effects of experiential learning encounters that challenge learners to engage, through music, with community members outside the academy are being reported throughout the world (Ball & Shreeve, 2008; Kautsky, 2017; Triantafyllaki, 2016). Incorporating meaningful service learning and community engagement projects in the curriculum should also promote creativity and self-reflection, thus enhancing metacognitive skills (Bennett & Ferns, 2016; Myers, 2016; Pike, 2017).

American music scholars have studied creativity in music through the lens of creative thinking (Balkin, 1990; Webster, 1990). Webster suggests that the four broad phases in creative thinking and activity are preparation, incubation, illumination and verification. These phases account for the path that an individual takes from the intent to produce a creative music work (a composition, performance or analysis), through the thinking process and to the final creative product. The incubation, illumination and verification phases feature creative thinking processes where individuals alternate between divergent and convergent thinking, apply enabling skills (musical aptitudes, craftsmanship and aesthetic sensitivities) and create conditions that enable successful experimentation (subconscious imagery, personality traits, personal motivation and the environment). Individuals need time to reflect on creative practice during the creative process. Educators can facilitate thinking-in-action, but there also needs to be space in the curriculum (Guillaumier, 2016; Schön, 1987). Balkin (1990) suggests that because creative people tend to use logical processes for problem-solving (which might include both divergent and convergent thinking), they may be innovative in seeking a solution to the problem: they tend to persevere and are always product-oriented.

Despite the prevalence of scholarship on creativity, there are few reliable tests to measure creativity (Amabile, 1996; Running, 2008; Torrance, 1966). Amabile (1996) demonstrates that observers who have appropriate training in a specific domain are able to judge whether or not a work is creative. However, the issue is compounded by the fact that "creativity" is a buzzword in contemporary Western culture: for example, employers report that creativity is one of the most important attributes of employees (AACU, 2013; Adams, 2013; Benedictus, 2013; Soulé & Warrick, 2015).

In the US, concepts that can be measured empirically, usually on multiple-choice tests, tend to get the most attention during class due to the pervasive use of standardised testing. Indeed, even faculty productivity in the academy is often measured in terms of numbers of performances, citations or published research papers, rather than by the quality or level of creativity used to generate such works (CMS, 2015). In light of mass-media reporting about the importance of creativity, there is a trend in some US states to rate how well teachers teach creativity using a creativity index (Roblen, 2012). However, closer inspection reveals that measurement simply includes counting the number of creative enrichment activities in which students participate (Hennessey, 2015). One assumes that such a primitive measurement instrument, which neglects outcomes, does little to promote high-quality, prolonged or meaningful opportunities to engage in creative endeavours.

Despite persistent misconceptions about the nature of creativity among the general population (Baas, Nijstad, Koch, & DeDreu, 2015), educators and psychologists offer cogent arguments for how both pre-college and college students can be led to engage in creative activities (Amabile, 1996; Ball & Shreeve, 2008; Burnard & Hennessy, 2006; Guillaumier, 2016; Schön, 1983; Simonton, 2012; Soulé & Warrick, 2015; Sternberg, 2015). These scholars argue that students can develop domain-specific skills, creativity-relevant skills, and intrinsic motivation in tandem, while seeking creative solutions to challenging, ill-defined tasks if there are spaces to explore such skills and attributes in the curriculum.

Music Advocacy

Musicians note the inherent tension between teaching music for its own sake and justifying music study for utilitarian reasons, such as to teach social and cultural values and to enhance educational and economic outcomes (Carruthers, 2008; Logsdon, 2013). Indeed, music education was introduced in American schools for utilitarian purposes in the 19th century (Austin & Reinhardt, 1999). While using music participation to boost academic, social and motivational success raises concerns (see Gee, 2002; Libman, 2004), there is a shift towards such advocacy again (Logsdon, 2013). Evidence suggests that this justification no longer serves musicians or the art form.

In the US, music schools and conservatories are experiencing increased pressure to demonstrate the value of degree programmes for graduates and universities (CMS, 2015). In the past, showing that students and faculty met minimum performance goals and standards, many of which were imposed by administrators with little or no understanding of music or performing arts, has addressed this need; such assessments are no longer serving their purpose. In January 2016, the College Music Society (CMS), a national organisation comprised of music faculty, administrators and students, gathered for a summit, entitled "Shaping institutional expectations for national benchmarking of faculty and music unit accomplishments". The stated goals of this conference were: (a) to create a short-term toolkit of quantitative metrics to address the value of music; and (b) to devise "a long-term plan that will involve new means for the collection and analysis of data not currently available" (CMS, 2015, n.p.). In 2014, the US National Coalition for Core Arts Standards set forth four standards that artists and educators determined were central experiences for all pre-college students. In music, these are creating, performing, and responding. 'Connecting', the fourth standard, is embedded in the three other processes (NAfME, 2015). It appears as though educators set standards, while administrators, parents and the public wish to see quantitative metrics in order to assess the value of music.

Is it possible, or even desirable, to show quantitatively how students are creating, performing and responding to music? It might be easy to measure and increase the number of student performances. However, without ample incubation periods (Webster, 1990), opportunities to reflect-in-action (Schön, 1987) or time to explore increasingly complex musical problems, the quality and value of these endeavours may suffer in the effort to tally high numbers. Although American music administrators identify ways to supply performance metrics, doing so in the way that engineering or mathematics departments do may further devalue the true worth of music.

Even if the "art for art's sake" argument seems esoteric to those uninitiated in the arts, Libman (2004, p. 33) advocates for honestly promoting "what we do and why we do it". Musicians should become adept at explaining how humans benefit from active participation in or experiencing music aesthetically (Bowman, 2005; Elliott, 1995; Reimer, 2002). Indeed, cogent arguments that clearly articulate goals and ideals should be enough to justify music's existence; these are the narratives that musicians need to convey.

Arts organisations around the world report that the arts help people to make meaning of complex situations, our shared humanity and contemporary society (Mowiah, Niblett, Blackburn & Harris, 2014). In line with this, Gee (2002, p. 3) reminds us that "arts advocacy is what we proclaim arts will do for the individual and society in return for investments of time, love and money". Arguably, many educators will not have considered how to guide students to advocate for the intrinsic and societal value of music, which they will surely need to do. The case for the value of art in society or for the individual has not been made, nor has the contribution "between art, artists, education in the arts … and the public good" (Gee, 2002, p. 4) been made, which is perhaps why when economic growth slows, the arts lose funding (Ross, 2006).

There is an evident need to advocate for music programmes at all educational levels and within society. Musicians must find ways to express the value of high-quality, creative musical experiences and not take the path of least resistance, quantifying musical events with little aesthetic value. Music majors will need to advocate for the role of music in society as they create innovative performance spaces, although they may graduate without having thought about such critical issues. If they become teachers, they will need to advocate for the role of music in children's lives. Recent data show that many music educators across the US are successful because they have clearly and compellingly advocated for their music programmes and for their students to various stakeholders including principals, parents and community partners (Abril & Bannerman, 2015; Miksza, 2013).

Arguably, engaging all constituents requires considerable leadership skills on the part of the teacher. Miksza (2013, p. 31) acknowledges that "the types of skills and characteristics that arts specialist teachers employ to negotiate within … their schools are important to understand and could represent valuable information for the preparation of arts teachers". Ross (2006, p. 4) adds that "the absence of arts education that connects creation of art to its primary 'raison d'être' – the reflection or leadership of society – reinforces the dull approach of teaching that leads, inevitably, to lack of public support for the arts".

Hawkins (2012) believes that artists and organisations must make the connection between the "arts' civic and community impact" (p. 131) and she recommends that individuals leverage social networks to advocate for the arts in contemporary society. Hawkins argues for arts agencies to develop visionary goals, create tools, and lead social media efforts for advocacy. Since these efforts should be undertaken by all 21st-century artists and musicians, they should be learned by students prior to graduation. Music entrepreneurship is integrated into some undergraduate curricula. In such classes, students learn to leverage technology and to advocate for creativity and art when interacting with different constituents. This becomes especially crucial in light of troubling reports about how arts teaching is considered to be a "non-creative role" when reporting to arts and funding agencies (Bennett & Bridgstock, 2015). In light of the previous discussion, results of a recent survey of professional musicians will be explored through the lens of indirect leadership, creativity and advocacy.

Method

A survey was sent to 50 professional musicians who were active in an American state-affiliate of a national music teacher organisation. Compared with the other 49 state associations, the organisation is typical; it has members from across the state in both large and small communities and is considered to be mid-sized, based on membership. It may be atypical in terms of demonstrated teaching and professional development programming success, as it has been named state affiliate of the year twice in the past eight years.

Thirty-six musicians completed the survey. Respondents included pianists, vocalists, guitarists and violinists. Individuals had earned music degrees (BA 19 per cent, BMus 36 per cent, MM 28 per cent, DMA/PhD 17 per cent of respondents) and had been working as professional musicians from two to 35 years. The in-depth survey consisted of Likert-type and open-ended questions about professional skills used regularly. The survey was developed following a small study of early-career piano graduates (Pike, 2014). Data were analysed for the entire subject pool. Additionally, comparisons were made between recent graduates (42 per cent of respondents) and established musicians (58 per cent). The primary purpose of the survey was to find out in which areas professional musicians were earning their income, to learn which skills they used on a daily or weekly basis during the past year and to discover which skills from their degree programmes they believed were most beneficial. Open-ended questions encouraged the musicians to reflect upon skills they deemed important and which could have been, but were not, developed during their formal music studies.

Findings and Synopsis of the Results

The primary income source for all respondents, regardless of graduation date or highest degree earned, was teaching. Because the respondents were selected from a music teacher organisation, this result is not surprising. However, 92 per cent of the degrees earned by the respondents were not in music education or pedagogy but in performance. This finding is similar to research of early-career professional musicians in other countries (for example, Juuti & Littleton, 2012). Church musician roles were the second most frequently reported source of income. The most common church positions were accompanist, choral director and seasonal or substitute positions. Not all of the respondents had formal training in choral directing: they learned these skills "on the job" and many were using a secondary instrument (that is to say, organ) in their church employment.

Fourteen per cent of respondents were engaged in regular paid orchestral or band work, although these sources of income were secondary to teaching. While many of the respondents had engaged in collaborative classical music performances in their communities during the past several years, few of these were paid; nor were there any reported paid solo concerts. This finding was even seen among those who had earned doctoral degrees in performance, where the majority of formal training was in solo repertory. No respondents were working full-time in academia, although several held adjunct positions at universities, either as teachers or accompanists.

Respondents identified regularly used playing and teaching skills shown in Figure 10.2. The most commonly reported playing-related skills were (in descending order of use) technique, collaborative performance, efficient practising and sight-reading. Teaching skills, again ranked from most to least frequently used, included choosing and assigning appropriate technique and repertoire; teaching practice strategies; student performance preparation; and business management such as bookkeeping, maintaining communication with students and families, arranging studio performances, overseeing teaching assistants, and studio publicity or marketing to build studio profile and increase enrolment.

Studio maintenance (running the teaching business) occupied a large proportion of time among teachers who had graduated within the past five years. Although this finding was not unexpected, a number of more established teachers also reported high time commitments for business related to running the studio. Closer inspection revealed that these experienced teachers had re-envisioned and reinvented how they operated their studios during the previous five years. These innovations included entering into teaching consortiums with colleagues and opening new learning and performance spaces or arts academies within their communities. Some long-time teachers were engaging in group teaching and music-making activities with students for the first time. The new business models were undertaken as a result of changes in student demographics, declining student enrolments and decreased annual income.

Among educators who had been teaching for more than ten years, those who had changed their teaching situations, business model and/or teaching procedures reported higher degrees of satisfaction with teaching activities than their peers. In fact, teachers who reported teaching much as they had ten years earlier referenced involuntary enrolment decreases, less satisfaction with daily teaching endeavours and less time devoted to seeking out new teaching repertoire or professional development opportunities. Closer inspection of open data revealed that many of the satisfied and self-reported successful teachers were more likely to:

- engage in creatively solving business or teaching problems;
- seek out creative performance and educational activities for their students;
- collaborate and work with organisations within the community; and
- advocate for the importance of music and music lessons in the lives of their students.

Finally, those musicians who reported high levels of satisfaction with daily professional pursuits and whose activities included self-described high levels of creativity and advocacy, regularly assumed leadership roles within various local, state or national music organisations.

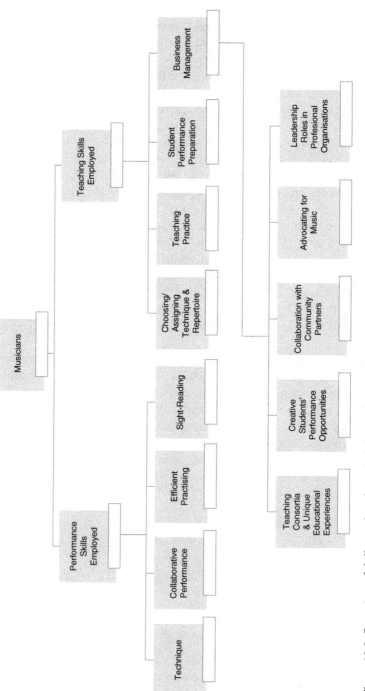

Figure 10.2 Overview of skills employed regularly by professional musicians

Even though the terms "leadership", "creativity" and "advocacy" were not used by any respondents, these surfaced as important professional skills as the themes were being fleshed out. No one reported learning about these skills during their degree programmes. Those who reported higher levels of career satisfaction, however, noted that they had reflected upon teaching and other career options during their formal music study. Although the design of the survey precludes making a clear connection between leadership and creativity, critical components of indirect leadership roles that these musicians played cannot be ignored. The satisfied musicians engaged members of their community in meaningful ways, advocated for the arts, and led creatively by example, through performing and teaching.

Discussion and Implications for Music Education

The results of this small study, viewed in light of the background discussion highlighting the intersection between creativity, advocacy and leadership among professional musicians, suggest that tertiary educators should consider implications for curriculum design. Some faculty have little experience with structuring activities and assignments that call for the use of creative thinking or creativity; others suggest that assessment of creative activities is difficult. Moreover, inexperienced teachers may be less adept at designing and assessing assignments that develop creative skills and generate musical products (Kokotsaki & Newton, 2015). Perhaps, after addressing domain-specific skills development in traditional music courses, there is little time within a student's schedule for incubation, illumination and verification to occur. Yet, students can develop creativity, leadership and advocacy skills (concurrent with domain-specific skills) through:

- undergraduate-led chamber rehearsals and concerts;
- creative projects in theory and history classes;
- entrepreneurship and service-learning projects that take students outside the academy where they interact with the broader community, learn to communicate effectively or explore innovative technologies; and
- meaningful concert programmes and bringing them to constituents unlike themselves.

A curricular paradigm shift is necessary if students are to meaningfully engage in creative activities, transformational leadership practices and reflect on professional identities beyond that of performer or teacher. Educators should look at how frequently and in what contexts students are presented with problems for which they must use divergent and convergent thinking, generate new ideas, and find novel solutions to musical problems. Having time to engage in reflective practice is critical, not only for creative development (Webster, 1990) but also for development of professional musical identities (Bennett, 2007; Freer & Bennett, 2012; Purves, Marshall, Hargreaves, & Welch, 2005; Schön, 1987; Triantafyllaki, 2016), which might include performing, teaching, leading and advocating for the arts, both in and out of the music profession.

Fortunately, there is a growing body of literature supporting the creative and educational benefits of integrating such creative and service-learning projects into current courses (for example, Bartolome, 2013; Burton & Reynolds, 2009;

Figure 10.3 Interwoven connection between leadership, creativity, teaching and advocacy among professional musicians

Kautsky, 2017; Pike, 2015, 2017). When creative activities, service-learning and community engagement projects require students to solve real-world problems and find novel solutions to musical problems, they develop skills vital for creativity and advocacy. As students engage in small-group projects with peers, mentors and superiors, they learn how to function as effective followers and leaders; they develop skills indispensable for professionals who teach, collaborate with peers in chamber performances, and engage with community members within their cities and regions.

Space should be created in music curricula for students to engage in new types of coursework, teaching practice, internships or informal performances where they avail of notation, web tools, and other music technologies and use verbal, visual and online communication to network with community constituents. Project-based courses, which require students to hone music skills, create marketing materials, practise advocacy, and interact with community members help students to develop critical creative and leadership skills alongside domain-specific techniques that they will need upon leaving the sheltered walls of the academy.

Conclusions

Most music educators or graduating performance majors are not prepared to work creatively in the 21st-century musical context. Since few will rely solely on performances like those experienced during their studies for income, other musical ventures, some perhaps yet to be imagined, will need to be pursued. If music is not valued within the broader culture, creating professional opportunities may prove difficult. A persuasive argument for the value of music has yet to be agreed upon, even though these issues are critical (Austin & Reinhardt, 1999; Elpus, 2007; Hawkins, 2012). Although creating and disseminating promotional materials, embracing new technologies, being savvy about business practices and other important 21st-century skill sets are still not being taught in many tertiary schools (Slaughter & Springer, 2015), there is growing evidence that such skills could be practised in meaningful ways throughout the undergraduate curriculum.

Future research might work with practising musicians to share best practice and emerging trends so that pedagogy and curricula can be transformed to meet the needs of emerging music professionals. Shown in Figure 10.3, by thoughtfully interweaving creativity, teaching, advocacy and leadership skill development in courses and projects throughout the undergraduate curriculum, students have the opportunity to create a tapestry of musical meaning that has the power to transform their learning and musical experiences and engage musicians within their broader communities.

References

Abril, C. R., & Bannerman, J. K. (2015). Perceived factors impacting school music programs: The teacher's perspective. *Journal of Research in Music Education, 62*(4), 344–361. doi: 10.1177/0022429414554430.

Adams, S. (2013, October). The top 10 skills employers want in 20-something employees. *Forbes*. Retrieved from www.forbes.com/sites/susanadams/2013/10/11/the-10-skills-employers-most-want-in-20-something-employees/.

Amabile, T. M. (1996). *Creativity in context: Update to the social psychology of creativity.* Boulder, CO: Westview Press, Inc.

Association of American Colleges and Universities (AACU). (2013). Top ten things employers look for in college graduates. Retrieved from www.aacu.org/leap/students/employers-top-ten.

Austin, J. R., & Reinhardt, D. (1999). Philosophy and advocacy: An examination of preservice music teachers' beliefs. *Journal of Research in Music Education, 47*(1), 18–30.

Baas, M., Nijstad, B., Koch, S., & DeDreu, C. K. W. (2015). Conceiving creativity: The nature and consequences of laypeople's beliefs about the realization of creativity. *Psychology of Aesthetics, Creativity, and the Arts, 9*(3), 340–354. doi: 10.1037/a0039420.

Balkin, A. (1990). What is creativity? What it is not? *Music Educators Journal, 76*(9), 29–32.

Ball, L, & Shreeve, A. (2008). *Bold resourcefulness: Redefining employability and entrepreneurial learning.* Project Report: University of Arts London. Retrieved from http://ualresearchonline.arts.ac.uk/671/.

Bartolome, S. J. (2013). Growing through service: Exploring the impact of a service-learning experience on preservice educators. *Journal of Music Teacher Education, 23*(1), 79–91. doi: 10.1177/1057083712471951.

Benedictus, L. (2013, April). Top 10 things employers are looking for: UK Perspective. Retrieved from www.theguardian.com/money/2013/apr/22/top-10-things-employers-looking-for.

Bennett, D. (2007). Utopia for music graduates. It is achievable, and how should it be defined? *British Journal of Music Education, 24*(2), 179–189. doi: doi.org/10.1017/S0265051707007383.

Bennett, D., & Bridgstock, R. (2015). The urgent need for career preview: Student expectations and graduate realities in music and dance. *International Journal of Music Education, 33*(3), 263–277. doi: 10.1177/0255761414558653.

Bennett, D., & Ferns, S. (2017). Functional and cognitive aspects of employability: Implications for international students. In G. Barton, & K. Hartwig (Eds.), *Professional learning in the work place for international students* (pp. 203–223). New York: Springer. Retrieved from www.springer.com/gp/book/9783319600574?wt_mc=Internal.Event.1.SEM.ChapterAuthorCongrat.

Bowman, W. (2005). To what question(s) is music education advocacy the answer? *International Journal of Music Education, 23*(2), 125–29.

Burnard, P. (Ed.). (2014). *Developing creativities in higher music education: International perspectives and practices.* New York: Routledge.

Burnard, P., & Hennessy, S. (Eds.). (2006). *Reflective practices in arts education.* Dordrecht, Netherlands: Springer.

Burton, S., & Reynolds, A. (2009). Transforming music teacher education through service learning. *Journal of Music Teacher Education, 18*(2), 18–33. doi: 10.1177/1057083708327872.

Bújez, A. V., & Mohedo, M. T. D. (2014). Creativity in the music classroom. *Procedia: Social and Behavioral Sciences, 141*, 237–241. doi: 10.1016/j.sbspro.2014.05.041.

Campbell, D. (2013). *The leader's code.* New York: Random House.

Carruthers, G. (2008). Educating professional musicians: Lessons learned from school music. *International Journal of Music Education, 26*(2), 127–133. doi: 10.1177/0255761407088487.

Csikszentmihalyi, M. (1996). *Creativity: Flow and the psychology of discovery and invention.* New York: HarperPerennial.

College Music Society (CMS). (2015). CMS Summit. Retrieved from www.music.org/index. php?option=com_content&view=article&id=2096:cms-summit-overview-shaping-institutional-expectations-for-national-benchmarking-of-faculty-and-music-unit-accomplishments&catid=185&Itemid=1765
Deliège, I., & Wiggins, G. A. (Eds.). 2006. *Musical creativity: Multidisciplinary research in theory and practice*. Hove, UK: Psychology Press.
Elliott, D. J. (1995). *Music matters*. New York: Oxford University Press.
Elpus, K. (2007). Improving music education advocacy. *Arts Education Policy Review, 108*(3), 13–18. doi: 10.3200/AEPR.108.3.13-18.
Freer, P. K., & Bennett, D. (2012). Developing musical and educational identities in university music students. *Music Education Research, 14*(3), 265–284. doi: 10.1080/14613808.2012.712507.
Gardner, H. (1995). *Leading minds: An anatomy of leadership*. New York: Basic Books.
Gee, C. B. (2002). The "use and abuse" of arts advocacy and consequences for music education. *Arts Education Policy Review, 103*(4), 3–21. doi: 10.1080/10632910209600294.
Guillaumier, C. (2016). Reflection as creative process: Perspectives, challenges and practice. *Arts & Humanities in Higher Education, 15*(3–4), 353–363. doi:10.1177/1474022216647381.
Hall, J. L. (2008). The sound of leadership: Transformational leadership in music. *Journal of Leadership Education, 7*(2), 47–68.
Hawkins, J. (2012). Leveraging the power of individuals for arts advocacy. *Journal of Arts Management, Law & Society, 42*(3), 128–140. doi: 10.1080/10632921.2012.729497.
Hennessey, B. A. (2015). If I were Secretary of Education: A focus on intrinsic motivation and creativity in the classroom. *Psychology of Aesthetics, Creativity, and the Arts, 9*(2), 187–192. doi: 10.1037/aca0000012.
Juuti, S., & Littleton, K. (2012). Tracing the transition from study to a contemporary creative working life: The trajectories of professional musicians. *Vocations and Learning, 5*(1), 5–21. doi: 10.1007/s12186-011-9062-9.
Kautsky, C. (2017). Keys behind bars. *American Music Teacher, 67*(2), 24–25.
Kelley, R. (1988). In praise of followers. *Harvard Business Review, 66*(6), 142–148.
Kokotsaki, D., & Newton, D. P. (2015). Recognizing creativity in the music classroom. *International Journal of Music Education, 33*(4), 491–508. doi: 10.1177/0255761415607081.
Kouzes, J. M., & Posner, B. Z. (2002). *The leadership challenge* (3rd edn). San Francisco, CA: Jossey-Bass.
Libman, K. (2004). Some thoughts on arts advocacy: Separating the hype from reality. *Arts Education Policy Review, 105*(3), 31–33.
Logsdon, L. F. (2013). Questioning the role of "21st-century skills" in arts education advocacy discourse. *Music Educators Journal, 100*(1), 51–56. doi: 10.1177/0027432113499936.
McManus, R. M., & Perruci, G. (2015). The five components of leadership. In R. E. Riggio (Ed.), *Becoming a better leader: Applying key strategies* (pp. 50–57). London: Routledge.
Miksza, P. (2013). Arts education advocacy: The relative effectives of school-level influences on resources in arts education. *Arts Education Policy Review, 111*(1), 25–32. doi: 10.1080/10632913.2013.744245.
Mowiah, A., Niblett, V., Blackburn, J., & Harris, M. (2014). *The value of arts and culture to people and society: An evidence review*. Report, Arts Council England, London). Retrieved from www.artscouncil.org.uk/sites/default/files/download-file/Value_arts_culture_evidence_review.pdf.
Myers, D. (2016). Creativity, diversity and integration: Radical change in the Bachelor of Music degree. *Arts & Humanities in Higher Education, 15*(3–4), 293–307. doi: 10.1177/1474022216647378.
Myers, D., & Sarath, E. (2014). *Transforming music study from its foundations: A manifesto for progressive change in the undergraduate preparation of music majors*. Report of College Music Society Task Force on the Undergraduate Music Major. Retrieved from www.mtosmt.org/issues/mto.16.22.1/manifesto.pdf.

National Association for Music Education (NAfME). (2015). *The core music standards.* Retrieved from www.nafme.org/my-classroom/standards/.

O'Brien, M., & Walton, M. (2011). *Music & creativity: Music can spark creativity in math and science.* Report from National Science Foundation. Retrieved from www.nsf.gov/news/special_reports/science_nation/musiccreativity.jsp.

Pike, P. D. (2014). Newly minted pianists: Realities of teaching, performing, running a business and using technology. In G. Carruthers (Ed.), *Relevance and reform in the education of professional musicians. Proceedings of the 20th International Seminar of the Commission on the Education of the Professional Musician* (pp. 85–92). Malvern, Australia: ISME.

Pike, P. D. (2015). The ninth semester: Preparing undergraduates to function as professional musicians in the 21st century. *College Music Symposium Online, 55.* doi: 10.18177/sym.2015.55.sr.10852.

Pike, P. D. (2017). Improving music teaching and learning through service: A case study of a synchronous online teaching internship. *International Journal of Music Education, 35*(1), 107–117. doi: 10.1177/0255761415613534.

Puccio, G. (2014). *The creative thinker's toolkit.* Chantilly, VA: The Teaching Company.

Purves, R., Marshall, N. A., Hargreaves, D. J., & Welch, G. (2005). Teaching as a career? Perspectives from undergraduate musicians in England. *Bulletin of the Council on Research in Music Education, 163,* 35–42.

Reimer, B. (2002). *A philosophy of music education: Advancing the vision* (3rd edn). Upper Saddle River, NJ: Pearson.

Roblen, E. W. (2012). Coming to schools: Creativity indexes. *Education Week, 31,* 12–13.

Ross, J. (2006). Arts education and the newer public good. *Arts Education Policy Review, 106*(3), 3–7.

Running, D. J. (2008). Creativity research in music education. *Update: Applications of Research in Music Education, 27*(1), 41–48.

Ruggio, R. E. (Ed.) (2015). *Becoming a better leader: Applying key strategies.* London: Routledge.

Sawyer, R. K. (2006). Group creativity: Musical performance and collaboration. *Psychology of Music, 34*(2), 148–165. doi: 10.1177/0305735606061850.

Schön, D. (1983). *The reflective practitioner: How professionals think in action.* New York: Basic Books.

Schön, D. (1987). *Educating the reflective practitioner: Toward a new design for teaching and learning in the professions.* San Francisco: Jossey-Bass.

Simonton, D. K. (2012). Teaching creativity: Current findings, trends, and controversies in the psychology of creativity. *Teaching of Psychology, 39*(3), 217–222. doi: 10.1177/0098628312450444.

Slaughter, J., & Springer, G. (2015). What they didn't teach me in my undergraduate degree: An exploratory study of graduate student musicians' expressed opinions of career development opportunities. *College Music Symposium Online, 55.* doi: 10.18177/sym.2015.55.sr.10889.

Soulé, H., & Warrick, T. (2015). Defining 21st century readiness for all students: What we know and how to get there. *Psychology of Aesthetics, Creativity, and the Arts, 9*(2), 178–186.

Sternberg, R. J. (2015). Teaching for creativity: The sounds of silence. *Psychology of Aesthetics, Creativity, and the Arts, 9*(2), 115–117.

Torrance, E. P. (1966). *The Torrance tests of creative thinking: Norms-technical manual.* Lexington, MA: Personnel Press.

Triantafyllaki, A. (2016). The role of "creative transfer" in professional transitions. *Arts & Humanities in Higher Education, 15*(3–4), 401–406. doi: 10.1177/1474022216647387.

Vendler, H. (2012, Nov–Dec). Writers and artists at Harvard: How to welcome and nurture the poets and painters of the future. *Harvard Magazine,* 27–29.

Webster, P. (1990). Creativity as creative thinking. *Music Educators Journal, 76*(9), 22–28.

XI

The Leadership Role of Instrumental Teachers in Students' Career Development: Negotiating Professional Identities

CHRISTINE NGAI LAM YAU

As undergraduate students enter higher music education, they often go through a pivotal transition in their need for guidance and leadership. Instrumental and vocal teachers, in particular, can discover a wealth of opportunities to extend their influence over their students, leading them through periods of personal and professional transformation as they speculate on possible career positioning within their musical communities. Based on a case study of a first-year undergraduate piano student in a UK music conservatoire, this chapter explores the construction of professional identity experienced by the student and the ways in which his piano teacher led that reflective process. The findings suggest that students' professional identity negotiations involve a reflective process of envisioning a future career. These reflections are drawn from subjective and objective factors as well as from internal and external dialogues, most notably with instrumental teachers. The influences combine to arrive at a vision that is grounded in students' personal interests and musical identities. The case described here illustrates a potential leadership role for instrumental teachers in supporting the transition and complex identity work of conservatoire students. Recommendations are offered regarding the ways in which teachers and institutions might facilitate students' professional identity formation and career development.

Leadership and the Master–Apprentice Model

One-to-one instrumental tuition is a widespread aspect of music education, employed with diverse populations of students in various settings. Of these settings, higher music education is arguably where one-to-one teachers play the most central role in the professional training of future performers and musicians. This involves the coming together of a teacher and a student to build a pedagogical relationship wherein the teacher leads students in the process of becoming a member of a professional music community.

This chapter describes the findings of a qualitative research project that explored the leadership role of a piano teacher in a first-year undergraduate student's construction of his professional identity. The study was conducted over a period of five months in 2012, in a UK music conservatoire. The chapter begins by providing a brief literature review, followed by a description of research methods and context. It closes with discussion of the findings and implications for instrumental teaching practice from the perspectives of both teachers and institutions.

When aspiring musician-students embark on their conservatoire undergraduate education, they experience a transitional process from school life to a higher education environment and the professional community. During this process, commencing performance students are likely to experience apprehensions and fears about their futures (Burt & Mills, 2006).

Some students feel the pressure of being expected to adopt greater responsibility for their learning and time management (Creech et al., 2008). Other students may find that their aspirations of becoming a soloist-performer are disrupted by their growing awareness of the international and competitive nature of musical careers, which is such that a soloist's career is realised by very few graduates (Juuti & Littleton, 2012). Also, having lost their "star" status as the prominent performer within their previous school and community contexts (Pitts, 2002), many students start to doubt their own musical abilities when surrounded by talented peers (Kingsbury, 2010). These pressures add to student-musicians' feelings of insecurity and worry, in addition to their performance anxiety (Kokotsaki & Davidson, 2003). Juuti and Littleton (2010, p. 487) suggest that conservatoire students' insecure feelings can be described as part of the transformative process of becoming professional musicians, where the construction of artistic practices, self-narratives and professional identities are inextricably interwoven.

Indeed, such a transformative process is part of what conservatoire students might experience as they navigate career options for themselves as musicians. As Mills (2004) suggests, a career for musicians is both objective and subjective. It is *objective* as a musician is involved in a particular professional activity for an objective measure of time and money. It is also *subjective* as it encompasses how one sees oneself in relation to others and a vision for the future (Mills, 2004). Based on a study conducted at the Royal College of Music London (RCM) to explore the role that identity and vision play within students' career development, Perkins (2012) suggests that students' objective (that is to say, time and money) and subjective (that is to say, identity and vision) facets of career shift over time during their undergraduate programme. Moreover, they might particularly feel insecure when there is a significant gap between one's objective career (for example, piano soloist) and subjective career (for example, being a well-rounded musician) (Perkins, 2012).

During these unsettling learning experiences, then, who plays the supportive role in guiding undergraduate students to make sense of their experiences while being challenged with intense identities development? Many scholars agree that it is instrumental teachers who take on the most influential role in this transformative process (see Gaunt, Creech, Long, & Hallam, 2012; Nielsen, 2006; Persson, 1994). For example, Persson (1994, p. 80) purports that one of the fundamental elements for the identity formation of professional musicians seems to be the musical and personal dialogue they have with instrumental teachers who believe in the musical potential and talents of their students, and who support their students emotionally in their professional and personal endeavours.

Specifically, instrumental teachers may powerfully influence their students' professional identities. Juuti and Littleton (2012), for example, give an enlightening example of how one student-participant's vocational position-taking process was powerfully mediated by her instrumental teacher. As an "outcast" within the institution, this student's teacher acted as a role model by sharing her own strategies and encouraging the student to do the same. With support and encouragement from this teacher, the student felt empowered to make unconventional professional choices, opening up new directions and finding a balance "between negotiating independence from and dependence on authorities" (Juuti & Littleton, 2012, p. 13). Here, instrumental teachers' critical role within students' identity formation might be magnified due to the isolated nature of one-to-one teaching, given that this model of teaching is often "sealed, sound-proofed or placed at a distance" from the rest of the institutional activities (Burwell, Bennett, & Carey, 2017, p. 2).

The conservatoire one-to-one teachers' critical role within students' identity development within the isolated nature of one-to-one teaching is also evident in Nielsen's (2006) investigation of conservatoire learning in a Danish music conservatoire. Nielsen (2006, p. 1) found that one of the ways in which conservatoires' performance culture is made transparent is through students' learning by imitation within the context of one-to-one teacher–student relationships. As such, teachers act as student role models by setting "benchmarks" for what is being followed, therefore mediating the established standards and traditions within the musical profession. Similarly, Jørgenson (2000, p. 68) describes this apprenticeship model as the arrangement "where the master usually is looked upon as a role model and a source of identification for the student, and where the dominating mode of student learning is imitation". This description of master–apprentice model gives a strong image of a leader and a follower.

Undeniably, there are many similar qualities to be found between this master–apprentice model and leadership. According to Northouse (2013), despite the many ways in which leadership has been defined, there are at least four components that can be recognised as central to the concept of leadership:

1. Leadership is a process;
2. Leadership entails influence;
3. Leadership involves common goals; and
4. Leadership occurs in groups.

As such, leadership can be defined as "a process whereby an individual influences a group of individuals to achieve a common goal" (Northouse, 2013, p. 5). Northouse suggests that many people define leadership in terms of the power relationship that exists between leader and followers, where the leader has the power to effect change in others.

The master–apprentice model commonly recognised in conservatoire teacher–student relationships contains all these components. That is, there are dynamics of power invested in the masters, and the master influences apprentices in the learning process, with the common goal of them becoming professional performers. However, despite such similarities, relatively little research has sought to understand the leadership role of conservatoire instrumental teachers within the process of students' professional identity negotiations. Against this backdrop, in this chapter I explore the construction of professional identity as experienced by a first-year undergraduate piano student in a UK music conservatoire and the leadership role of his piano teacher within that process.

Method and Context

Framed within a social constructivist epistemology, this chapter draws on nine semi-structured interviews conducted over the course of a term with a pair of individuals who shared a one-to-one teacher–student relationship at a UK conservatoire known here as the British Conservatoire (this pseudonym is hereafter referred to as BC). The interviews were transcribed, analysed inductively and then triangulated with lesson observations. Inductive analysis was based on an interpretative phenomenological analysis (IPA) approach (Smith & Eatough, 2007). This meant not imposing any existing analytical categories onto the data, but rather allowing the data to speak for itself.

The primary purpose of the IPA approach was to pinpoint leadership themes regarding participants' perceptions of the teacher–student relationship. Specifically, there were four steps involved in the IPA process for this study, based on guidelines derived from Smith and Eatough (2007). First, during the

Table 11.1 Themes and subthemes for the dyad

Pierre : Being a leader
A "convincing" leader Role-model Search students' best qualities
Carl: Reflective process
Reality checks Possibilities Approval Emergent professional identity

transcribing process, initial thoughts and potentially important points were noted in the left-hand margin. The second step involved returning to the transcript and using the right-hand margin to transform initial thoughts into more specific preliminary themes. The third step consisted of further synthesising the data by clustering preliminary themes appropriately. Finally, a table was produced (Table 11.1) to illustrate subordinate and superordinate themes for the dyad.

The choice of the dyad as a case study – a piano teacher and his first-year undergraduate piano student in a UK music conservatoire – reflected my interest in their specific situation. That is, the transition process of the first undergraduate year, during which students might negotiate professional identities both as musicians and aspiring professional pianists. This is because such a transition period is characterised by intense identity work involving many internal dialogues with the self and external dialogues with instrumental teachers and others, in attempts to reconcile multiple discourses and identity positions. This dyad case thus constitutes an ideal opportunity to explore how the construction of professional identity by a conservatoire student is potentially influenced and led by his instrumental teacher.

The conservatoire piano teacher known as Pierre (see Box 11.1) and his first-year undergraduate student referred to here as Carl (see Box 11.2), were each interviewed on a one-to-one basis by the author, with the interviews lasting between one and two hours. Teacher Pierre was recommended by the head of the keyboard department at BC as an ideal participant for this project, mainly due to his interest in reflecting on his own pedagogy and relationship with his students. Carl was subsequently recommended by Pierre as a suitable participant in terms of the purpose of this study and the stage of his learning. Pierre

> *Box 11.1* Pierre
>
> Pierre is 49 years old and six feet tall, with a solid build and medium-length brown hair. On his profile on the piano department web page, Pierre highlights his own pedagogical lineage by foregrounding his educational experience in one of the most prestigious music conservatoires in the US: he learned piano with a number of eminent piano teachers, themselves students of some of the great pianists of the 20th century. Pierre also accentuates his current interest in piano pedagogy: after a successful soloist career, he decided 15 years earlier to devote himself entirely to his work as a piano pedagogue, prompted by the enrichment and knowledge that he receives from human exchange with his students. At the time of the fieldwork, having spent five years as a conservatoire piano teacher at BC, Pierre had ten BC students studying piano as a principal musical instrument. Pierre had 25 years' teaching experience and over ten years' performing experience.

> *Box 11.2* Carl
>
> Carl is a 19-year-old male Chinese piano student from Hong Kong. At the time of the research he was in the first year of his undergraduate degree, having been studying at the institution with Pierre for six months. His policeman father and housewife mother were both amateur pianists, who arranged for Carl to have piano lessons from the age of five. Then, at 11 years old, Carl came to the UK to undertake secondary education at a boarding school, where he received a music scholarship and enjoyed a very active musical life in various choirs, bands, orchestras and other chamber groups, in addition to winning many local piano competitions. Because of this positive school experience, he became interested in becoming a professional musician and subsequently applied to study at the BC.

and Carl were interviewed separately about Carl's possible future career development and Pierre's guidance in this speculative process.

The Institution

Regarded as one of the most prestigious and prominent music institutions within the UK and internationally, BC was in founded in the 19th century. BC promotes itself as one of the UK's oldest conservatoires, with a long history and tradition and many successful and world-renowned alumni. BC aims to provide pre-professional training of the "highest international standards" in the Western classical style. Located in the central and most prestigious part of a major cosmopolitan city in England, BC's two buildings are close to restaurants, bars, cafés and famous performance venues. The buildings were constructed in the early 20th century, with red brick and terracotta exteriors, interior spaces featuring white marble flooring, and a main staircase decorated with stained-glass windows in bright colours.

The piano department at BC has 27 teaching staff, including 14 piano teachers and 13 piano accompaniment and ensemble coaches. The principal study piano teachers come from diverse backgrounds and include accomplished performers, soloists, pedagogues, recording artists and festival directors. A review of the departmental profiles of the 14 piano teachers again shows that most teachers portray themselves in terms of their musical success and accomplishments as performers and pedagogues. Among the accomplishments are positions within vertical pedagogical lineages. These teachers often depict themselves as descendants in a long musical tradition, citing their own eminent teachers from earlier generations. One teacher, for example, presents herself as a distinguished supporter of the Russian school of piano playing, while another identifies as a former student of an eminent teacher who was in turn a student of Artur Schnabel.

Pierre and Carl's self-perceptions are situated within the context of the institution and the piano department as described above. Pierre's perceptions, followed by Carl's ongoing reflective process in constructing his professional identities as supported by Pierre, form the basis for this chapter.

Findings

A "Convincing" Leader and Role-Model

Pierre describes his perceptions of himself as a teacher in this way: "[as a teacher], you have to be convincing, they have to really follow you and trust you". This idea encapsulates the importance Pierre places on being a convincing leader to his followers, who become his students and disciples by following and trusting his leadership. Moreover, throughout the interviews, Pierre shows that he is aware of his power as a successful professional and role model for his students. For example, he sees his dream to move to a big terraced flat in the city as an opportunity to position himself as a role model.

> I dream! I know what I want right now, I'm thinking of new things – I want to move to a new big terrace flat, I want to organise cultural

activities at home ... That's why some students like me, because they see me: "uh-uh, uh-uh, where is he going now? Okay, he's going [to do this]." [I am] always [doing something] better.

(Pierre, fourth interview, April)

Pierre sees himself as a convincing role model and discusses how his various personal and professional endeavours contribute to this position. For example, he showcases his new flat for his students as an example of a social and cultural hub. During his piano lessons, Pierre makes students aware of his high-profile professional engagements, such as giving masterclasses abroad, adjudicating for international piano competitions, co-writing piano tuition books and recording sonatas for a record label. These engagements show what it means to be a successful professional – something to be admired and emulated by his students.

Pierre's status as someone who models success is certainly what attracted his student Carl to choose Pierre as his piano teacher. Carl states that Pierre "studied at [prestigious conservatoire in US] and he has students who won competitions all over the world". Most importantly, Carl sees Pierre as his role model when it comes to a possible future career: "I would hope to become a professor here [at BC] one day ... I see myself being a person or a teacher that's really pushy and just try to get things out of people – which Pierre is in a way". This seems to validate Pierre's perception that in order to become a convincing leader he needs to pose as a role model: someone who can demonstrate his professional capability both as a performer and a well-rounded musician through the projects in which he is involved.

Given both Pierre and Carl's perceptions, Carl's reflective process in developing his professional identities seems in many ways to express the nature of the relations explored in this dyad. In the space of five months (from March to July inclusive in 2012), Carl experienced a period of doubts, reflections and speculation on his hopes, wants and professional aspirations. This process included internal and external dialogues, the latter with Pierre, who guided and influenced this process in a way that was intricately interwoven with Carl's personality, interests, and musical strengths.

Dreams, Reality Checks and Possibilities

Carl started to consider a professional career in music in his senior high school years, when he was regarded a talented young performer in his own town: "So at the time I was thinking that: 'okay, yeah, I'm one of the best now'." This gave him the confidence to dream of becoming a concert pianist. Yet, that dream was at odds with his later realisation of "what it's like in the real world". Indeed, having studied at BC for six months, Carl's understanding of his own position within the institution emerged and he became increasingly aware of the competitive context within and outside of the institution: "The competition in general for that field of work is very, very competitive because you're not just competing with people from BC, you're competing with people from the world."

In addition, Carl recognised his own weaknesses and preferences as a pianist: "I also realised [that] when I performed solo I got really nervous, whether that is playing for an hour or only ten minutes, and I can't see myself going through that as my career." These "reality checks" and Carl's increased self-understanding triggered his doubts and raised questions about his future in music: "So, I'm not going to be a concert pianist. What am I going to do?" Carl was experiencing a period of internal dialogues about possibilities in his musical and professional future. At the beginning of the research study, when being asked about his professional future, he seemed both uncertain and excited about these possibilities.

> That's the thing! I'm not quite sure what I want to do, just yet. ... So, I'm thinking of being a piano accompanist because I've been doing that quite a lot now. I want to be a conductor at the same time, whether it's an orchestral conductor or a conductor in the opera house or for a musical, which I've thought about. I would love to put a show or be a musical director in Covent Garden or one of the West End shows ... And I thought about piano teaching of course. I would hope to come back to BC or some conservatoire to teach there.
>
> (Carl, first interview, March)

Here, Carl lists possible music-related careers with hopes, dreams and desires. He includes recognition of the need to do something pragmatic as a piano accompanist ("I've been doing"), the desire to be a conductor (for example, "want to be"), the hope of becoming a conservatoire instrumental teacher (for example, "I would hope"), and the passion for musical theatre (for example, "I would love to"). Alongside Carl's internal dialogues, external dialogues with piano teacher Pierre contributed towards his exploration of his position within the professional community.

Guidance and Reassurance from Instrumental Teacher

At the time the research was conducted, Carl had been studying with Pierre at BC for about six months. When asked about his specific teaching aims, Pierre spent considerable time discussing his role in actively imagining and guiding students towards realistic and suitable careers based on each student's qualities and personality. This, he explained, was necessary due to the harsh reality of performance careers: "not everyone can become a concert pianist. It's impossible." He continued:

> I try to search what are the best qualities [of each student]. They could become accompanists, they could maybe teach. [...] I try to see what kind of personalities they are. They can become maybe music critics, you know? You can work at the BBC [British Broadcasting Corporation], why not? You never know: in a record company? I try to see what they would be good for.
>
> (Pierre, first interview, January)

Pierre sees his role as being to search for students' best qualities and to get a sense of students' personalities while encouraging them to consider options beyond the traditional soloist career. His perception of the dialogues he had with Carl may illustrate the nature of Carl's speculative process. Pierre began the process by hinting that it would not be possible for Carl to become a concert pianist since at his age he had not already launched a solo career. Pierre then offered his opinion on what might suit Carl.

> I said [to Carl], "You might have a big chance one day in musical theatre and you can maybe play for them, maybe direct one day and that might be your world." He said to me, "How do you know? Because I am actually interested in this". I said, "Well, you have got the look and the personality; you are going to get the experience of being a good classical pianist. So, you are going to have very good training – and very solid – and maybe you will like it and you are going to be great, or maybe not!"
>
> (Pierre, fifth interview, July)

Based on Carl's "look" and "personality", Pierre foresaw Carl's professional self by projecting a positive future for him, while putting Carl's classical piano training into context as the foundation of this future career.

It is interesting to note that Carl's appearance is considered as one of the factors. The quote below, from Pierre, might help to contextualise what he means. When asked how he might come to know a suitable career for Carl, Pierre replied that he had been "watching" and "listening to" Carl a lot, and this led to a conclusion: "It's the energy around him: the way he acts, the way he looks. And I heard him play Gershwin also and I enjoyed it a lot, but I knew that he was enjoying it a lot." Hence, it was Carl's musical style and strength that shone through his piano playing and inspired Pierre. Moreover, this was a musical genre that Carl appreciated and expressed well. In other words, it was not just Carl's appearance that indicated a suitable career but his "energy" or way of being towards music and people. In this sense, by relating to Carl as a person and musician over a period of time, Pierre envisioned the kind of professional musician he might become in the future, all the while searching for the personal qualities, interests and musical strengths to position Carl in a suitable career. Asked how he perceived his career dialogues with Pierre, Carl reflected:

> Pierre mentioned it [the theatre career] to me first out of the blue. He said to me, "I've been thinking about you. What are you going to do later on with your life or career? I think theatre would be very suitable". I was like, "Interesting", because that's what I've been thinking as well.
> (Carl, fourth interview, July)

Indeed, Carl was pleasantly surprised as Pierre made the suggestion soon after Carl's decision to give musical theatre a chance.

> Probably halfway through this year, I wanted to do something more towards that side of work [in musical theatre] because I myself enjoy opera, musicals and ballets. So, if I like them and I want to do something similar to that, why not set my goal as that? Then not long after, two months later, Pierre mentioned that as well and I was like, "Mmm, interesting".
> (Carl, fourth interview, July)

Carl found it "reassuring" to hear that Pierre's suggestions chimed with his own intentions; it helped him to feel more secure in this regard. When asked whether it was important that Pierre agreed with his thinking, Carl asserts the importance of Pierre's agreement.

> So, I get his approval. So, it's not just me … It's nice to have someone who tells you, that's not your friend in a way, that they approve of what you are thinking, what you are doing. Maybe because most friends are like, "Oh yeah, I want to be like an astronaut or whatever". "Oh, yeah, yeah, go for it! Yeah". But it's like sometimes, although sometimes you can get your friends' approval, you don't actually whether they are being sincere or not. Whereas Pierre, he would tell you whatever he thinks. If I go up to him and say I want to be a concert pianist, he would be like: "You don't have what it takes."
> (Carl, fourth interview, July)

Carl's comments show that while it is important for Carl to receive approval from others regarding his professional intentions, he makes a distinction between approval from his friends and from Pierre as a teacher and role model. This implies a high level of trust, which stems from Pierre's professional experiences and knowledge of what it takes to succeed in music and also from Pierre's sincerity in giving Carl the realistic picture. Most importantly, Pierre's agreement with Carl carries certain authority as a form of approval.

Emerging Professional Identity

Towards the end of the academic year, during our final interview, Carol was prompted to reflect on his future and expressed his professional dream.

> That I would be able to work in big shows, whether that will be opera or musical. Musicals in [the] West End or Broadway like *Wicked* or *Les Miserables* or *Sister Act* on Broadway, or *Phantom of the Opera* or something like that. That would be the musical side. And in opera, I would hope to go to Glyndebourne opera house in Covent Garden and Amsterdam and Germany, or wherever. That would be the big dream for the opera world.
> (Carl, fourth interview, July)

This narrative shows Carl's vivid visualisation of his future successful professional self. It evolved from the early fantasy of being a concert pianist to a more grounded choice in musical theatre that was closer to his own musical style, personality and interest. Carl went through a journey in developing his thoughts on his professional positioning. While there is still a long way to travel before Carl can actualise this goal, he will have at least his undergraduate years and beyond to seek out relevant professional and musical experiences. These experiences could both verify and substantiate Carl's choice and enable him to start developing his professional career and contacts in the area of musical theatre.

Discussion

The findings of this study are consistent with the previous literature on music students' experiences of losing their "star-soloist" status when entering higher music education (Burland & Pitts, 2007), realising the competitive nature of the music profession (MacNamara, Holmes, & Collins, 2008), and the realisation that a soloist's career is available to very few graduates. In Carl's case, such experiences led to a reflective process of envisioning a future career during his first year of study, led by his teacher Pierre. This process drew from internal dialogues with himself, external dialogues notably with Pierre, subjective aspects of career (for example, career aspirations) and objective aspects of career (for example, competitiveness of profession). These were weighed up against one another in order for Carl to arrive at a career vision that was grounded in his personal interest and musical identity. Carl's reflective journey echoes with Juuti and Littleton's (2012) study, which suggested that students' transition from conservatoire into professional life involves intensive identity considerations and is a balancing act using one's own inner resources grounded in reality, while following one's individual needs supported by meaningful others.

Most importantly, the skills modelled by Pierre in supporting Carl's identity work in this case study contained all four components of leadership as defined by Northouse (2013): process, influence, common goals and groups. It was obvious that Pierre has considerable influence over Carl's thinking process and that he played a strong role in reaffirming Carl's career thinking. Similar to many other leader–follower relations, this dyad had its inherently asymmetrical nature rooted in the dynamics of power invested in the leader.

Power Dynamics Invested in Leaders

Institutionally, conservatoire teachers possess "institutional authority" by virtue of their formal positions as teachers (Nerland & Hanken, 2004) and also through their contributions to student assessment panels (Gaunt, 2008). Professionally, due to their high status and accomplishments as successful performers, teachers' "professional authority" is associated with the high level of performing standards accepted within the profession. Accordingly, one-to-one tuition is seen as giving students access to a practitioner's method of carrying out the profession within a community of practice (Nerland & Hanken, 2004). Given their professional network, teachers could also potentially open doors for the students by offering them professional work. Such institutional and professional power has as yet unrealised impacts as a productive resource for students' development.

From this productive dimension, the power dynamics invested in the teachers are possibly anchored within students' trust and dependency on their teachers, as evident in Carl's trust for Pierre. Nerland and Hanken (2004, p. 5) suggest that teachers' authority is both needed and necessary for learning as such authority is embedded in students' ambitions to learn from "the standards and values of a broader professional community", as mediated by teacher interactions. Thus, students are said to "deliberately subject themselves to the teacher's ideas and acknowledging his or her legitimacy" (2004, p. 5). Such ambition becomes a critical factor in driving students' trust in their teachers, who are seen to be representative of professional knowledge. In this way, one-to-one tuition provides students the opportunities "to come close to practitioners who master the procedures defining the discipline" (Nerland and Hanken, 2004, p. 5).

Conversely, teacher-leaders' power over students can act as an inhibitive force on the development of students' autonomous learning and artistic voices, as argued by Gaunt (2008, 2010, 2011). To understand how one-to-one tuition and pedagogical relationships are conceptualised by conservatoire teachers, Gaunt (2008, 2010, 2011) conducted a qualitative study in which she explored the perceptions of 20 teachers and 20 students from a diverse range of instrumental specialisms in a UK conservatoire. Her analysis revealed the inhibitive dimension of such invested power in teachers. This occurred when students became overly dependent on their teachers for motivation rather than developing their own intrinsic motivations and self-confidence through independent learning, and/or when they trusted their teachers unquestionably without any analytical reflection (Gaunt, 2010). Gaunt (2010, p. 186) concluded that this could create a situation in which students were "utterly accepting of the teaching styles of their current teachers", believing that it was "up to them as the student to learn as much as they could from the teacher" without any attempts to negotiate the teaching process, even if they struggled to understand the teaching or perhaps preferred a different teaching approach.

Gaunt (2010) argued that such power dynamics illustrate a "'halo' effect" which seems to colour students' perceptions of their current teachers, explaining why the students tend to be so willingly uncritical in their learning as they become lazy and overly dependent on one-to-one tuition as a "safe" and "easy" learning environment. In this environment, students are enabled to remain comfortably in the passive role as learners, relying on the teachers to help them sustain their motivation and the pace of their learning without active engagement in gathering, reflecting on and integrating knowledge and skills. This is risky when a student becomes reluctant to take advantage of other forms of relationships and interactions.

Overall, Gaunt (2008, 2010, 2011) argues that such power dynamics, when misused, can impede the students' long-term development as autonomous learners and also the expression of their own artistic voice. Therefore, despite the fact that the productive dimension of power dynamics is undoubtedly evident in the case study reported here, one-to-one teachers should be cautious in exercising their power and authority, and mindful of helping students to develop their independence.

Recommendations

The findings inform several recommendations for instrumental and vocal teachers and for institutions. To begin with, given these productive and inhibitive dimensions of power dynamics, for conservatoire teachers to achieve the full potential of their leadership role in guiding students' identity work they could consider exercising their power and authority with reflexivity and awareness, to bring about "mutual learning and growth" (Gaunt, 2011, p. 176). In that sense, it is crucial that conservatoire instrumental teachers reflect on the values that underpin their teaching and the specific roles of teacher and learner (Yau, 2010).

To encourage reflexive thinking as a form of leadership, more professional development opportunities could be encouraged for instrumental teachers to ask questions that enable students "to think reflectively and reflexively about their artistic, personal and professional development" (Gaunt et al., 2012, p. 40). Indeed, in guiding the development of students' reflexivity in their identity, there is much scope to explore how teachers and students might work together to support their reflective thinking.

It is not always easy for instrumental teachers and students to find the language of reflection for the purpose of "bringing hidden treasure to the surface" and communicating their reflections to others (Gaunt, 2013, p. 50). For aspiring and practising musicians to find the appropriate reflective verbal language, they need to be equipped with the tools to articulate their thoughts. One such example may be the notion of "sources", with musicians asked to find materials (for example, poems, music or photos) to represent the source of their inspirations and the core influences on their artistic practice and possible career aspirations (Gaunt, 2013).

Another possibility is the use of a "life river": a critical incident charting method through which people can draw out significant influences on their professional growth and speculate on what such influences might mean for their future professional development (Burnard, 2000). These innovative methods could potentially be utilised by institutions and teachers to lead conservatoire students' creative process of professional identity formation and career directions in a number of ways.

At the institutional level, it would be beneficial if institutions offered space for students to reflect on their vision and identity (Perkins, 2012). For example, there could be regular career development workshops where students could voice their ideas on certain important questions (Perkins, 2012). But what kind of questions? Based on a framework developed by Mills (2004) from her extensive research on the careers of RCM alumni, Perkins (2012) proposes a set of questions which can form the foundation of such workshops, and where concept of career is based on subjective factors (that is to say, vision, identity) and objective factors (that is to say, time and money). Such workshops could aim to create an accepting and safe atmosphere based on values of empathy, trust, mutual respect, honesty and risk-taking (Renshaw, 2009). Further, there is great potential for such workshop atmospheres to be gradually transformed into an institution's culture such that the leadership team and teachers model similar values, creating an empowering institutional discourse of trust and exploration.

Indeed, collaborations between teachers and institutions are essential for such institutional cultures to be sustainable. For example, ideas gathered from students' career development workshops could potentially be shared with instrumental teachers, informing their teaching meaningfully and enriching explorations with their students' aspirations. Vice versa, just as students require support to develop their thinking, instrumental teachers would also require support as they "too often lack access to the communities of practice that might help them to develop their engagement – with pedagogy, with one another, and with the institution to which they contribute" (Burwell et al., 2017, p. 16). But what kind of initiatives can institutions offer to reduce the isolated nature of one-to-one teaching and enhance teachers' communities of practice? Burwell et al. (2017, p. 14) provided a number of good examples. For instance, the Royal Conservatory of The Hague offers teachers opportunities to be involved with curriculum development through creating and implementing a programme that encourages peer learning for students (van Zelm, 2013, p. 181).

At an international level, the Innovative Conservatoire (ICON) group holds seminars and workshops in different regions (for example, Europe and Australia) with an aim to accelerate collaborations and reflections among practitioners and administrators worldwide (Gaunt, 2013). Finally, a sustained and consistent institutional effort is required to provide a support structure for instrumental teachers and students to ensure an ever-growing creative foundation to encourage students' professional identity work.

Future research might analyse both teachers' and students' perceptions over a longer period of time and for both the beginning and advanced student within the context of master–apprenticeship model. This would generate a greater sense of students' development and professional identities negotiation enabled by instrumental teachers' guidance at different stages of the students' learning process. This would help to enhance our understanding about instrumental teachers' role as leaders in students' career development from a long-term perspective.

Conclusion

The dyad for Carl and Pierre illustrates a leadership role that instrumental teachers could play in supporting the identity work and career direction of a first-year conservatoire student. This relationship resembles a master–apprenticeship model, where the teacher is regarded as a role model and a source of knowledge for the student. This master–apprenticeship model contains many similar components when compared with the definition of leadership, where the master possesses much power over the student. Regardless of teaching models or styles, it is ethically and professionally essential that conservatoire teachers develop awareness and reflexivity in the process of supporting their students' long-term development, to ensure that they are achieving common goals and mutual purposes.

References

Bennett, D. (2012). *Life in the real world: How to make music graduates employable*. Champaign, Illinois: Common Ground Publishing LLC.

Burland, K., & Davidson, J. W. (2004). Tracing a musical life transition. In J. W. Davidson (Eds.), *The music practitioner: Research for the music performer, teacher and listener* (pp. 225-249). Aldershot: Ashgate.

Burland, K., & Pitts, S. (2007). Becoming a music student investigating the skills and attitudes of students beginning a music degree. *Arts and Humanities in Higher Education, 6*(3), 289-308. doi: 10.1177/1474022207080847.

Burnard, P. (2000). How children ascribe meaning to improvisation and composition: Rethinking pedagogy in music education. *Music Education Research, 2*(1), 7-23. doi: 10.1080/14613800050004404.

Burt, R., & Mills, J. (2006). Taking the plunge: The hopes and fears of students as they begin music college. *British Journal of Music Education, 23*(1), 51-73. doi: 10.1017/S0265051705006741.

Burwell, K., Bennett, D., & Carey, G. (2017). Isolation in studio music teaching: The secret garden. *Arts and Humanities in Higher Education*. Published online first, October 2017. doi: 10.1177/1474022217736581.

Creech, A., Papageorgi, I., Duffy, C., Morton, F., Haddon, E., Potter, J., … Welch, G. (2008). From music student to professional: the process of transition. *British Journal of Music Education, 25*(3), 315-331. doi: 10.1017/S0265051708008127.

Gaunt, H. (2008). One-to-one tuition in a conservatoire: The perceptions of instrumental and vocal teachers. *Psychology of Music, 36*(2), 215-245. doi: 10.1177/0305735607080827.

Gaunt, H. (2010). One-to-one tuition in a conservatoire: The perceptions of instrumental and vocal students. *Psychology of Music, 38*(2), 178-208. doi: 10.1177/0305735609339467.

Gaunt, H. (2011). Understanding the one-to-one relationship in instrumental/vocal tuition in Higher Education: Comparing student and teacher perceptions. *British Journal of Music Education, 28*(2), 159-179. doi: 10.1017/S0265051711000052.

Gaunt, H. (2013). Promoting professional and paradigm reflection amongst conservatoire teachers in an international community. In H. Gaunt & P. H. Westerlund (Eds.), *Collaborative learning in higher music education* (pp. 49-61). Surrey, England UK: Ashgate Publishing Company.

Gaunt, H., Creech, A., Long, M., & Hallam, S. (2012). Supporting conservatoire students towards professional integration: One-to-one tuition and the potential of mentoring. *Music Education Research, 14*(1), 25-43. doi: 10.1080/14613808.2012.657166

Jørgenson, H. (2000). Student learning in higher instrumental education: Who is responsible? *British Journal of Music Education, 17*(1), 67-77.

Juuti, S., & Littleton, K. (2010). Musical identities in transition: Solo-piano students' accounts of entering the academy. *Psychology of Music, 34*(4), 481-497. doi: 10.1177/0305735609351915.

Juuti, S., & Littleton, K. (2012). Tracing the transition from study to a contemporary creative working life: The trajectories of professional musicians. *Vocations and Learning, 5*(1), 5-21. doi: 10.1007/s12186-011-9062-9.

Kingsbury, H. (2010). *Music, talent and performance: A conservatory cultural system*. Philadelphia: Temple University Press.

Kokotsaki, D., & Davidson, J. W. (2003). Investigating musical performance anxiety among music college singing students: A quantitative analysis. *Music Education Research, 5*(1), 45-59. doi: 10.1080/14613800307103.

MacNamara, A., Holmes, P., & Collins, D. (2008). Negotiating transitions in musical development: The role of psychological characteristics of developing excellence. *Psychology of Music, 36*(3), 335-352. doi: 10.1177/0305735607086041.

Mills, J. (2004). Working in music: The conservatoire professor. *British Journal of Music Education, 21*(2), 179-198. doi: 10.1017/S0265051704005698.

Nerland, M., & Hanken, I. M. (2004, June). *Apprenticeship in late modernity: Trust as a critical but challenged dimension in teacher-student relationships.* Paper presented at the Professionalism, Trust and Competence Conference, Oslo University College, Centre for the Study of Professions.

Nielsen, K. N. (2006). Apprenticeship at the Academy of Music. *International Journal of Education and the Arts, 7*(4), 1–15. Retrieved from www.ijea.org/v7n4/.

Northouse, P. G. (2013). *Leadership: Theory and practice*. Los Angeles, CA: Sage Publications.

Perkins, R. (2012). Rethinking "career" for music students: Identity and vision. In D. Bennett (Ed.), *Life in the real world: How to make music graduates employable* (pp. 11–26). Champaign, IL: Common Ground LLC.

Persson, R. S. (1994). Concert musicians as teachers: on good intentions falling short, *European Journal for High Ability, 5*(1), 79–91. doi: 10.1080/0937445940050108.

Pitts, S. E. (2002). Changing tunes: Musical experience and self-perception amongst school and university music students. *Musicae Scientiae, 6*(1), 73–92. doi: 10.1177/102986490200600104.

Renshaw, P. (2009). *Lifelong learning for musicians: The place of mentoring*. Groningen, Netherlands: Lectorate Lifelong Learning in Music and the Arts. Retrieved from www.hanze.nl/assets/kc-kunst-samenleving/lifelong-learning-in-music/Documents/Public/theplaceofmentoring2009peterrenshaw.pdf.

Smith, J. A., & Eatough, V. (2007). Interpretative phenomenological analysis. In E. Lyons & A. Coyle (Eds.), *Analysing qualitative data in psychology: A practical and comparative guide* (pp. 35–50). London: Sage Publications.

Yau, C. N. L. (2010, July). Culturally reflective voice: The "Cultural Models of Self" of a conservatoire's instrumental music professor. In M. Hannan (Ed.), *The musician in creative and educational spaces of the 21st century*. International Society for Music Education (ISME) 18th International Seminar of the Commission for the Education of the Professional Musician. Shanghai, China. Retrieved from www.isme.org/sites/default/files/documents/proceedings/2010%2BCEPROM%2BProceedings.pdf.

van Zelm, G. (2013). From competitors to colleagues: The experience of devising a peer learning environment in a vocal department. In H. Gaunt & P. H. Westerlund (Eds.), *Collaborative Learning in Higher Music Education* (pp. 179–186). Surrey, UK: Ashgate Publishing Company.

XII
Leadership and Conducted Improvisation: Connections and Opportunities in Undergraduate Music Programmes

JANIS F. WELLER

This chapter explores concepts of leadership through the theoretical lenses of transformational and shared leadership, and through the metaphorical lenses of musical improvisation, composition and performance. In particular, conducted improvisation, with its liminal intersections between controlled composition and spontaneous improvisation, serves as metaphor for examining these leadership concepts. The distinct elements of conducted improvisation provide a means to examine leadership topics from two perspectives: individual roles of conductor-composers in conducted improvisation groups; and the shared, collaborative leadership within an improvising orchestra of diverse, changing personnel and instrumentation. The chapter begins by providing historical context and framing commonalities and differences between 21st-century musician careers and historical realities. Theoretical context follows, focused on leadership definitions and theories to establish the choice of transformational and shared leadership theories. The next two sections provide musical context, examining relationships between composition and improvisation and the distinct history and techniques of conducted improvisation. This theoretical and musical background combines to establish the case study of a young conductor-composer who leads an improvising orchestra. The case study illustrates transformational and shared leadership principles in practice and exemplifies the concepts and connections between these theories and creative musical endeavours. The final section summarises the research, suggesting potential applications in the education and career preparation of music students preparing for diverse and multifaceted 21st-century careers.

Framing 21st-Century Musician Careers

Whether in 17th-century Europe or 21st-century Chicago, a do-it-yourself (DIY) quality has defined musicians' careers through the ages as musicians have continually diversified their skill sets and income sources to create viable, sustainable and richly meaningful career paths (Hahn, 2011; Weber, 2004). Multiple income streams requiring heterogeneous musical, entrepreneurial and personal skills, help provide financial stability and allow musicians to take advantage of divergent artistic opportunities.

Among the many necessary career-building proficiencies and attributes cultivated by musicians, leadership skills often play a central if under-recognised role in launching and developing various income streams. For example, church musicians have historically held implicit leadership positions by composing, planning and performing music for each Sunday's services, by rehearsing and directing choirs and by booking guest artists. During the week, they have taught lessons and played for weddings, and they have perhaps toured to raise their artistic profile and network with artists in other locations, illustrating career realities remarkably similar to today's professionals (Weber, 2004).

A variety of skills in the performance and creation of music, both composed and improvised, informed by the traditions and historical expectations of their culture and geographic region, has enabled composite careers with the varied array of income streams necessary to create a sustainable life (Hahn, 2011; Weber, 2004). Leadership skills – the ability to lead, collaborate with and inspire others – serve as an essential thread connecting many disparate activities and income streams.

In spite of historical career continuities for musicians, the rapid pace of social change, evolving economic realities, the pervasiveness of technology and the resulting global intercultural connectivity, music students today will build careers significantly different from those their teachers experienced (Covach, 2015; Cutler, 2012; Freeman, 2014; Sarath, Myers, & Campbell, 2017). In recognition of this emerging reality, the College Music Society (CMS) Task Force on the Undergraduate Music Major (TFUMM) created a manifesto in 2014, strongly encouraging significant curricular changes and outlining three pillars for curricular reform: creativity, diversity and integration.

In the first pillar, creativity, the CMS manifesto suggests expanding current practice beyond technical proficiency in the service of interpretive performance to encompass and integrate composition and improvisation throughout the curriculum. This recommendation represents a return to a broader definition of the performing musician from earlier centuries (Sarath et al., 2017). The authors suggest that greater emphasis on original creativity – improvisation and composition – can help reinvigorate the current interpretive performance model, providing young performers with broader skill sets, deeper musicality and enhanced creativity (Sarath et al., 2017).

In the artistic, DIY reality of musicians' careers, musical excellence is assumed but not sufficient, especially as the core definition of artistry often morphs to include a wide array of genres and methods. For the past century or more, the education of classical musicians has focused on developing virtuoso soloists, vocalists and orchestral players who are thoroughly trained in the Western canon. As musical aesthetics have broadened and intertwined for artists and audiences in recent years, expectations and opportunities continue to shift and increasing numbers of emerging artists integrate their eclectic musical tastes in traditional and non-traditional ensembles. Increasingly, many performers write or arrange original music and may incorporate electronics or other technology in performance. Composer Libby Larsen anticipated the growing importance and embedding of "produced sound" 20 years ago in a keynote address to the National Association of Schools of Music, proposing that from the late 20th century and into the 21st the integration of both acoustic and produced sound has required increasing sophistication with technological tools and an expanded aural palette (Larsen, 1997).

Performers specialising in Western classical music may also utilise skills in improvisation and composition, incorporating popular music and diverse music styles from around the world, sometimes incorporating technological tools as well. For example, members of the ground-breaking, Grammy award-winning vocal group Roomful of Teeth are graduates of high-level traditional music programmes. As a group, they study a rich, worldwide palette of vocal techniques and styles ranging from Tuvan throat singing, yodelling and Hindustani music through to belting and Korean *p'ansori*. These diverse vocal styles are incorporated into powerful, newly commissioned pieces. Outside their commitment to this busy, but not full-time ensemble, the artists pursue a range of musical activities from operatic roles to early music performance and teaching. Several of the singers also perform professionally as instrumentalists.

Such diverse, organic and practical approaches to career building have grown over recent times. Numerous musical collectives have emerged, for example, where musicians create nimble, innovative ensembles which are flexible in personnel, repertoire, instrumentation, genre and geography, ranging from contemporary concert music (for example, International Contemporary Ensemble, ICE) to hip-hop (Doomtree, Wu-Tang Clan) to world music (Silk Road Ensemble).

Self-employed performer-composer-teachers, in addition to developing a high level of artistry and expertise, must devote considerable time and resources to the very different skills of self-promotion, event planning, financial management and developing professional relationships. Learning the basics of contracts, booking, promotion, record-keeping and more can spell the difference between continuing in the field and leaving for more stable employment.

These realities and skill sets are not new for most independent artists, but many are learned on-the-job as the circumstances require.

Should the skills and attitudes necessary for such diverse careers be learned primarily on the job, or should they have a prominent place in the formal curriculum for undergraduate music majors? Expanding career expectations have led an increasing number of music colleges and conservatories to recognise a need to expand the approach to educating future professionals for sustainable careers (Covach, 2015; Cutler, 2012; Freeman, 2014; Herstand, 2017), but change often moves slowly in higher education. The recognition of evolving needs provides an important first step. Aligning the rapidly changing requirements of the music industry with college curricula, already constrained by tradition, accreditor expectations and regulations, can prove daunting, but Sarath et al. (2017) and others make compelling arguments in favour of pushing ahead with curricular changes.

Many music schools acknowledge a need for both entrepreneurial training in the business elements of independent artistic careers along with more diverse musical experiences for performers, including composition/arranging, improvisation, genre and stylistic variety, and technology driven methods (Beeching, 2010; Herstand, 2017). An increased knowledge of, and facility with, broad business, media and leadership expertise have become necessary and expected career skills, and gradually, more music schools include this training as part of their curricular and co-curricular offerings. These efforts are highly tailored for each institution and range from curricular tweaks adding business or career development skills to prominently funded branded institutes sponsored by wealthy donors, such as those at the Eastman School of Music, DePauw University and University of Colorado, Boulder.

Independent and entrepreneurial careers require broad business knowledge and skills together with diverse artistic expertise, but what roles do leadership skills play in career development? The chapter continues, first with a brief overview of leadership definitions and theories establishing a focus on transformational and shared leadership theories. The following two sections provide musical context, examining relationships between composition and improvisation, and the distinct history and techniques of conducted improvisation. These theoretical and musical backgrounds combine to frame the case study of a young conductor-composer who leads an improvising orchestra. Finally, I summarise the research, suggesting potential applications in the career preparation of music students in higher education.

Leadership Roles

Scholars, generals, business gurus, self-help authors and journalists have attempted without consensus to define the most salient concepts of leadership

(Northouse, 2007; Winston & Patterson, 2006). One study claimed to identify more than 26,000 articles using the term "leadership" (Winston & Patterson, 2006). Definitions of leadership typically centre on two perspectives – aspects of individual leaders or organisational leadership issues (Morgan, 1986; Mayer-Schonberger & Oberlechner, 2002; Winston & Patterson, 2006). Based on diverse and extensive scholarly literature examining leadership theories, Northouse (2007, p. 3) suggests a broad and simple definition of leadership combining both individual and organisational aspects: "Leadership is a process whereby an individual influences a group of individuals to achieve a common goal".

For this chapter, I have selected transformational and shared leadership theories to help tease apart the intriguing relationships between organised and spontaneous composition and for examining the seemingly incongruous but necessary role of a conductor in improvised performance along with the shared leadership roles of the ensemble musicians.

Transformational leadership theory, a vertical leadership style, emerged in the early 1980s, and emphasises intrinsic motivation and strong interpersonal connectivity (Noonan & Fish, 2007; Northouse, 2007). In individuals, transformational leadership is characterised by an inspirational, charismatic and highly individualised style, frequently grounded in morality or social justice (Morgan, 1986; Noonan & Fish, 2007; Northouse, 2007). Unlike its diametric opposite, transactional leadership, where an exchange of money, status, grades or other external commodity occurs, transformational leadership focuses on building relationships, trust, ideals and shared ethical and moral purpose between leaders and followers (Bolman & Deal, 2003; Northouse, 2007).

Kuhnert and Lewis (1987, p. 649) describe the transactional leader as "influential because doing what the leaders want is in the best interests of the followers". In a traditional conducted ensemble such as a symphony orchestra, there is a clear hierarchy of power and clarity of roles between the conductor and musicians, defined by the conductor's musical imagination and the players' ability to realise that singular vision. The conductor ideally inspires great performances from the players, but ultimately leads an essentially transactional relationship focused primarily on the conductor's goals rather than those of the individual musicians or the musician collective (Northouse, 2007; Seifter & Economy, 2001).

Transformational leaders work differently, moving beyond a transactional role and engendering a group spirit focused on the whole, with motivation and inspiration helping to maximise capacity, creativity and innovation in the players (Northouse, 2007). The case study later in this chapter illustrates how a transformational leader in a conducted improvisation ensemble creates both a unified musical structure and form, while highlighting the individual strengths of each musician.

Shared leadership, also known as distributed, collective or collaborative leadership, is a horizontal style of leadership that draws on the expertise and ideas of the team in partnership with the designated leader and focuses on collective outcomes (Carson, Tesluk, & Marrone, 2007; Pearce & Conger, 2002; Suk Bong, Kihwan & Seung-Wan, 2017). As in transformational leadership, shared leadership relies on relationships and shared goals and has been shown to result in effective and innovative results, although it has proved inefficient and time-consuming at times (Hoch, 2013; Pearce & Conger, 2002; Ulhoi & Müller, 2014; Wood & Dibben, 2015). Studies have shown shared leadership is highly process-oriented and enhances the team members' engagement and ownership (Pearce & Conger, 2002; Ulhoi & Müller, 2014; Wood & Dibben, 2015).

While the literature on shared leadership focuses primarily on work teams in traditional business settings, it can provide a clear complementarity to the transformational aspects of the conductor-composer in conducted improvisation. Some researchers view shared leadership as a process-based activity, driven by the relational aspects of the team rather than a designated individual (Pearce & Conger, 2002; Wood & Dibben, 2015). Such studies show that shared leadership encourages engagement, empowerment and innovation among the team members, along with opportunities to develop the individual voices of participants (Carson et al., 2007; Hoch, 2013; Suk Bong et al., 2017; Verrico & Reese, 2016). The pairing of transformation and shared leadership provide insights for the case study below.

With the theoretical lenses of transformational and shared leadership described, the next section compares the distinctions in purpose and method between two creative methods encouraged by the 2014 CMS manifesto: composition and improvisation. Examining the intersections of composition and improvisation highlights liminal aspects of the creative process and potential new creative opportunities. Together, the roles of the leader and players along with the creative contrasts and overlaps of composition and improvisation come together to illustrate a process-oriented, intersectional style of leadership and music-making.

Intersections of Composition and Improvisation

In Western art music, typically, a single composer creates a composition and then musicians interpret the work through performance. This process of composition is generally solitary and structured by the composer within prescribed parameters including length, instrumentation or style. Improvisation has its own wide-ranging rules, depending on the tradition, for creating music "in the moment". In jazz, for example, chord progressions and stylistic, melodic, rhythmic and form conventions provide a framework for improvisation. Other forms of improvisation work within their own designated rules, encompassing form, harmonic or melodic progressions, cultural traditions, instrumentation and so on.

Improvisation is, of course, not only a centrepiece of jazz, but deeply embedded in the fabric of classical and folk music traditions around the world (Colwell & Richardson, 2002). In Western art music, improvisation has played an important role historically through the centuries, from figured bass, cadenzas, preludes and, of course, American jazz. Today, with technology fostering cross-fertilisation of styles, the fusion of musical genres has further expanded the art and expectations of improvisation. In an effort to support this diversity, the International Society for Improvised Music provides a definition exemplifying improvisation for the 21st century without genre or stylistic implications.

> Improvisation is spontaneous interaction between musicians from the most disparate backgrounds, dissolution of boundaries between performers and listeners, and access to the transcendent dimensions of creative experience. Improvisation is at the heart of a new musical paradigm that uniquely reflects contemporary life.
> (International Society for Improvised Music, n.d.)

In the spirit of evolving notions of improvisation in the musical genres of the world and the melding of many styles, the National Association of Schools of Music (NASM) recognised the core importance of improvisation when educating professional musicians and began, from 1999, to require its inclusion in the curriculum of American higher education institutions (NASM, 1999, rev. 2010). Describing improvisation broadly, the methods and integration of incorporating improvisation in traditional programmes were left open for institutions to determine. Some higher education curriculum for performers provides credits to accommodate the learning of creative activities (such as composition and improvisation); more rarely, student performers access opportunities for continuous creative skill development alongside the traditional focus on developing technical proficiencies and interpretive performance (Sarath et al., 2017), but such activities may be relegated to a course or two rather than being integrated throughout the programme. In fact, Myers proposes further expanding the definition of entrepreneurship to encompass innovation in creativity as well as business-related pursuits (Myers, in Sarath et al., 2017).

Completing a brief contextual overview, the next section provides background on a specific subset of improvisation – conducted improvisation – to provide a historical context for the intersections of structured and improvised composition as a lens for viewing leadership.

Conducted Improvisation: Liminal Musical Spaces

> Improvisation is not composition … It is a work in progress. It is performer's music.
>
> (Foss, 1962, p. 684)

In the 1960s, composer Lukas Foss experimented with improvised chamber music, but he quickly became disenchanted by the results. Foss (1962, p. 684) described improvisation as equivalent to an artist's initial sketch rather than a completed painting, calling it "raw material exposed, rather than composed". Ultimately, the random nature of open improvisation simply held little interest for Foss as a composer. However, Foss, perhaps anticipating the CMS manifesto of 2014, promoted in 1962 the value and importance of incorporating creative training and practice into musicians' education (Foss, 1962).

Foss's experimentations with improvisation hold particular relevance for an examination of conducted improvisation with his observation that "Chance … becomes musically interesting only when it rubs against the will, when musical selectivity enters into the picture correcting the chance formations" (Foss, 1962, p. 684). Foss's statement aligned with the directions of pioneering composers interested in these compositional intersections between chance and will: the liminal spaces. The role of the composer-conductor in conducted improvisation ensembles meets Foss's dual goals of making musical choices within chance formations.

Initially, composer-musicians testing the waters with these concepts emerged from the free jazz and the avant-garde experimental music scene of the 1960s and 1970s, experimenting with control of the compositional process and of leadership within the art of performance. Early innovators in structured improvisation ranged widely and included diverse artists such as the pioneer of free jazz and central influence, Sun Ra, through to Butch Morris, Ornette Coleman drummer Charles Moffett, and eclectic avant-garde musician Anthony Braxton (Larsen, 2015; Smith, 1995).

Composer John Zorn created highly collaborative and semi-structured, improvisational games in the late-1970s, where the leader used cue cards and an anarchic set of rules to organise the resulting improvisation, giving players the latitude to follow or rebel against these instructions (Sisario, 2013). Zorn never published a complete score or rules for the performance of his work *Cobra*, considering the work part of an oral tradition; he intentionally relinquished most control over the results and yet it remains his most frequently performed work (Brackett, 2010).

During this same richly experimental period, Frank Zappa embraced free jazz and sound experiments while he simultaneously created music as a spontaneous improviser and a composer of traditional notated music. As a composer, Zappa created complex and meticulously notated scores and brought a perfectionist leadership style to realising these pieces with his ensembles. Zappa resisted, however, any kind of codifying of the improvisation, whether by practised repetition, recordings or transcriptions (Friedman, 2014). Zappa's precise distinctions between composition and improvisation clearly defined these two compositional methods and also determined his leadership approaches.

Moving from the "extreme openness" of Zorn's artistic approach to the generally clear-cut boundaries between composition and improvisation practised by Zappa (Sisario, 2013), we finally arrive at the niche genre of conducted improvisation, which can be defined as a hybrid compositional method with distinct leader–follower goals. Conducted improvisation is evident in the work of Zappa, who experimented with directed or conducted improvisation with classically trained players, "using the *Ensemble Modern* 'like an instrument'" by teaching them gestures and hand signals to shape compositional improvisations (Carr, 2013, p. 197).

Influenced by the innovative artists described above and others, Lawrence "Butch" Morris emerged as a seminal pioneer of conducted improvisation (Stanley, 2009). Morris explored the liminal intersections of composition and improvisation in distinct ways, creating structures, rules and aesthetic goals as composer-conductor with a distinct leadership style. In the 1980s, Morris created *conduction*®, a carefully predetermined set of hand gestures used by a conductor-composer to organise and compose with an improvising ensemble (Bynum, 2013; Foss, 1962; Morris, 2006). Morris (2006, p. 233) described conduction as "a vocabulary of ideographic signs and gestures activated to modify or construct a real-time musical arrangement or composition". Conduction serves as conceptual compositional inspiration for exploring conducted ensemble improvisation, providing a structure to meld performer-generated improvisation with a composer's purposeful intention: in Foss's terms, "chance … rubbing against the will" (Foss, 1962, p. 684).

The conductor-composer moulds and balances unknown and unpredictable musical elements as they unfold, working with the individual and collaborative contributions of the musicians (DePree, 1992; Goleman, Kaufman & Ray, 1992). The completely improvised yet expertly guided results meet in the intersection between composition and improvisation. In this process-oriented music-making, "the 'working' becomes as important, perhaps more so, than the resulting 'work'" (Turner, 1988, p. 8). Turner describes this intersection or threshold state as liminality: a complex, ambiguous zone of possibilities particularly suited to creative artistic activities (Burnard, 2012; Turner, 1988). The liminal space provides rich opportunities for the conductor-composer-leader and also for the musicians to create and innovate together (Dobrian, 1991; Turner, 1988). Worldwide, contemporary composers and musicians continue to develop various approaches to conducted improvisation, drawing many diverse musical traditions to compose in real time. Some of these grow out of the conduction model; others experiment using similar principles and develop their own sound-language. Conducted improvisation provides a unique perspective on leadership in the moment while also serving as a vivid metaphor for leadership and leader–follower dynamics in general.

With context provided by broad definitions and descriptions of leadership and by an overview of the history, people, methods and influences of structured improvisation, we turn next to a case study of a young composer-conductor in the US. Aaron's initial inspirations and training came from a musician who had worked directly with Butch Morris. His experiences as the leader of an improvising ensemble illustrate the growth of creative, intersectional boundaries between improvisation and composition, forming an apt metaphor for leadership and interpersonal interaction.

Case Study: Aaron and Improvestra

On a wintery Monday evening in the community room of a hip bowling alley in Northeast Minneapolis, Aaron and his ensemble, Improvestra, have launched their monthly "Potted Meet Monday" event: a multimedia, mixed-art extravaganza. In an extraordinary example of staying power and continuity, tonight is the 31st consecutive monthly Potted Meet event. The audience of nearly a hundred people is dominated by people in their twenties and thirties, with a few older couples and some multigenerational families. Audience members mill about, drinking beer and chatting, while small children run around between the tables as the musicians set up.

Serving as a rowdy arts event, composers' lab and opportunity for collaborative leadership, a typical Potted Meet night includes performances by Improvestra – a conducted, improvising orchestra of flexible instrumentation – and often includes other small, eclectic ensembles. A local composer may showcase a reading of a new work, and the events often highlight a visual artist, perhaps a poet, and include raffle drawings for original works by selected neighbourhood visual artists and even gift certificates to local restaurants. The lights are low and the energy level high as the audience eagerly anticipates an evening of ephemeral new art, created in the moment and dissipating just as quickly.

When Aaron was an undergraduate music student, a composition instructor recruited him to work with an improvising ensemble of students and faculty assembled for an interdisciplinary visual art and music event planned on campus. In preparation, Aaron received training in improvisational conducting from a former member of Butch Morris's band. He initially developed his new craft working with a group of musicians, many of whom had a background in jazz improvisation and were willing to experiment and play with new ideas.

At Improvestra's first performance, the audience was mesmerised by the unexpected but engaging sounds; three years later, Aaron continues to lead a fluid collective of 20 to 30 improvising musicians while blossoming as a conductor-composer and charismatic leader.

Aaron's evolving perceptions of the distinct but interrelated musical realms of composition and improvisation inform both his musical decision-making and his broader career directions as an artist and a leader. In his work with Improvestra, Aaron's personal evolution as a musician, leader, composer, conductor and colleague has sparked reflection and heightened self-awareness, enhancing his evolving transformational leadership style. Artistically, Aaron lives at the liminal intersections of spontaneous and controlled composition. As a leader, Aaron inspires and energises the players, freeing them to take musical risks. Aaron as composer shapes the resulting improvised music into clearly discernible musical forms with emotional energy and impact.

With a romanticist's aesthetic and a film composer's vision and process, Aaron consciously describes his musical goals as a "tonal, groove-oriented" style of improvisation rather than the "out there, random, atonal" sounds of free jazz or new music ensembles (personal communication, 2015). Acknowledging his debt to pioneers in conducted improvisation, Aaron creates his own artistic vision, prioritising musical accessibility along with musician and audience engagement as central goals for Improvestra performances (Bynum, 2013; Morris, 2006). Initially, he learned an array of hand signals from Morris' *conduction*® repertoire, incrementally adding new signals and signs developed collaboratively with the musicians. Over time, Aaron learned to shape the improvisations with the deliberate intentions of a composer, growing as both a musician and as a leader.

Out of the initial somewhat chaotic and unstructured potential in an Improvestra performance, Aaron now responds to the emerging musical material. He may start with a solo instrument, setting an evocative or energised mood, or he might launch the music by providing a tempo and feel, allowing an original groove to emerge. As both conductor and composer he plays with instrumental colour, juxtaposing unusual combinations of instruments or non-traditional voicings. He listens closely for melodic fragments that catch his ear, signalling players to create duets or instrumental sections. He plays with contrasts of dynamics, texture, mood and form, shaping the improvised composition by balancing expectation and surprise. Aaron uses his distinct and focused aesthetic and transformational leadership style to "make my voice heard through everyone else" (personal communication, 2015).

Aaron can only work his transformational musical magic in collaboration with the musicians of Improvestra. While a group of core players performs at most events, the membership of the ensemble remains fluid, creating a substantial pool of musicians with the knowledge, skills and attitudes necessary for creating innovative and engaging music using conducted improvisation. At a typical Improvestra event, the instrumentation includes rhythm section players (drum set, other percussion, electric and/or acoustic bass, keyboards), guitars, horns, woodwinds and strings in various configurations. Sometimes a dozen players perform, while at other events over 30 players may convene. Improvestra musicians represent a variety of musical training and traditions, from classical to jazz, rock to fusion and world traditions. Each of the musicians has developed their craft to a high level musically, technically and creatively.

With few or even no verbal exchanges, conducted improvisation requires a sophisticated level of shared leadership between the conductor-composer and the musicians and also among the musicians. Relying on hand, body, facial and gestural signals from the conductor-composer to convey musical ideas and directions requires deep musicianship, good ears and inventive spirits. The process opens both the leader and players to diverse interpretations, freeing them for spontaneous creativity and innovation. Dependent on careful listening and observation in the moment, conducted improvisation builds on the artistic vision of the conductor-composer leader enhanced by the musical languages of the performers.

Most musicians have significant experience in self-directed ensemble playing. This experience comes from their involvement in chamber music, jazz or rock, or indeed any type of small ensemble that functions autonomously without a designated conductor or leader. Because of this, musicians have arguably developed highly effective methods to achieve their shared goals. Depending on the genre or style of the music, however, written scores, lead sheets, chord progressions and other performance conventions have often helped to drive the musical goals and the rehearsal and performance process. In the more open and uncharted (literally) waters of conducted improvisation, those conventions no longer serve as the common musical language; rather, they require an enhanced level of mutual trust (leader with players and player to player) combined with open stylistic creativity, careful listening and mutual support.

Aaron's role as leader, conductor and *de facto* composer for Improvestra continues to grow and evolve. Earlier in his development as a leader, he shared his emerging transformational approach to leadership: "the ability to lead a situation depends on reading personalities (overall and in the moment) to bring out the best in people and communicate effectively". Today, Aaron's sophisticated philosophy about conducted improvisation also includes "empowering musicians, not dictating what they play". As a conductor-composer, he sees his role as a "giver of context" deciding who plays, when they play, how and why they play, with each musician choosing what they play (personal communication, 2015).

Unlike the solitary nature of most composers' work, this compositional activity takes place on stage with an audience present. A high potential for failures, small and large, elevates the level of musical unpredictability and inspiration for Aaron and the ensemble: Will the ideas come together to create order out of chaos, or will the performance fall apart? While some efforts occasionally fail, Aaron's willingness to experiment and his excitement about the inherent risks inspire and unite the players. Aaron embraces the risks and rewards of leadership, modelling both for the ensemble: "I don't know if you can call someone a good leader unless they take a risk and you see them come out of a hole. If you're afraid of that, man, you've got a rough life ahead of you" (personal communication, 2015).

Uncertainty, risk-taking and the potential for satisfying musical results inspires focus and attention in both the players and the listeners. Audiences appreciate the musical tightrope of an Improvestra performance, remaining both engaged and moved by the music. This consistently positive connection with the musicians and the audience demonstrates a full circle of creative expression: the ultimately social nature of creativity (Goleman et al., 1992). General audiences of non-musicians respond enthusiastically to witnessing the birth of thoughtful but transient musical ideas which emerge and then dissipate, in a Zappa-esque tribute to the power and intentions of improvisation.

Composing in the moment as the conductor of an improvising ensemble, and responding to the composer/conductor and fellow performers as a player, illustrates empowering, transformational and shared leadership and demonstrates the liminal, transitional nature of leadership.

Summary and Recommendations

This chapter explored connections between the musical expertise required of conducted improvisation and complementary transformational and shared leadership abilities, to illustrate how these skill sets can provide useful tools addressing the challenges of creating sustainable music careers in the 21st century.

Every year, new students arrive on our campuses with a passionate desire to study music. In the college where I work, focusing on contemporary popular music, some creative students may enter a programme with years of formal instruction, while others come in largely self-taught. Whether trained formally or informally, students enter college creating and playing music intuitively, eager to further develop musical and entrepreneurial skills they have learned through traditional instruction, personal exploration and collaborative interactions. Increasingly, we find that students begin higher education studies less as specialists and more as generalists, with broader and deeper musical and artistic interests and experiences. These young musicians are driven to create their own unique music and already recognise the necessities of producing, promoting and performing their music online and in live performances.

New students may find choosing a major baffling when they are already active and interested in virtually all possibilities offered across majors. Traditional music tracks or majors (for example, performance, music business, composition, production and technology) have merged for this generation, and their careers will require these diverse skills along with the tools and attitudes to foster lifelong learning. As Claire Chase, founder of the International Contemporary Ensemble (ICE) said recently, "The 20th century was the century of specialisation; the 21st century is the century of integration and collaboration" (Sarath et al., 2017, p. 131).

Creating a substantive, current and effective curriculum not bound by traditional silos of learning presents considerable challenges within traditional music programmes. Curriculum changes tend to unfold slowly, bound to some degree by accreditor demands and faculty experiences, but are also driven forward by student expectations and the rapid and inexorable pace of change within society and the music industry. In a time of cultural and curricular change made more challenging by limited budgets, however, career proficiencies in improvisation and leadership can provide opportunities for student development and growth with little direct financial cost.

The CMS manifesto noted the importance of embedding critical learning and career experiences within curricular and co-curricular opportunities rather than simply adding courses and credits (Sarath et al., 2017). Establishing a consistent culture which notices and values both overt and subtle forms of leadership and which includes opportunities to apply and practise these skills can help students internalise expectations and encourage growth throughout their education and beyond. In addition, well-developed and broadly integrated musical, intellectual and spoken improvisation skills serve the development of leadership attributes. A well-honed ability to improvise supports expanded income streams such as teaching artistry, engages audiences in settings ranging from concert halls to living rooms to bars, and enhances the ability to provide clarity of purpose and musical intent. Myers describes this integration of musical and life improvisation as "spontaneous creative adaptation" (Myers, 2016, in Sarath et al., 2017, p. 137), an invaluable skill set in 21st-century life.

In higher education, instructors can look for opportunities to define leadership organically in the curriculum, providing or encouraging leadership opportunities in class, rehearsals, on campus and in the community (see also O'Neill, Chapter VII, this volume). We can bring attention to leadership moments, telling stories from our experiences and encouraging students to do the same. Challenging student musicians by giving them significant responsibilities with real consequences appropriate to their level of experience can help the development of both prepared and spontaneous leadership styles.

Aaron's experiences of melding conducted improvisation with an expanding leadership persona were tested and grew first within the safe space of the classroom. Supported and mentored, he practised technical musical skills in conducted improvisation and composition while honing his abilities to lead, motivate and inspire others. After graduation, Aaron's charisma was combined with his experience and growing confidence, and this enabled him to retain and build a core ensemble of committed players while expanding to include musicians from the broad professional community.

Success in engaging audiences in the earliest performances provided Aaron with the self-assurance to reach out and connect with eager, new audiences. Leadership is not always a designated, titled role; it might be temporary or project-based, like Aaron's first exposure to conducted improvisation, or it might emerge from within ensembles or teams as shared leadership. However they evolve, leadership opportunities can provide career turning points with powerful and long-lasting results and they need to be an integral part of the higher music education curriculum.

References

Beeching, A. M. (2010). *Beyond talent: Creating a successful career in music* (2nd edn). New York: Oxford University Press.
Bolman, L. G., & Deal, T. E. (2003). *Reframing organizations: Artistry, choice, and leadership* (3rd edn). San Francisco, CA: Jossey Bass, John Wiley and Sons, Inc.
Brackett, J. (2010). Some notes on John Zorn's Cobra. *American Music, 28*(1), 44–75. doi:10.5406/americanmusic.28.1.0044.
Burnard, P. (2012). *Musical creativities in practice*. Oxford: Oxford University Press.
Bynum, T. H. (2013, January 30). Postscript: Butch Morris (1947–2013). *New Yorker*. Retrieved from www.newyorker.com/culture/culture-desk/postscript-butch-morris-1947-2013
Carr, P. (Ed.) (2013). *Frank Zappa and the And*. London: Routledge.
Carson, J. B, Tesluk, P. E., & Marrone, J. A. (2007). Shared leadership in team: An investigation of antecedent conditions and performance. *Academy of Management Journal, 50*(5), 1217–1234.
Colwell, R., & Richardson, C. (2002). *The new handbook of research on music teaching and learning: A project of the Music Educators National Conference*. New York: Oxford University Press.
Conrad, A. (2015). *Conductor-led improvisation for orchestra*. TEDxEdina. Retrieved from https://youtu.be/7lZ3dBShP-Y.
Covach, J. (2015, February 2). Rock me, maestro. *The Chronicle of Higher Education*. Retrieved from http://chronicle.com/article/Rock-Me-Maestro/151423/?cid=cr&utm_source=cr&utm_medium=en.
Cutler, D. (2012, June 19). Re-imagining arts in higher education. *The Savvy Musician Blog*. Retrieved from www.savvymusician.com/blog/2012/06/re-imagining-arts-higher-education/.
DePree, M. (1992). *Leadership jazz*. New York: Dell Publishing.
Dobrian, C. (1991). *Thoughts on composition and improvisation*. Retrieved from http://music.arts.uci.edu/dobrian/CD.comp.improv.htm.
Foss, L. (1962). Improvisation versus composition. *The Musical Times, 103*(1436), 684–685.
Freeman, R. (2014). *The crisis of classical music in America: Lessons from a life in the education of musicians*. Lanham, MD: Rowman & Littlefield.
Friedmann, J. L. (2014, October 1). *Improvisation and origination*. Retrieved from https://thinkingonmusic.wordpress.com/tag/frank-zappa/.
Goleman, D., Kaufman, P., & Ray, M. (1992). *The creative spirit*. New York: Penguin Books USA, Inc.

Herstand, A. (2017). *How to make it in the new music business: Practical tips on building a loyal following and making a living as a musician*. New York: W.W. Norton.

Hahn, D. (March 9, 2011). How to actually make $50,000 a year as a musician. *Music Thinktank blog*. Retrieved from www.musicthinktank.com/blog/how-to-actually-make-50000-a-year-as-a-musician.html.

Hoch, J. (Oct. 2013). Shared leadership and innovation: The role of vertical leadership and employee integrity. *Journal of Business and Psychology*, 28(2), 159–174. doi: 10.1007/s10869-012-9273-6.

International Society for Improvised Music. (n.d.). Retrieved from www.improvisedmusic.org/overview.html.

Kuhnert, K. W., & Lewis, P. (1987). Transactional and transformational leadership: A constructive/developmental analysis. *Academy of Management Review*, 12(4), 648–657.

Larsen, L. (1997). *The role of the musician in the 21st century: Rethinking the core*. Retrieved from https://libbylarsen.com/as_the-role-of-the-musician.

Larsen, N. P. A. (2015). *Conducted improvisation: A study of the effect of the concept of signs on musical creativity*. Unpublished Master's thesis. Lund University, Malmö: Sweden.

Mayer-Schonberger, V., & Oberlechner, T. (2002, October).*Through their own words: Towards a new understanding of leadership through metaphors*. KSG Working Papers Series RWP02-043. doi: org/10.2139/ssrn.357542.

Morgan, G. (1986). *Images of organization*. Newbury Park, CA: Sage Publications, Inc.

Morris, L. D. (2006). Conduction is. *Contemporary Music Review*, 25(5/6), 533–535.

National Association of Schools of Music (NASM) (1999, rev. 2010). *Notes for music faculty and administrators: standards for composition/improvisation and history/repertory in undergraduate professional degrees in music*. Retrieved from http://nasm.arts-accredit.org/site/docs/NASM%20Faculty%20Advisories^Standards/Notes-StandardsCompilation.pdf.

Noonan, S., & Fish, T. (2007). *Leadership through story: Diverse voices in dialogue*. Lanham, MD: Rowman & Littlefield Education.

Northouse, P. G. (2007). *Leadership: Theory and practice* (4th edn). Thousand Oaks, CA: Sage Publications, Inc.

Pearce, C. L., & Conger, J. A. (2002). *Shared leadership: Reframing the hows and whys of leadership*. Thousand Oaks, CA: Sage Publications.

Sarath, E., Myers, D., & Campbell, P. (2017). *Redefining music studies in an age of change: Creativity, diversity, and integration*. New York: Routledge.

Seifter, H., & Economy, P. (2001). *Leadership ensemble: Lessons in collaborative management from the world's only conductorless orchestra*. New York: Henry Holt and Company.

Sisario, B. (2013, July 10). Lionized, but restless as ever. *The New York Times*. Retrieved from https://nyti.ms/1aWYeXr

Smith, C. (1995). *Broadway the hard way: Techniques of allusion in the music of Frank Zappa*. College Music Symposium, 35. Retrieved from http://symposium.music.org/index.php?option=com_k2&view=item&id=2114:broadway-the-hard-way-techniques-of-allusion-in-the-music-of-frank-zappa&Itemid=124.

Stanley, T. T. (2009). *Butch Morris and the art of conduction*. Unpublished doctoral dissertation. College Park, MD: University of Maryland.

Suk Bong, C., Kihwan, K., & Seung-Wan, K. (2017). Effects of transformational and shared leadership styles on employees' perception of team effectiveness. *Social Behavior & Personality: An International Journal*, 45(3), 377–386. doi: 10.2224/sbp.5805.

Turner, V. (1988). *The anthropology of performance*. New York, NY: PAJ Publications.

Ulhoi, J. P., & Müller, S. (2014). Mapping the landscape of shared leadership: A review and synthesis. *International Journal of Leadership Studies*, 8(2).

Verrico, K., & Reese, J. (2016). University musicians' experiences in an iPad ensemble: A phenomenological case study. *Journal of Music, Technology & Education*, 9(3), 315–328. doi: 10.1386/jmte.9.3.315_1.

Weber, W. E. (Ed.) (2004). *The musician as entrepreneur, 1700–1914: Managers, charlatans, and idealists*. Bloomington, IN: Indiana University Press.

Winston, B., & Patterson, K. (2006). An integrative definition of leadership. *International Journal of Leadership Studies, 1*(2), 6–66.

Wood, M., & Dibben, M. (2015). Leadership as relational process. *Process Studies, 44*(1), 24–27. doi: 10.5840/process20154412.

XIII
Student Commentary: Leadership at the Undergraduate Level; Cultivating Collective Ownership

KELLY BYLICA

Leadership in musical practice offers foundational complexities such as the roles of individual and collective leadership and leadership that progresses beyond autonomy. These complexities are multifaceted and become even more so when considering the development of leadership dispositions within undergraduate settings. Reflecting on my own experiences as a music educator and future teacher-educator, my main concern often turns to how undergraduate students can more carefully and practically consider the role of leadership skills as they enter the profession, as well as how higher education can support such dispositions.

The Initiative to Lead

The chapters in this volume explore and develop ideas surrounding a variety of skills, knowledge, practices and leadership types employed by individuals and collectives. These include the development of vision (Berger, Chapter IX) and risk-taking (Weller, Chapter XII) as well as the role of leadership in the development of both professional and personal identity (Yau, Chapter XI). While each of these is important, leadership, particularly at the undergraduate level, should be grounded in developing a sense of self-concept, with a foundation in critical thinking, which leads students to interrogate the status quo and creatively lead, work and advocate in the domain of musical practice within and beyond higher education.

The nucleus for the development of musical practice in higher education often occurs in studio lessons and ensemble rehearsals, where students hone their practical craft. This places the relationship between students and studio teacher-conductor at the centre of both musical and leadership development. Upon entering higher education, music students go through a "pivotal transition in their need for guidance and leadership" (Yau, Chapter XI) and the instrumental teacher has the potential to play a substantive and influential role in their lives. It is within the co-creation of learning in the studio or rehearsal setting that students can learn from a master teacher and take an active role in their own musical education, eventually leading to engagement in the musical life of society.

While variations on leadership styles are presented in this volume, including the traditional role of the master teacher (Yau, Chapter XI), it is transformational leadership that most clearly demonstrates the fluid relationship that can exist in studio lessons and rehearsals. Weller describes transformational leadership in the guise of conducted improvisation, giving the example of a young musician and his practice as an innovative and transformational leader. Similarly, in the second leadership volume in this series, Mitchell (Chapter V) attributes transformative leadership to the "sharing of responsibilities and diminished hierarchical boundaries". Both authors contend that transformational leadership goes beyond modelling leadership that students might learn through observation. Rather, transformational leadership takes the further and critical step of involving all players in experiential learning by generating an exchange of mutual stimulation and elevation. In this environment, leadership skills can be created and nurtured, and boundaries of the "teacher" and the "taught" are dissolved. This dissolution is essential as the very goal of higher education is to prepare the student to become the teacher: to lead in performance, studio and classroom.

Why Does Leadership Matter?

While each author presents different arguments for the need and value of leadership skills within undergraduate education, "the belief that individuals need to exhibit leadership qualities is a common refrain in numerous first-world cultures" (Pike, Chapter X). As a young scholar and educator, I resonate with Mitchell's statement: "Whether conductor, performer, teacher or composer, the musician must exhibit some level of leadership." However, it also concerns me that leadership roles are often thrust upon individuals rather than earned or developed (Pike, Chapter X), particularly when growing expectations for enacting leadership are part of hiring and evaluative practices in many work environments. Not only are graduating musicians expected to be technically proficient, they are also expected to present creative teaching strategies, develop innovative plans for audience engagement and devise new ways to connect with the needs and interests of an ever-changing, musically engaged society.

Higher education needs to be where leadership skills are explicitly taught and nurtured rather than where students are expected to absorb or adapt leadership as needed. Leadership proficiencies help to produce stronger musicians who are poised to advocate for themselves and their careers. Leadership proficiencies also help to build the skills and self-efficacy that encourage musicians to become agents of change, critical thinkers and engaged citizens who think and speak for themselves and who advocate for music and music education as critical art forms in society (see also Reid, Bennett & Rowley, Chapter VIII; Berger, Chapter IX).

The Roles of Teacher and Curriculum

The co-creation of learning and the implementation of a transformative leadership approach begins with the teacher. In order to develop leadership skills that lead graduates to innovative societal engagement, the environment facilitated in studio lessons and rehearsals needs to encourage critical thought and provide space for creativity. We must ask ourselves in what ways graduating musicians might be expected to fulfil roles in a changing society and how we might equip them "to contribute musically toward the public good and to adapt their roles amidst constant change" (Myers, 2016, p. 296). The role of the musician in society is changing, but higher education curricula have not kept up. Whereas graduates are expected to engage in careers "marked by initiative, flexibility and artistry ... engaging audiences as co-creators, managing their own careers, collaborating with other artists, and crossing roles among creators, performers, and producers of music" (Myers, 2016, p. 295), curricula have remained stagnant in terms of capabilities that prepare students to be self-reflective leaders and problem-solvers.

Musical creativity, independence and active initiative, all trademarks of leadership, are absent when the power relationship is defined in such a way that there is no space for dissonance (Jørgenson, 2000). In contrast, the relationship between studio teacher or conductor and student musician has historically been grounded in a master-apprentice model (Burwell, 2012, 2016; Burwell, Bennett, & Carey, 2017; Callaghan, 1998; Jørgenson, 2000; Lebler, 2007; Nielsen, 2006; Persson, 2000; Uszler, 1992), and the definition of these roles is not always clear.

Uszler (1992, p. 584) describes the master–apprentice model as follows: "The master is the model who demonstrates, directs, comments, and inspires. The apprentice is the disciple who watches, listens, imitates, and seeks approval." Manturzewska (1990, p. 135) claims that the master takes command of almost every aspect of the student's life: for example, in terms of "personality, aesthetic attitudes, life philosophy, professional standards and attitudes". This level of command does not foster independence, critical thought and initiative or, consequently, transformational leadership. Several authors in the volume acknowledge and identify the master–apprentice model (or versions of it) as an area of concern in both studio and rehearsal relationships (see Berger, Chapter IX; Pike, Chapter X; Yau, Chapter XI). In order to embrace transformational leadership, we must begin to deconstruct power relationships in favour of a relationship that supports and cultivates collective ownership and co-creation of learning.

In the standard master–apprentice model, the master performer often dominates both lesson activity and initiative. Persson's (2000, p. 32) study, which followed a "master performer" in his role as a teacher, found that the professor "dominated lessons completely … instructions were clear and to the point … students were rarely allowed to take initiative or make suggestions", thereby impacting students' sense of competency. Given that self-competency and opportunities to question and critically explore repertoire, pedagogy and performance practice further the development of leadership skills, limited opportunities to pose questions creates followers rather than leaders. Beyond fundamental (and important) technical training, students must be able to engage as communicators and problem-solvers, to dynamically attract new audiences, to create new artistic experiences and to seek out innovative collaboration in order to engage a 21st-century audience. This begins in the studio and ensemble relationship.

Learning communication and collaboration skills and participating in real-world experiences that link student musicians to the community helps to explicitly engage students in leadership development. Transformational leadership is not about one person leading all others in a common goal, it is about sharing a collective consciousness that moves us forward, creating space for growth and change. The teacher's role, then, is not to dictate, nor is it simply to offer alternative approaches. It is to explore interpretations and ideas alongside the student, each contributing to the dialogue and opening space for collective learning.

In the traditional teaching model, much of the knowledge constructed in music classes is "procedural and declarative" (Pike, Chapter X) rather than creative and/or critical. As Myers (2016, p. 296) states, music education is often an "information-based, didactic process including imitative technical training that incorporates little creativity and does even less to nurture students' individual and collaborative creativity". Jørgenson would agree, asking: "Is the student given opportunity to develop his [sic] *independence and active initiative in learning*, or is he restricted to develop his *ability to receive, absorb and transform teacher influences*?" (2000, p. 68, emphasis in the original). This includes leadership skills that help students plug into "the values of music in society" and to understand "how to share those values and embed them within the core issues and questions of a twenty-first century global-technical society" (Myers, 2016, p. 295). The challenges faced both in society as a whole as well as within the music profession cannot be solved in isolation; they require collaboration and creativity, both of which can, and should, be taught through the co-creation of learning.

Collective Ownership

Collective ownership suggests that the responsibility for development of leadership skills lies equally with teacher and student. Whereas the teacher's responsibility is to facilitate a welcoming, collaborative environment, the student's responsibility is to take advantage of it: to share his or her goals, to engage in dialogue, to not rely solely on an imitative approach to music-making and to participate creatively in the musical process. The development of independence and active initiative, coupled with critical thought, creates change and forward motion, both within and outside of music, and higher education often promotes these capacities as being central to undergraduate development. However, Burwell (2016, p. 508) points out that the "rather unique setting of studio apprenticeship ... gives rise to a paradox: that the development of critical or evaluative thinking would seem to conflict with the trust and authority essential to success". When viewed through a lens of transformative leadership, the paradox disappears and critical thinking works in partnership with the relationship built between the student and teacher/conductor.

The relationship built through the sharing of responsibility leads to co-creation of learning and development of leadership skills that move beyond musician autonomy, confidence and competence towards students "extending their artistry and creativity toward engaging others in socially and aesthetically fulfilling experiences" (Myers, 2016, p. 300). Leadership skills should not be confined to an elective (co-curricular) course taken at the end of a degree programme. Rather, they should form a cohesive part of the existing curriculum, intentionally integrated both with technical skills and with what Myers (2016, p. 299) describes as "contemporary problems and issues in music and society".

While the chapters in this section of the first leadership volume focus on performance and the teaching studio, there are also linkages with the more traditional conception of music education as seen in a classroom environment. Within the more traditional construction of music education, educators working with a "one-size-fits-all" curriculum are striving to develop ways to nurture creativity and student voice in curricular decisions. Student investment in both classroom dialogue and musical engagement is deepened when responsibility and choice are shared. This suggests that elements of transformative leadership can, and should, be enacted at all levels. The intentional, purposeful development of leadership capacities in the realm of higher education has the potential to generate more performers and educators who can engage in reciprocal relationships with younger musicians both in and outside of the classroom. Lebler (2007, p. 206) argues that:

> If the modern conservatorium is to prosper in a rapidly changing cultural and economic landscape, it will need to provide a learning experience that

is musically inclusive and likely to produce multi-skilled and adaptable graduates who are self-monitoring and self-directed in their learning, able to function across a range of activities that can constitute a portfolio career.

Because the musical and societal world are inherently connected and neither is static, leaders must be prepared to promote growth. The world is rapidly changing and, if we are to graduate students prepared to advance opportunities for musical engagement across societal boundaries, transformational leadership skills must be central to curricular development.

References

Burwell, K. (2012). Apprenticeship in music: A contextual study for instrumental teaching and learning. *International Journal of Music Education, 31*(3), 276–291. doi: 10.1177/0255761411434501.

Burwell, K. (2016). Dissonance in the studio: An exploration of tensions within the apprenticeship setting in higher education music. *International Journal of Music Education, 34*(4), 499–512. doi: 10.1177/0255761415574124.

Burwell, K., Bennett, D., & Carey, G. (2017). Isolation in studio music teaching: The secret garden. *Arts and Humanities in Higher Education*. Published online first, October 2017. doi: 10.1177/1474022217736581.

Callaghan, J. (1998). Singing teachers and voice science – an evaluation of voice teaching in Australian tertiary institutions. *Research Studies in Music Education, 10*, 25–41. doi: 10.1177/1321103X9801000103.

Jørgenson, H. (2000). Student learning in higher instrumental music education: Who is responsible? *British Journal of Music Education, 17*(1), 67–77. doi: 10.1017/S0265051700000164.

Lebler, D. (2007). Student-as-master? Reflections on a learning innovation in popular music pedagogy. *International Journal of Music Education, 25*(3), 205–221.doi: 10.1177/0255761407083575.

Manturzewska, M. (1990). A biographical study of the life span development of professional musicians. *Psychology of Music, 18*(2), 112–139. doi: 10.1177/0305735690182002.

Myers, D. E. (2016). Creativity, diversity, and integration: Radical change in the bachelor of music curriculum. *Arts & Humanities in Higher Education, 15*(3–4), 293–307. doi: 10.1177/1474022216647378.

Nielsen, K. (2006). Apprenticeships at the academy of music. *International Journal of Education and the Arts, 7*(4). Retrieved from http://ijea.asu.edu/v7n4/.

Persson, R. S. (1996). Studying with a musical maestro: A case study of commonsense teaching in artistic training. *Creativity Research Journal, 9*, 33–46. doi: 10.1207/s15326934crj0901_4.

Persson, R. S. (2000). Survival of the fittest or the most talented? Deconstructing the myth of the musical maestro. *Journal of Secondary Gifted Education, 12*(1), 25–39. doi: 10.4219/jsge-2000-638.

Uszler, M. (1992). Research on the teaching of keyboard music. In R. Colwell (Ed.), *Handbook of research on music teaching and learning* (pp. 584–593). New York: Schirmer Books.

XIV
Institutional Leadership and Musician Development in Higher Music Education

DAWN BENNETT, JENNIFER ROWLEY AND PATRICK SCHMIDT

Traditional, hierarchical approaches to leadership are unable to meet the needs of a higher education sector so adversely impacted by volatility, uncertainty, complexity and ambiguousness. Higher music education is no exception; indeed, music schools and conservatoires in many countries are now subsumed into larger university departments and governed by more or less the same processes as any other discipline. Although the impact of these changes on artistic research, academic careers and identity has been the subject of fairly consistent commentary and research, the leadership of higher music education has been less discussed. Similarly, the development of leadership abilities among students has focused largely on graduate attributes while little has been written about the need for student musicians to learn how to lead and manage their future practice. In this chapter we bring together key concepts and challenges addressed by the authors and suggest how these might be addressed across higher music education. We pay particular attention to institutional leadership and the development of musicians.

This is the first of two volumes which address leadership in and through higher music education. In this volume, authors explored institutional leadership and musician development in higher music education; in volume two the authors turn their attention to pedagogical and curricular leadership. The volumes include short chapters from students, who provide a novel and important perspective on the development and application of leadership both within educational institutions and in the profession.

Highlighting the essential qualities needed by the next generation of music graduates and leaders, this volume presents compelling arguments for greater attention to be paid to the leadership development of student musicians and faculty. Through numerous examples, the authors help us to understand how we might benefit from the existing spaces where *hard* and *soft* policies have been designed and implemented, and how we might envision a space in which to develop leadership so that others can become agentic contributors.

Music graduates who know how to create and sustain their careers also know how to lead, for it is leadership – of self, career and others – which enables graduates to negotiate their transition into the professional world. In this final chapter we bring together the authors' key concepts and challenges and suggest how these might be addressed across higher music education. We begin with a focus on developing student musicians as leaders and then we address the often-fraught issue of how to engage faculty. There follows a discussion of leadership today and tomorrow, including the challenges of effecting change. A compelling feature of the authors' accounts is that they begin to frame how the leadership qualities of graduate musicians might be developed within higher music education. We draw on their accounts to suggest strategies for moving forward.

Leading the Development of Student Musicians

There is no universal definition or formula for leadership in and through higher music education; however, there is a critical need to challenge the central practices and theories that underpin the preparation and practice of musicians, defined in the broadest sense as people who work in music within one or more specialist roles (Bennett, 2018).

The authors of this volume agree that leadership is a core graduate attribute and an essential element in the identity formation of emerging music professionals. Its development within the constraints of higher education systems, however, presents particular challenges relating to rigid curricular structures, limited finances, a heavily casualised workforce, hierarchical notions of success in music, and music's position within a commodified higher education sector ranked according to research outputs, grant funding, "efficiency" measures and inadequate graduate destinations metrics.

Ironically, one of the answers to the leadership challenge lies within the practice of music itself: developing leadership and reflective practice through "approaches that are embedded within real and daily practice experiences" (Smith & Trede, 2013, p. 632). Pamela Pike (Chapter X) gives the example of transformational leadership, which is inherent in students' creative convergent and divergent thinking. This is the thinking that underpins the creative phases of preparation, incubation, illumination and verification. Janis Weller (Chapter XII) illustrates convergent and divergent thinking in action. She does so with a case study that exposes the liminal intersections between the control of composition, the spontaneity of improvisation and the blend of transformational and shared leadership inherent in performances of conducted improvisation.

Similarly, Anna Reid (Chapter III) finds that the distributed leadership in musicians' ensemble work can inform their understanding of collaborative forms of leadership. Writing from the perspective of institutional leadership, Reid describes the need to translate broader institutional changes so that they "work in meaningful ways for us and our students". This, she contends, demands that the musical and non-musical expertise, experience and views of diverse stakeholders is leveraged through a distributed leadership approach.

All three authors expose the leadership in which student musicians already engage, whether as performers, creators, technologists, directors or pedagogues. However, Reid emphasises the need for students and faculty to become far more aware of the non-musical qualities of their activities. These include issues of sameness, difference and context, the influence and impact of their actions, and "how the 'real politick' of the specific situation enables or restricts [their] activities". The same argument can be made for the engagement of faculty, both as educators developing students' leadership capacities and as peers developing their own leadership within a distributed model.

Leadership can only be articulated, refined or further developed if it is mindful. Trede and McEwen (2016, p. 7) articulate this as the behaviour of a deliberate professional: a "thinker and a doer, where the thinking informs the doing and the doing informs the thinking". For student musicians to recognise and articulate their confidence and abilities as leaders – to become deliberate professionals – curricular space must be made. We note, however, that the need for curricular *space* should not be conflated with the need for additional curricular *time*. As Anna Reid, Dawn Bennett and Jennifer Rowley explain in Chapter VIII, within-curriculum strategies include ensuring that both "every day" and work-integrated learning experiences such as internships incorporate the critical thinking necessary for students to make cognitive connections between their class, community or industry engagement and their future lives and careers in music.

The arguments for active or experiential learning carry still more weight when considering that the majority of tertiary (post-secondary) student musicians are from "Generation Z". These are people born between 1995 and 2010, who tend to "demand a voice in the decisions that affect their lives" (O'Neill, Chapter VII). Generation Z students are inclined towards being change agents, and yet they experience a higher education system where "the concept of student voice can be passive and disempowered, governed and operated by the institution rather than by students themselves" (Kay, Dunne, & Hutchinson, 2010, p. 1, in O'Neill, Chapter VII, this volume).

Community engagement and student voice is a prevalent theme in the authors' accounts. Martin Berger (Chapter IX) gives as his example the work of choral conducting graduates, who because of the diverse cultural contexts of their work can find themselves working as social change agents almost by default. The same could be said for most music graduates and yet many student musicians graduate without having experienced music-making in their own communities, let alone in diverse community contexts. This needs to change.

Students and faculty benefit from observing and engaging in leadership which is inclusive and which challenges dominant stereotypes. Provided with a framework within which to reflect on and explore their leadership experiences, and given the language with which to articulate their thinking, student musicians should be challenged to consider their leadership development within the context of their artistic and scholarly practice. There is, after all, compelling evidence that mindful or deliberate artistic practice has academic, artistic and career benefits for the artist and musician (see, for example, Barrett & Bolt, 2014). Glen Carruthers (Chapter II) observes that students' leadership development promotes a richer and more agentic student experience. These benefits signal a far more constructive positioning of leadership than that of leadership as an "employability skill" or graduate attribute.

The authors agree that higher music education is incomplete without the inclusion of equitable opportunities for students to develop transformational leadership, transcultural understanding, diverse creativities and an awareness of the contexts within which music work takes place. As Patrick Schmidt (Chapter IV) contends, change requires leaders to adopt more robust, pervasive and effective leadership development in higher education. This might include leadership that is committed to democratic engagement and which seeks, as Euridiana Silva Souza attests in Chapter VI, both fairer outcomes and more apt and equitable processes. The engagement of faculty is absolutely crucial and it is to this engagement that we turn next.

Leading Faculty Engagement

A common theme across the chapters is that the responsibility for developing leadership lies equally with student and teacher. There will inevitably be some people in higher music education who view student musicians' leadership development as outside their role, interest or capacity. Similarly, there will be students for whom time away from technical work is considered time wasted. This is where institutional leaders need to create opportunities to engage their constituents in elements of transformational leadership, and in transformative leadership which reviews (see Carruthers's model, for example) not only the curriculum but the values and hierarchies which underpin institutional schema (see Kappler Hewitt, Davis, & Lashley, 2014).

Hierarchical notions of success in music and in higher education cannot be ignored. Here, explicit celebrations of success beyond the norm have the potential to be transformative to the thinking and cultural milieu of both students and faculty. Think, for example, of the performance-centric messages encountered by aspiring students and current students on open days and in yearbooks and websites: how many of these "success" stories feature students and graduates who win teaching awards, run successful businesses or lead crucial work in the community?

Leadership development is better thought of as a driver of what Bennett (2018, p. 5) terms employABILITY thinking: "students' cognitive and social development as capable and informed individuals, professionals and social citizens". Cognitive approaches to employability help educators to embed employability within the curriculum and they motivate students and faculty to engage metacognitively. Approaches such as this (see also the deliberative professional work of Trede and McEwen) demand the explicit and metacognitive engagement of students *within* the curriculum, in this case *within* the everyday practice of student musicians. There are, however, three ubiquitous challenges that must first be overcome if educators are to engage.

- First, educators cite a *lack of time* due to overcrowded curricula, content-heavy programmes and the perception that embedding employability requires them to do more.
- Second, educators refer to a *lack of resources* in that to embed employability they need to develop appropriate teaching resources and understand the theoretical basis of that work.
- Third, educators voice their *lack of expertise*. Educators rightly state that they are neither career coaches or careers professionals. Moreover, a nuanced understanding of contemporary industry is an unrealistic expectation of academic staff in higher education's research-focused and metrics-driven environment (adapted from Bennett, 2018).

These challenges demand a systematic and collaborative approach to realising sustainable change in both thinking and practice. At the forefront of this is the need to position leadership as a core aspect of the musician's practice: to make clear the relevance of leadership to musicians' development and practice.

Writing about the trends and framing of higher music education, Minors, Burnard, Wiffen, Shihabi and van der Walt (2017, p. 467) agree that relevance is a key ingredient and that relevance is learned through active student engagement. As such, student musicians:

> not only need to get involved in the world around them, they particularly need to know how and why they need to get involved. Opportunities

to seek things out need to be provided, nurtured and encouraged, and this needs to begin as soon as possible as part of their overall student experience.

As Weller elucidates, the need for leadership is far from new: musicians have been responsible for leading their own practice for centuries. Drawing on Weller's observation, Kelly Bylica (Chapter XIII) asks in her student commentary why, if this is the case, leadership is not already an essential and valued component of higher music education. In Chapter XI, Christine Ngai Lam Yau emphasises the enormous influence of instrumental and vocal teachers and the potential for them to lead the development of aspiring musicians who think beyond hierarchies of success. In line with Gaunt (2008), Yau agrees that many instrumental and vocal teachers inhibit rather than develop such thinking. These are the cultures and behaviours which need our immediate attention; their persistence in the modern conservatoire goes some way to answering Bylica's question.

Higher music education change and renewal, then, requires a whole-of-community approach in which reciprocal learning processes drive reflection and action; the buy-in of faculty is crucial. The process should begin with the adoption of a reflective stance, first considering the development and experiences of personal and collective schema and then articulating these to others. A constructivist approach to building and reframing leadership capacities is equally valid at the individual, curricular and institutional levels. As such, the following approach could underpin our change leadership at every level.

- Analyse the current schema.
- Understand the nature and effectiveness of current practice.
- Construct meaning and knowledge dialogically.
- Frame and implement new directions, actions and practices (new schema) (adapted from Lambert, 2002).

Applied in a cyclical way, a constructivist approach creates continuous learning interactions within a culture of trust and consultation.

Leadership and Policy Thinking

Embedded in many of the questions posed in this volume is the notion of tension. Leadership exists, is developed and made present, in the midst of tensions. This is how leadership and policy thinking and action intersect very well. Policy emerges from questions, from the need to engage in resolution or strategic planning. And leadership adds a human quality to this work, bringing the structural tension to intersect with the personal tensions present in complex settings such as education or cultural environments.

Carruthers, after analysing data from programme reviews in Canadian universities, invites us to consider basic, yet unresolved tensions in higher music education, asking:

1. Should university music curricula focus on career-preparedness, aesthetic values, or skills development? What is the relationship between these goals and objectives?
2. There can be a tension between the "elite" nature of many music schools – students are admitted only after passing a rigorous audition, a battery of theory and aural skills tests, and so on – and the responsibilities universities have to serve the needs of the local community. How can this tension be resolved?

Carruthers highlights that there are often disparities between what leaders intend to achieve and what they are able to achieve; that is, how effectively they can establish vision and implement action. Often these issues are understood only managerially; that is, poor execution is blamed. However, being able to reflect, in curricular and programmatic ways, the multiple needs of a changing music profession requires more than apt management.

Schmidt is concerned with how policy can become less about rule-making and streamlining, and more about a cyclical engagement with framing in order to address relevance. Rather than shy away from developing their own *framing capacity* as illustrated in the constructivist approach above, leaders and leaders-in-the-making should practise leadership just as we engage in our musicianship and teacher-ship, constructing it as a form of agency. The implication here is that higher music education needs to help foster *leadership-in-the-world* as much as and perhaps more than it develops the *formal leader* by virtue of a post or position.

Reid, Bennett and Rowley expand the notion of leadership-in-the-world by evidencing how leadership emerges in the "liminal space between formal music study and internship work experiences". Their work shows students becoming young musicians, educators and cultural workers by virtue of transforming their thinking from situation to situation: adopting a metacognitive view such as employABILITY thinking. This carries with it significant implications for higher music education, where these kinds of work-integrated learning opportunities are, puzzlingly, still not ubiquitous. The authors illustrate how multiple experiences are a way to practically foster one's framing dispositions. And they point us to the questions of how our curricula might become more open and porous, and how higher music education might create the spaces where both approaches can supersede extant structures.

Pamela Burnard (Chapter V) links tension to the intersection between the personal and the political by focusing on gender challenges as a way to better understand the challenges of leadership. She asks us to consider how institutions challenge gendered trends in music careers while also linking the larger, more abstract aspects of this issue to the individual responsibility aligned with the idea of leadership-in-the-world. Burnard asks how we are going about creating opportunities to challenge and improve the ways in which diverse musical groups engage in purposeful and inclusive ways so that all voices can contribute to decision-making.

Returning to the earlier point about reward, value and hierarchy, Burnard also asks how our institutions reward inclusive behaviour and interventions among faculty and students. Taken together, the authors' narratives indicate that leadership development must address and contend with the many ways in which discrimination is made manifest, how and where it operates, and how we might be able to better navigate both its overt and insidious/structural presence.

Leading for Today and Tomorrow

> We all want heroes. Having individuals undertake heroic duties relieves us of the time, energy, and thought needed to lead change. It is less stressful, less demanding, easier. But when knowledge, its development, dissemination, sharing, and growth is at stake, individual leaders are mythical creatures. We need to develop parables for the collaborative future that engage all of us, enable us to develop, and encourage us to share the expertise within us. What this requires is a new leadership approach to guide us to the future.
>
> (Jones, 2017, p. 65)

Higher education is beset by volatility, uncertainty, complexity and ambiguousness. The traditional hierarchical approach to leadership, with its emphasis on the heroic leader in a position of power, is simply unable to meet the needs of higher education or the community with which it is invested; neither is that model appropriate to the needs of graduate musicians. And yet leadership has a long history of being thought of as a personal trade. The tendency to both naturalise and personify leadership established it as an attribute, a capacity that would emerge even in the absence of guidance or structural preparation. Today, industry, the military and government alike take the notion of fomenting and nurturing leadership seriously, recognising the need for institutional commitment which is sustainably designed and implemented at the structural level. Leadership as an explicit consideration in higher education, and even more specifically in higher music education, has been slow to emerge.

Many universities have invested in auxiliary programming aimed to support faculty labelled as leaders – usually by virtue of a post or position such as chair or dean. Leadership workshops and mentoring programmes are also growing and have become institutional fixtures in some locations. In North America, organisations such as the College Music Society (CMS) or the National Association of Schools of Music (NASM) have come to recognise and address the professional development needs of today's leadership; similar leadership programmes exist, albeit with a more generic focus than music, in multiple countries. Systemic and systematic engagement with tomorrow's leadership in higher music education, however, is still lacking.

We have argued that few higher music education institutions explicitly address the qualities required for graduates to negotiate their future careers and how these might be developed within the core curriculum of higher music education. Leadership is one such quality and its development in student musicians is vital for the longevity of the profession and its actors. Naturally, leadership development is not simple. Leadership, particularly when it is distinguished from and understood as more than management, requires a disposition toward complexity and nuance. As with everything else, and evidenced by the authors in this volume, leadership development requires thoughtful thinking and theory, careful practice, and lots of questions. It also requires a collaborative approach. As Carruthers emphasises, a substantive part of the time and efforts of people in formal leadership positions is consumed by priority setting and external response. This leaves many of the proactive change agendas unrealised unless they are approached collaboratively.

The authors engage in meticulous thinking and theory alongside careful practice, and from these experiences they pose questions to stimulate further debate. Authors' questions and evidence point to the ways in which the leadership development of higher music education faculty and students can be developed through mindful practice, community engagement and research efforts, and by undertaking and sharing with students a complex view of real-world experiences. Readers who are interested or curious about leadership might find ourselves – or our future selves – reflected in the cases, stories, voices and theories. We can also be guided by questions and actions such as the ones posed below.

Pike challenges us to consider just one undergraduate music class and to create just one semester-long assignment that engages students in the development of creativity and leadership. This is a similar approach to Bennett's employABILITY approach, which embeds a single, manageable touchpoint within each class. Pike also emphasises the benefits of including both formative and summative assessment tasks. In line with Boud, Cohen and Sampson (2001), this approach demands ample time and opportunity for self-reflection and reflective feedback so that stakeholders can explore, practise, innovate and validate their creative experiences (see also peer-to-peer connectivity as described by Tosey, 2006).

Several authors challenge us to think of a story that would emerge from our own professional practice and to evaluate the story in terms of how it outlines a balance or imbalance. Where were the imbalances felt, and why? In what ways was balance achieved? Many such examples can be found within the collaborative process which enable music, whether within the context of rehearsals, the recording studio or the classroom. As such, they need not be isolated from the passions that led students to select a career pathway in music.

Authors also challenge us to consider how we might engage undergraduate students in considering the role of music in society, specifically within their local communities. Is there a community engagement project through which students could work with people who do not share their musical and/or cultural background, so that their assumptions about music, culture and education might be challenged? Music has a language that is uniquely positioned to enable shared expression and dialogue. There is nothing similar in other disciplines, and yet students will only realise the strength of their music in community settings if they have opportunities to engage. We would add that many examples of superb community partnerships in higher music education exist as teacher-driven initiatives which are reliant on the good will of individuals. Such initiatives are precariously positioned and should be supported and embedded in a sustainable format.

Finally, we are challenged to think of a recent, difficult decision made by or made for us – at work or in our personal life – and ask: were complex elements of leadership present in the decision-making process? Would it have been possible or desirable to adopt a leadership process? Might the outcomes or the process been different had we done so? These might seem small changes and challenges, but if students encountered just one class and just one assessment every semester in which they made the explicit link between their learning and their development as musician leaders, cultural change would surely follow.

Concluding Comments

Higher music education has experienced profound changes in the structure and funding of higher education, the vocational expectations of graduates and employers, and the challenges of sustaining work within a globalised and diverse music workforce. These changes prompted the authors to consider how higher music education leaders might enact individual, curricular, institutional and policy changes within the often-rigid traditional higher education curriculum and assessment processes. Although the challenges are addressed daily, in and through our own experiences, they also require some level of structural organisation. If we see formative value in leadership development and desire for musicians and educators to find the enterprise compelling and impactful, institutional and dispositional spaces must be designed, supported and sustained.

The notion of policy thinking and action is significant here, particularly when policy is understood broadly as the realm in which vision is constructed and actualised. *Hard* policies which can see leadership development instituted in curricula, or those which establish carefully designed mentorship or economically foment professional development, are critical, particularly for long-term sustainability. However, *soft* policies – those that are constructed in our interactions, guided by our assumptions or established tradition, by unspoken rules – are equally powerful. A culture of leadership development is thus formed by both tangible, clearly articulated structures and also by changes in language and relations; that is, through dispositions.

As discussed, the tensions exposed in this volume can be addressed in various ways. In fact, part of what emerges from these chapters is that we, as a community, are well on our way. And while we clearly have the collective know-how with which to enact towards positive change, we can do more in terms of naming what we do and advocating for stronger institutionalisation of these ideas: by sharing cases, talking about models, engaging in further research, asking questions, and fostering dialogue. Anna Reid names this disposition as a willingness to adopt a distributed leadership approach. The question that emerges from her work is one that we all should contemplate: What is impeding us from adopting (or demanding) a leadership approach where we have greater autonomy to invent, criticise, change and mould processes? We hope that the two leadership volumes provide a compelling starting point from which to address these questions.

References

Barrett, E., & Bolt, B. (Eds.). (2014). *Practice as research: Approaches to creative arts enquiry*. London: I. B. Tauris.

Bennett, D. (2018). *Embedding employABILITY thinking across higher education*. Sydney: Australian Government Office for Learning and Teaching.

Boud, D., Cohen, R., & Sampson, J. (Eds.). (2001). *Peer learning in higher education: Learning from and with each other*. London: RoutledgeFarmer.

Gaunt, H. (2008). One-to-one tuition in a conservatoire: The perceptions of instrumental and vocal teachers. *Psychology of Music, 36*(2), 215–245. doi: 10.1177/0305735607080827.

Jones, S. (2017). *Leading the academy: Distributed leadership in higher education*. Sydney: Higher Education Research and Development Society of Australasia.

Kappler Hewitt, K., Davis, A. W., & Lashley, C. (2014). Transformational and transformative leadership in a research-informed leadership preparation program. *Journal of Research on Leadership Education, 9*(3), 225–253. doi: 10.1177/1942775114552329.

Kay, J., Dunne, E., & Hutchinson, J. (2010). *Rethinking the values of higher education – students as change agents?* Quality Assurance Agency (QAA) for Higher Education. Retrieved from www.qaa.ac.uk/en/Publications/Documents/Rethinking-the-values-of-higher-education-students-as-change-agents.pdf.

Lambert, L. (2002). *Building leadership capacity in schools*. Melbourne: Australian Principals Centre Ltd.

Minors, H., Burnard, P., Wiffen, C., Shihabi, Z., & van der Walt, S. (2017). Mapping trends and framing issues in higher music education: Changing minds/changing practices. *London Review of Education, 15*(3), 457–473. doi: 10.18546/LRE.15.3.09.

Smith, M., & Trede, F. (2013). Reflective practice in the transition phase from university student to novice professional: Implications for teaching reflective practice. *Higher Education Research & Development, 32*(4), 632–645. doi: 10.1080/07294360.2012.709226.

Tosey, P. (2006). Interfering with the interference: An emergent perspective on creativity in higher education. In J. Jackson, M. Oliver, M. Shaw, & J. Wisdom (Eds.), *Developing creativity in higher education* (pp. 49–62). London and New York: Routledge.

Trede, F., & McEwen, C. (2016). Scoping the deliberate professional. In F. Trede & C. McEwen (Eds.), *Educating the deliberate professional* (pp. 3–14). Switzerland: Springer.

The International Society for Music Education (ISME)

Mission

The International Society for Music Education (ISME) believes that lived experiences of music, in all their many aspects, are a vital part of the life of all people. ISME's mission is to enhance those experiences by:

- building and maintaining a worldwide community of music educators characterised by mutual respect and support;
- fostering global intercultural understanding and cooperation among the world's music educators; and
- promoting music education for people of all ages in all relevant situations throughout the world.

Core values

To build and maintain a worldwide community of music educators the ISME affirms that:

- there is a need for music education in all cultures;
- effective music education depends on suitably qualified teachers who are respected and compensated properly for their work;
- all teacher education curricula should provide skills in and understandings of a selection of both local and international musics;
- formal and informal music education programmes should serve the individual needs of all learners, including those with special needs and exceptional competencies; and
- music education programmes should take as a point of departure the existence of a wide variety of musics, all of which are worthy of understanding and study.

With respect to international and intercultural understandings and cooperation, the ISME believes that:

- the richness and diversity of the world's music provides opportunities for intercultural learning and international understanding, cooperation and peace; and
- in music education everywhere, respect for all kinds of music should be emphasised.

In its promotion of music education worldwide, the ISME maintains that:

- access for all people to music learning opportunities and to participate actively in various aspects of music is essential for the well-being of the individual and society;
- in teaching the musics of the world, the integrity of each music and its value criteria should be fully respected; and
- access to music, information about music, and opportunities to develop musical and related skills can occur in a range of ways, that are essential in satisfying peoples' diverse musical needs, interests, and capacities.

For more information, visit www.isme.org.

The ISME Commission on the Education of the Professional Musician

The seven ISME Commissions and the ISME Forum offer members opportunities to explore a specialised area in greater depth than might otherwise be possible. Through the Commissions and Forum, ISME members share mutual interests and gather, collate and disseminate information on developments in their specialised fields within music education.

For more information on the ISME Commissions and Forum, visit www.isme.org/our-work/commissions.

Vision

Undergirding the vision of the ISME Commission on the Education of the Professional Musician is the belief that any discussion or action pertaining to the education and training of professional musicians must be sensitive to the roles and status that musicians have in various societies and cultures. Of equal importance is the attention to the value systems in those societies and cultures that drive the choices concerning music, education, and the arts in a broader sense.

Mission

The mission of the ISME Commission on the Education of the Professional Musician is to engage in and promote a variety of activities in international and local settings that:

- focus on the professional musician as one who accepts responsibility for advancing and disseminating music as an integral part of life, and whose engagement with music; reflects perception, understanding, appreciation, and mastery in a manner that conveys meaning to people;
- foster the recognition of the many modes of educating and training musicians as practised by various societies and cultures;
- emphasise strategies through which educators can prepare musicians for the continually changing role of the musician in various contexts, societies and cultures; and
- raise awareness and develop an appreciation of matters pertaining to the general health and welfare of musicians.

Contributors

Dawn Bennett is John Curtin Distinguished Professor of Higher Education and Director of the EmployABILITY and Creative Workforce Initiatives with Curtin University in Australia. Dawn is a National Senior Australian Learning and Teaching Fellow and Principal Fellow with the Higher Education Academy in the UK. She is editor-in-chief of two Routledge series, Global Perspectives in Music Education and Specialist Themes in Music Education, produced in partnership with the International Society for Music Education. Recent grants relate to the characteristics of work in music, career-capable graduates and employability in a global context. Her metacognitive model for employABILITY thinking (see developingemployability.edu.au) has been widely adopted in Australia, the UK, Europe and the US. Publications appear at Researchgate.

Martin Berger is Head of Choral Studies at Stellenbosch University, South Africa. He graduated in church music performance, music education, musicology, German literature and choral conducting from the Universities of Saarbrücken and Düsseldorf. As Professor for Choral Pedagogy at the Robert Schumann Music University in Düsseldorf, Berger further developed modern teaching methods for choral music. In 2013 he joined Stellenbosch University where he is developing new concepts for choral conducting training in South Africa. Apart from practical tuition, the university aims to pioneer new concepts of music-making and research in a multi-ethnic environment by combining musical excellence, research and social awareness.

Pamela Burnard is Professor of Arts, Creativities and Education at the Faculty of Education, University of Cambridge, in the UK. She co-convenes the British Educational Research Association (BERA) Special Interest Group, Creativities in Education, the Creativities in Intercultural Arts Network and the biennial international conference, Building Interdisciplinary Bridges Across Cultures and Creativities. She has published widely with 15 books and more than 100 articles on the expanded conceptualisation and plural expression of creativities across diverse learning contexts and cultures. Pamela is co-editor of *Thinking Skills and Creativity* and *The Routledge International Handbook of Intercultural Arts Research*.

Kelly Bylica is pursuing a PhD in music education at Western University in the United States. Her research focuses on soundscape creation, composition and lived experience as a creative and critical pedagogy. Prior to her doctoral work, Kelly taught general music and choir in Illinois and Indiana. She holds degrees from Valparaiso University and Northwestern University, both in the US. Kelly has presented on her work at several conferences in North America and Europe.

Glen Carruthers is Dean of Music at Wilfrid Laurier University, Canada. He has published more than 50 articles and has presented conference papers and lectures in 20 countries. A past chair of the ISME Commission on the Education of the Professional Musician, Glen was recently named an honorary member of the Canadian University Music Society.

David Lines, PhD (Education), is Associate Professor of Music Education at the University of Auckland. His research is in the area of educational philosophy and the arts, particularly music, and music education philosophy. He has written on early childhood, improvisation and education, creativity, and music technology. David plays in an instrumental jazz ensemble and has contributed to five recorded albums and numerous performances. His music teaching career has spanned primary, secondary and tertiary levels and he has recently been Associate Dean Academic and Acting Head of School of Music at the University of Auckland.

Susan A. O'Neill is Professor and Associate Dean, Academic and Research in the Faculty of Education at Simon Fraser University. She is president-elect of the International Society for Music Education and has published widely in the fields of music psychology and music education. She has been awarded major grants for international collaborative research and has developed music education advocacy and intercultural programmes in several countries. Her current research includes a large survey and interview study of young people's music and creative technologies engagement in provinces across Canada and the social impact of music-making on young people's lives.

Pamela D. Pike, PhD is the Barineau endowed professor of piano pedagogy at Louisiana State University, USA where she directs the piano pedagogy and group piano programme. Pamela has authored the book *Dynamic Group-Piano Teaching: Transforming Group Theory into Teaching Practice* (Routledge), chapters in the Royal Conservatory of Music (Toronto) pedagogical materials and *High-Impact Practices in Online Education* (Stylus), and more than three dozen articles in peer-reviewed music education journals. She is sought after as a clinician and presenter on pedagogical topics for various teaching organisations. She has won awards for her pre-college and university teaching.

Anna Reid is the Dean of the Sydney Conservatorium of Music and plays the cello. A tertiary educator her entire career, she has worked as a director of music (1988–1994) and an academic developer (1996–2009). Her interest in higher education leadership developed during that time, and she gained a MEd. Admin from the University of New England. Her PhD on music in higher education explored variations in the ways that instrumental and vocal students and teachers learn and teach. She has research interests in creativity theory, informed performance, ethics, leadership, statistics and policy in higher education.

Jennifer Rowley is Associate Professor and Program Leader of Music Education at the Sydney Conservatorium of Music (SCM), The University of Sydney, and is the academic coordinator for the professional placement programme for SCM students into the arts industry, regional conservatoriums and schools. She is particularly interested in the areas of identity development, gifted musicians' talent development and the impact of the electronic portfolio for fostering enhanced work readiness. Jennifer is committed to musicians' professional learning and how the individual cognitive, social, emotional and behavioural needs of all learners can be met in a diverse range of educational settings. She is senior editor of the Routledge series Specialist Themes in Music Education, produced in partnership with the International Society for Music Education.

Patrick Schmidt is Chair of Music Education at Western University. His innovative work in critical pedagogy and policy is recognised internationally. Recent publications can be found in the *International Journal of Music Education*, *Theory into Practice*, *Arts Education Policy Review* and *Research in Music Education*. Patrick has led several consulting and evaluative projects including for the National YoungArts Foundation and the New World Symphony, US and the Ministry of Culture and Education, Chile. He co-edited the *Oxford Handbook of Music Education and Social Justice*, released in 2015. His *Policy and the Political Life of Music Education* was released by Oxford University Press in 2017.

Euridiana Silva Souza is PhD student at UFMG (Music Education programme), focusing on professional identity and higher music education. She is temporary teacher at UnB (Brasília University), and coordinator at Fábrica de Artes (Belo Horizonte, Minas Gerais state). She is also an active pianist performing on DuaAlismo, with Alysson Rodrigues (viola and piano). They explore an Iberian and Latin American repertoire mixing popular and erudite music. Euridiana currently works in collaboration with researchers from Chile and Colombia in a comparative research on public policy on evaluation of teacher training in music.

As a teacher, researcher and consultant, **Janis F. Weller** focuses on the intersections of personal and professional development, helping artists navigate transitions while building sustainable and meaningful careers and lives. She served as the former Associate Dean of Academic Affairs/Head of Liberal Arts at McNally Smith College of Music, where she also taught the senior capstone, Creating a Life in Music. As a flutist, Janis has premiered more than 100 new works ranging from traditionally notated pieces to graphic notation and sculptural scores.

Christine Ngai Lam Yau trained as a classical pianist in Beijing and the Shanghai Conservatory of Music in China. Christine previously worked as an accompanist, piano teacher and music director for music services in China, Australia and England. She worked at the Royal College of Music in London as a research associate before undertaking doctoral research at Cambridge University. Christine completed her PhD in 2015 with a thesis titled "The nature of one-to-one instrumental/vocal pedagogy in music conservatoire setting: Two cases from a UK conservatoire". She is currently a school administrator for an international school in China.

Index

Note: Page numbers in *italics* refer to figures.

Aaron, composer-conductor (case study) 176–179
academic administration, courses in 21
accessibility 55, 99, 177
accountability 9, 14–15, 31, 82
adaptability 11, 45, 50, 56, 58
advocacy, music education 94, 137–138
African culture 121, 124, 125
Agawu, V. K. 121
Ahmed, S. 77
Allsup, R. E. and Shieh, E. 123
ally approach 8, 97–99
Amabile, T. M. 134–135, 136
ambition 89, 161
anxiety 91, 150
apprenticeships 92; master-apprentice model 151–153, 164, 185, 186–187, 188
approvals processes 28–29
Arminio, J. 95, 97
art: arts sector internships 106–107; and policy 44, 50, 53, 57, 59; and politics 83, 85; primary and secondary education 2–3, 90
assumptions 49, 51, 57, 77, 200
audience engagement 34, 35; and improvisation 177, 178, 179, 180, 181, 185
audio sound designers 73–74
Australia 88, 164
authority 161, 162
authorship 74–76; *see also* composition
autonomy 8, 33, 41, 42, 84, 92
avant-garde music 174
awareness 12, 122–124, 162, 164, 177

"baby boomers" 87
Bachrach, P. and Baratz, M. S. 58
"balance" 120
Balkin, A. 136
Ball, S. J. 50
Bandino, R. et al. 34
Bathurst, R. and Ladkin, D. 34
being, sense of 38, 105
Bennett, Dawn 6–12, 64, 126, 190–200; and musician identity 9, 103–113, 192, 196
Berger, Martin 6, 115–127, 192–193; *see also* conductors, choral
bias 30, 58
Bjorck, C. 64
Boerner, S., Krause, D. and Gebert, D. 34
Boisot, M. 47
Bolden, R., Petrov, G. and Gosling, J. 41
Born, G. and Devine, K. 64
Boud, D., Cohen, R. and Sampson, J. 198
Boult, A. 119
boundaries 41, 98, 185
Bourdieu, Pierre 10, 62, 68
Brandon University 31–32
bridging 109, 110
budgets 19, 23, 82, 90, 180
Bull, A. 65
bureaucracy 84
Burnard, Pamela 10, 62–78, 85, 197; *see also* gender equality
Burwell, K. 8, 188; with Bennett and Carey 164
business administration/management 33, 84, 169–170; and career development 7, 130–145;

209

210 • Index

and creativity 143, 145; and musician income 141, *142*
Bylica, Kelly 8, 184–189, 195

Canada 88, 90
Canadian Association of Fine Arts Deans (CAFAD) 21
Canadian Broadcasting Corporation (CBC) 20
capital (Bourdieu) 40, 64, 65–68, 69, 70–77, 78
capitalism 82, 84
career development/preparation 12, 62–78, 92–93, 169–170; and business management 7, 130–145; career creativities 64, 65–68, 70, 73, 74, 76, 77; and conductors 177, 180–181; and curriculum 26, 83–84, 196; and identity 104, 108, 109–112, 150–151, 152–153, 191; and internships 26, 106–107; and musician identity 104, 108, 109–112, 150–151, 152–153, 191; and policy 53, 57–58; student-teacher relationship 157–159, 162–163; and sustainability 163, 168, 170, 179; *see also* gender equality; professional development
career satisfaction 141, 143
careers advice 70
careers, portfolio 73
caring 77, 99, 121
Carl, student (case study) 153–154, 156–161
Carruthers, Glen 9, 11, 14–32, 83, 193, 196, 198; *see also* leadership
case studies 16–30, 55–57, 153–161, 176–177
centralisation 40, 118, 119
Centre for Higher Education Research and Development (CHERD), University of Manitoba 20–21
certitude 48–49

chamber music 133, 143, 145, 174
change 85, 95; agents of 7, 93, 115–127, 186, 193; and choral conductors 6, 115–127, 193; and gender equality 72–78; and Generation Z 8, 88, 91–95, 98, 99–100, 192; and leadership 39, 44–59; and policy 11, 44–45, 47, 48, 50–51, 52, 57; social 7, 11, 96, 98, 167–181, 193; technological 87, 169
chaos 106, 111
charisma 119, 176, 181
Chase, Claire 180
children 2–3, 69, 134; youth choirs 119, 120
choices, curriculum 22–23, 24
choral singing 115, 117, 124, 126; *see also* conductors, choral
church musicians 130, 140, 168
citizenship, social 12, 94, 186, 194; and choral conductors 6, 116, 122, 124
Clarke, E. and Doffman, M. 7
classical music 65
classroom arrangements 98
cognitive approaches 194, 196
collaboration: and leadership 40, 187–188, 192, 194, 197; and music 93, 177–178, 187, 199
College Music Society (CMS) 137–138, 198; Task Force on the Undergraduate Music Major (TFUMM) 7, 45, 56–57, 168, 180
colleges 27
comfort zones 91, 111, 112
commerce, field of 75
Commission on the Education of the Professional Musician, ISME 204
commodification 82, 191
communication: and leadership 36, 81, 91, 109, 112, 187; of musical experience 4, 36, 131
Community Embedded Musicians 56

Index • 211

community engagement/involvement 81, 192, 196, 198, 199; and choral conductors 121, 126; communities of practice 104, 110, 163; community music 23, 24, 26, 28, 32, 56, 140; community partnerships 83, 105, 139, 141, 199; and creativity 85, 134, 136, 143, 145; and curriculum 28, 83, 134, 136, 139; and gender equality 76, 78; and Generation Z 90, 94; and policy 81, 83, 84, 85; and policy thinking 51–52, 54–55, 56
Community Leadership Council Initiative 55–56
compassion 89, 90, 94, 122
competency 92, 187
complexity 38, 39, 103, 105–106, 111
composers 69, 70, 73, 74–76
composition: and creativity 131, 134; and improvisation 7, 167, 168–169, 172–173, 174–179, 191
concert programmes 143
conduction (conducted improvisation) 175–176, 177
conductors: and charisma 119, 176, 181; and improvisation 171–172, 175–179; as leaders 34, 35, 36, 116–117, 118, 119; and reflexivity 126, 177
conductors, choral: and African culture 121, 124, 125; and change 6, 115–127, 193; choral conducting 119–120, 140; and citizenship 6, 116, 122, 124; and cultures/tradition 6, 120–121, 122, 124–126, 127; and democratisation 120, 123; and empowerment 122, 123–124, 125, 126; and excellence 115, 116, 122, 126, 127; and hierarchy 119, 120; and identity 117, 121, 122, 123, 125; and local relevance 122, 123, 126; and multiculturism 115, 122, 123, 124; and perception 123, 124–125; transdisciplinary approach 115, 121, 126; and Western music 120–121, 124
conductors, orchestral 34, 35, 36
confidence 67, 70, 78
connectedness, sense of 89, 90, 91, 94
conservatoires 45, 63–64; for non-university students 26, 32
constructivism 195, 196
control 39, 118
core abilities 130–145
courses: new 19, 24, 25; online 26; specialised 19, 22
craft 44, 50, 53, 57, 59
creative industries 64, 71, 73
creativity 130–145; and business management 143, 145; and choral conductors 6, 115–127; co-creation 56, 66, 88, 95, 185, 186–187; collaborative/group 63, 76, 88; and community engagement 85, 134, 136, 143, 145; and composition 131, 134; creative capital 69; creative disposition 47, 85; creative skills 130, 134–136, 137; creative thinking 131, 133, 136, 143; creativity networks 73; and curriculum 45, 136, 143–145, 168–169, 188; and domain-relevant skills 134–135, 137; and entrepreneurship 90, 139, 143; and gender equality 63, 64–68, 69–70, 71, 72–73, 74–77, 78; and Generation Z 90, 94, 99; and identity 105, 106, 144; and improvisation 131, 134, 135, 178–179; and innovation 103, 136, 141; and leadership 110, 133–137, 185, 186, 187, 198; and motivation 134, 135, 136,

137; musical 74–76, 122, 126, 131; and peers 133, 134, 145; and performance 130, 131; and problem-solving 130, 133, 135, 136, 145; and reflexivity 133, 136, 137, 191, 198
Csikszentmihalyi, M. 134
cultural production, field of 73, 75
cultures/tradition 134, 200; and conductors 120–121, 122, 124–125, 126, 127; and improvisation 169, 173; and ISME 202, 203, 204
Curlee, W. and Gordon, R. I. 106, 111
curriculum 14–32, 168–170, 194, 202; and career development 26, 83–84, 196; choice 22–23, 24; and community engagement 28, 83, 134, 136, 139; core 19, 22–23, 198; core abilities 130–145; and creativity 45, 136, 143–145, 168–169, 188; curriculum choices 22–23, 24; curriculum development 19–22, 95, 164; design 28, 143; and differentiation 27–28, 31; and Generation Z 94, 96; and improvisation 28, 168–169, 173, 180; and learning experiences 24, 25, 26–27; and learning outcomes 23–24, 28, 132; and music history 22, 25, 26, 116; and music therapy 23, 28; new courses 24, 25; "one-size-fits-all" 188; and partnerships 26, 27; and recruitment 18, 19, 22–23; reform 8, 14, 20, 22–30, 51, 168; and relevance 23, 31, 32; review process 9–10, 14–32, 83; and teachers 28, 117, 186–188
Curriculum Manifesto, College Music Society *see* Task Force on the Undergraduate Music Major (TFUMM)

Davies, B. and Ellison, L. 46
Davison, A. et al. 41
Day, D. and Antonakis, J. 118, 119
Dean, D. and Stanley, K. 95
decision-making 16, 72, 199; "decisionism" 48, 50; and Generation Z 94–95, 98; and policy 48, 49, 53
decolonisation 125
degrees, double 22
Dei, G. S. 123
deliberation 45–46, 48, 49, 51
democratisation 39, 59, 133; and choral conductors 120, 123; and education 11, 81–85, 193
Department of Culture, Media and Sport (DCMS), UK 64
DePauw University 170
dependency 161, 162
difference 36–37, 192
differentiation 27–28, 31
digital media 65, 70, 75, 89, 93
"digital natives" *see* Generation Z
discrimination 71, 197
diversity 24–25, 45, 169–170, 203, 204
domination 187; and conductors 118, 119; male 64, 74, 77, 92
doubt 110–111
Dunn, W. N. 48
Dunne, E.: with Kay and Hutchinson 88, 99–100; and Zandstra 95
Durrant, C. 7, 122
Dylan Smith, G. 64

Eastern philosophy 120–121
Eastman School of Music 170
economics 3–4, 45, 90; budgets 18, 19, 23, 82, 90, 180; and education 3–4, 82, 85; *see also* income of musicians
education: and capitalism 82, 84; and democratisation 11, 81–85, 193; and economics 3–4, 82, 85; primary 2–3, 90; secondary

70, 90, 132, 154; of teachers 28, 91, 202
effectiveness 84, 116, 117, 131
efficiency, leadership 112, 118, 120
ELISION ensemble 74–76
Elliott, D. 123, 124
employability 10, 54, 58, 67; employABILITY 194, 196, 198
empowerment 172; and choral conductors 122, 123–124, 125, 126; disempowerment 88, 192; and Generation Z 88, 94, 97, 192; and improvisation 178, 179; and instrumental teachers 151, 163
engagement *see* audience engagement; community engagement/involvement; students
ensembles 34, 133, 176–179
entertainment industry 73
entrepreneurship 21, 26, 85; and creativity 90, 139, 143; and gender equality 68, 76, 78; and Generation Z 90, 91, 92; and improvisation 168, 169–170, 173
equipment 18, 19
ethics 23; and leadership 77, 121, 171; and policy 49, 53
ethnicity 27–28, 55, 64, 90
Europe 88, 164
evaluation 95, 119
excellence, artistic 115, 116, 122, 126, 127, 169
expectation 66, 67, 70
experience, musical 25, 193; communication of 4, 36, 131; and identity 37–39, 105, 106–107, 109; and leadership 36, 37–38, 108, 112; value of 130, 137–139, 145
experience, professional 3, 38–39, 106, 108, 112, 159
experiential learning 24–27, 83, 111–112, 136, 185, 196

expertise: and Generation Z 88, 93, 95, 99; and leadership 39, 170, 172, 179, 194
expressivity 116
extroverts 132

facilitators 120
facilities 18, 19
family 69–70
Fear of Missing Out (FOMO) anxiety 91
fields (Bourdieu) 68, 73, 74, *75*
Finn, W. J. 119
Fischer, F. and Forester, J. 51
flexibility 22–23, 109
followers, mindful 7, 133, 151–153, 155–156
Forester, John 52–54, 57; with Fischer 51
Foss, L. 174, 175
Fowler, Robert 20
Freire, Paulo 83
friends 97–99, 159

Gade, C. B. N. 121
gaming industry 74
Gardner, H. 131, 133
Gaunt, H. 161, 162, 195
Gee, C. B. 138
gender equality 10, 62–78, 197; and capital 64, 65–68, 69, 70–77, 78; and career development 63–64, 67–68, 69, 70–71, 73, 74–77, 78; and change 72–78; and composers 69, 70, 73, 74–76; and confidence 67, 70, 78; and creative industries 64, 71, 73; and creativity 63, 64–68, 69–70, 71, 72–73, 74–77, 78; and digital media 65, 70, *75*; and entrepreneurship 68, 76, 78; and expectations 66, 67, 70; fields 68, 73, 74, *75*; and Generation Z 90, 92, 93; habitus 10, 62, 65, 68, 69–70; and leadership 70–71, 72–77,

197; and male domination 64, 74, 77, 92; and music industry 68, 73, 74, 75; and popular music 63, 64, 74; and role models 65–66, 78; and self-promotion 65, 66; and stereotyping 65–66, 67, 69–70; and Western music 63, 69; and workplace practices 71, 72
Generation X 87
Generation Y 87, 89
Generation Z 87–100; and career development 92–93; and change 8, 88, 91–95, 98, 99–100, 192; and community engagement 90, 94; and compassion 89, 90, 94; and connectedness 89, 90, 91, 94; and creativity 90, 94, 99; and curriculum 94–95, 96; and decision-making 94–95, 98; and digital media 89, 93; and empowerment 88, 94, 97, 192; and entrepreneurship 90, 91, 92; and expertise 88, 93, 95, 99; and inequality 90, 92, 93, 94, 99; and innovation 91, 94; and justice 90, 94, 99; and motivation 89, 92, 98; and peers 90–91, 93; and reflexivity 90, 94, 97; and student engagement 91, 95, 97, 98, 194–195; and technology 87, 89; and United States 88, 89, 90, 95–96; and "we-centricity" 89, 91
genres, musical 24, 39, 75, 173
globalisation 123
goals, common 34, 36, 120, 152, 178
governance 18, 19, 30
Grace, G. 44
"great man" theory 118
Green, L. 67
Gronn, P. 40

habitus (Bourdieu) 10, 62, 65, 68, 69–70
"halo effect" 162
Hamel, G. and Prahalad, C. K. 50
Hanson, Mark 55
harmony 34–35
Harris, A. 39, 40, 41
Harris, C. 93
Haussman, J. and Wise, D. 49
Hawkins, B. and Edwards, G. 110–111
Hawkins, J. 139
Healey, P. 50, 58–59
health 29–30
hegemony 66, 84
heritage 38–39
heroes 41, 63, 197
hierarchy: and choral conductors 119, 120; and leadership 118, 171, 190, 194, 197
honesty 163
Hope, J. 89, 91
Houston Symphony (HS) orchestra 55–56
human capital 64, 65–67, 68, 73, 77

idealisation 52
identity 8, 9, 92–93, 103–113, 115–127; and career development 104, 108, 109–112, 150–151, 152–153, 191; and choral conductors 6, 117, 121, 122, 123, 125; and complexity 38, 39, 103, 105–106, 111; and creativity 105, 106, 144; cultural 105, 121, 123; and leadership 37–39, 42, 103–105, 110; and musical experience 37–39, 105, 106–107, 109; and reorientation 108, 109–110, 111–112; student-teacher relationship 149, 151–152, 155–160, 163, 164
Improvestra ensemble 176–179
improvisation 7, 167–181; and audience engagement 177, 178, 179, 180,

181, 185; and composition 167, 168–169, 172–173, 174–179, 191; conducted 174–176, 177–178, 180–181, 185, 192; and creativity 131, 134, 178–179; and cultures/tradition 169, 173; and curriculum 28, 168–169, 173, 180; and empowerment 178, 179; and entrepreneurship 168, 169–170, 173; and inspiration 171, 175, 177, 179; and liminality 174–176, 177, 191–192
incentives 48–49
income of musicians 130, 140, 141, 142, 168
independence 151, 170, 186, 187, 188
Indigenous students 27
individualism 74, 76, 84
individuals 52, 53, 121; exceptional 118
inequality 11, 62–78, 81–85, 120; and Generation Z 90, 92, 93, 94, 99; LGBTQ 65, 72, 77; see also gender equality; justice, social
influence 39, 118, 192
information technology 89
initiative to lead 56, 93, 184–185, 186–187, 188
innovation: and creativity 103, 136, 141; and Generation Z 91, 94; and leadership 172, 185; and policy 45, 57
Innovative Conservatoire (ICON) group 164
insecurity 150–151
inspections, educational 46
inspiration 78, 171, 175, 177, 179
institutionalised practice 40–41
instrumental teachers 7–8, 149, 151, 153–155, 163, 184–185, 195; one-to-one teaching 149–150, 151–152, 161, 164; see also student-teacher relationship
intent, strategic 47, 85

interaction 56, 57, 76, 85, 120, 123; see also community engagement/involvement
International Society for Improvised Music 173
International Society for Music Education (ISME) 202–204
internships 26, 67, 92, 103, 106–112, 192; and liminality 9, 103, 105, 108, 110–112, 196
interpretative phenomenological analysis (IPA) 152–153
interrelatedness 120
intonation 124, 127
introverts, creative 132

jazz 31–32, 172–173, 174, 176
Jennings, B. 51
Johnson, Lyndon B. 49
Jones, S. 197
Jorgensen, E. R. 117
Jørgenson, H. 151, 187
Juneau, Pierre 20
justice, social 85, 171; and choral conductors 120, 122, 123; and Generation Z 90, 94, 99; see also gender equality; inequality
Juuti, S. and Littleton, K. 150, 151, 160

Kay, J., Dunne, E. and Hutchinson, J. 88, 99–100
Kelley, R. 133
Kertz-Welzel, A. 123
Khanna, N. and McCart, S. 98
knowledge, tacit 35
Kohler, R. A. 123, 124
Koivunen, N. and Wennes, G. 35
Komives, S. R. et al. 96, 97
Kuhnert, K. W. and Lewis, P. 171

labour market 71, 78, 84, 104
Lakehead University 31
language 50–52, 116, 163; tonal 124
Larsen, Libby 169

Latin America 81, 83–84
leadership 8–11, 81–85, 170–172, 190–200; and accountability 14–15, 31; and change 39, 44–59; and choral conductors 6, 115–127; and collaboration 40, 187–188, 192, 194, 197; and communication 36, 91, 109, 112, 187; and creativity 110, 131–132, 133–137, 185, 186, 187, 198; and curriculum 14, 188; definition 171; and efficiency 112, 118, 120; and ethics 77, 121, 171; and expertise 39, 170, 172, 179, 194; and gender equality 70–71, 72–77, 197; and governance 18, 19, 30; and hierarchy 118, 171, 190, 194, 197; and identity 37–39, 42, 103–105, 110; and initiative 56, 93, 184–185, 186–187, 188; and innovation 172, 185; leadership-in-the-world 197; and musical experience 36–38, 108, 112; and orchestras 34–36, 38–39; and priority setting 9, 14, 15–16, 198; process-based understanding of 48, 84; review process 18, 19; and stereotyping 118, 132, 193; theories of 39–41; workshops 198; *see also* creativity; curriculum; Generation Z; identity; policy thinking
leadership studies/leadership education 95–97
leadership styles: collaborative 10, 33–42, 91, 167, 172, 176; democratic 133; devolved 41; distributed 10, 33–42, 192, 200; indirect 7, 130–145; shared 167–181, 192; transactional 125, 171; transformational 7, 133, 167–181, 185–189, 191, 193–194; *ubuntu* leadership 121
learning, approaches to 36, 88
learning, experiential 24–27, 83, 111–112, 136, 185, 192, 196
learning outcomes 23–24, 28, 40, 132
learning processes 90, 195
Lebler, D. 188
Lees-Marshment, J. 46
Lewin, K. 111
Libman, K. 138
"life river" 163
lifewide learning 88
Lim, Liza 70, 74–76
liminality: and improvisation 174–176, 177, 191; and internships 9, 103, 105, 108, 110–12, 196
Lines, David 1–5
listening experiences 1
Locke, E. A. 111
Long, Jen 92–93
Lührmann, T, and Eberl, P. 112

Mahler, Gustav, 2nd symphony 38–39
Majone, G. 48
Manski, Charles 48–49, 57
Manturzewska, M. 186
marginalisation 67
Marion, R. 104–105
marketing 18, 19, 22–23, 28
master-apprentice model 149–153, 164, 185, 186–187, 188
McManus, R. M. and Perruci, G. 133
mentoring 73, 78, 198, 200
messaging, gender 65–67
Mills, J. 150, 163
Minas Gerais, Brazil 11, 81–85
mindfulness 192, 193, 198
Minors, H. et al. 194
Mintzberg, H., Ghoshal, J. and Quinn, S. 47
Mitchell, Annie 185
Mohr, K. A. J. and Mohr, E. S. 91
Morris, Lawrence "Butch" 175, 176

motivation 162, 171; and creativity 134, 135, 136, 137; and Generation Z 89, 98
multiculturalism 6, 115, 122, 123, 124
music history 22, 25, 26, 116, 143
music industry 68, 73, 74, *75*
music-making 4, 33, 38–39
music technology 74, *75*, 76, 92–93, 145, 169, 173
music theory 116, 143
music therapy 23, 28
musicians: becoming a musician 1–2; female 65–66, 71–72, 119; income of 130, 140, 141, 142, 168; *see also* creativity; identity
Myers, D. 57–58, 173, 180, 186, 187, 188

Nagel, A. 47
National Association of Music in Higher Education, UK 71
National Association of Schools of Music (NASM) 57, 173, 198
National Coalition for Core Arts Standards, US 138
needs: policy 52, *53*; of society 123–124, 185–186, 187, 199, 204
neoliberalism 3–4
Nerland, M. and Hanken, I. M. 161
New World Symphony, orchestral academy 56
Nielsen, K. N. 151
Noddings, N. 99
North axis 81, 82
Northouse, P. G. 118, 119, 152, 161, 171

O'Neill, Susan 8, 9, 87–100, 184–189; *see also* Generation Z
one-to-one teaching 149–150, 151–152, 161, 164
orchestras 119, 140, 167, 171; and leadership 34–36, 38–39; and policy 54, 55–56
outreach 18, 19, 26, 32

ownership, collective 184–189
Oxford Dictionary 34

parents 69–70
partnerships 98; community 83, 105, 139, 141, 199; and curriculum 26, 27; industry 19, 27
Pasler, J. 70
passion 91, 125, 133
passivity 41, 88, 162, 192
patriarchy 48, 73
peers 28, 104; and creativity 133, 134, 145; and Generation Z 90–91, 93, 98
perception 123, 124–125
perfection, technical 124
performance 70; and creativity 130, 131; and improvisation 7, 167–181; skills 140–1, *142*
performers 69, 105, 130, 150
Perkins, R. 150–151, 163; and Williamon 126
Persson, R. S. 151, 187
Pierre, teacher 153–154, 155–156, 157–159, 160–161
Pike, Pamela D. 7, 130–145, 185, 191, 198; *see also* creativity
Pippa, musician (case study) 71
placements 18, 26; *see also* internships
planning, strategic 46–47, 50, 95, 195
policy-making 71
policy thinking 11, 44–59, 195–197, 200; and adaptability 45, 50, 56, 58; and assumptions 49, 51, 57; and craft 44, 50, 53, 57, 59; and decision-making 48, 49, *53*; and deliberation 45–46, 48, 49, 51; and ethics 49, *53*; and individuals 52, *53*; and innovation 45, 57; and maps 44, 46, 47, 56; and needs 52, *53*; policy framing 45–48, 49, 51, 55, 57–58, 85, 196; and short change and shorthand 52, *53*,

57; and stories 52, 56, 57; and strategic planning 46–47, 50; traditional 44, 47
politicians 95, 96
politics 81–82, 85
popular music 63, 64, 74, 169, 179
Potted Meet events 176
power 161–162; fields of 75; power relations 8, 71, 152, 186, 187
practice, musician's 7, 167–181
Preparing Teachers and the Development of School Leaders for the 21st Century (OECD) 91
primary education 2–3, 90
priority setting 9, 14, 15–16, 198
problem-solving 89, 187; and creativity 130, 133, 135, 136, 145
pro bono work 78
productivity 82, 84, 137; research 16, 18
professional development 9, 91, 103–113, 198, 200; and experience 3, 38–39, 106, 108, 112, 159; and musician identity 108, 110–112; professional capital 67–68, 74, 76, 77, 78; see also career development/preparation
"public good" 3, 138, 186

quality 39, 126
quantification 137, 138

reciprocity 94, 99, 118, 188, 195
recommendations, review process 17–19
recruitment 18, 19, 22–23, 71
reflexivity 74–76, 107, 195; and conductors 126, 177; and creativity 133, 136, 137, 191, 198; and Generation Z 90, 94, 97; self-reflection 90, 94, 97, 136, 186, 198; student-teacher relationship 149, 155–160, 162–163, 164
reform, curricular 8, 14, 20, 22–30, 51, 168
Reid, Anna 9, 10, 33–42, 103–113, 192, 196, 200; with Solomonides 105; *see also* identity; learning, experiential
Rein, M. and Schön, D. 47
relevance 55, 194; and curriculum 23, 31, 32; local 122, 123, 126
reorientation 108, 109–110, 111–112
resources, lack of 194
respect 39, 67, 121, 163, 202
responsibility, shared 76, 120, 185, 188
review process 9–10, 14–32, 83; *see also* curriculum
risk 163, 178–179
Robertson, M. 123
role models 126; and gender equality 65–66, 78; student-teacher relationship 151–152, 155–156, 159, 164
Roomful of Teeth, vocal group 169
Roshi, singer-songwriter 69
Ross, J. 139
Rowley, Jennifer 6–12, 9, 103–113, 125, 190–200; *see also* identity; internships
Royal College of Music (RCM), London 150
Royal Conservatory of The Hague 164
rules 74, 76, 134, 174, 200

Santos, B. S. 84
Sarath, E. et al. 169–170
Scharff, C. 65
scheduling, coordinated 29
Schleicher, A. 91
Schmidt, Patrick 6–12, 11, 44–59, 83, 190–200; *see also* policy thinking
schools of music 45
secondary education 90
Seemiller, C. and Grace, M. 89, 90, 92, 95–96
self-awareness 12, 177
self-concept 8, 184–189
self-help books 95
self-knowledge 133
self-monitoring 73, 189

self-promotion 65, 66, 169
self-reflection 136, 186, 198; and Generation Z 90, 94, 97
self-regulation 135
self-understanding 156–157
Senge, P, 104
sexual equality 65, 72, 77
sexualisation 66
Shamir, B. and Eilam, G. 125
short change and shorthand 52, 53, 57
shows, musical 2–3
singers 122, 125
skills: creative 130, 134–136, 137; domain-relevant 130, 134–135, 137; musical 42, 106, 130; performance 140–141, *142*; skills training 78, 130
small groups 94, 133, 145
Smith, J. A. and Eatough, V. 152
social capital 40, 66, 68
Social Change Model of Leadership Development 96
social networking 88, 93, 139
society, needs of 123–124, 185–186, 187, 199, 204
soloists 150, 158, 160, 169
Solomonides, I. and Reid, A. 105
Soulé, H. and Warrick, T. 136
sound 2, 34, 37, 124, 127
South Africa 125
Southern philosophy 121
Souza, Euridiana Silva 11, 81–85, 193
specialisation: institutional 64, 66; music 41–42, 126, 135, 179, 180; performance 70, 169; specialised courses 19, 22
special needs 202
staffing: academic 18, 19, 194; administrative 18, 19, 21, 30
standardisation 82
standard setting 92, 123, 137
stereotyping: and gender equality 65–66, 67, 69–70; and leadership 118, 132, 193
Stone, D. 51

stories 52, 56, 57
streamlining 25–26
students 81–85, 179–180; ethnic/Indigenous 27; Generation Z 8, 87–100; health and wellbeing 29–30, 91, 150; international 27; non-music 23, 28; non-university 26; student engagement 91, 95, 97, 98, 194–195; student leaders 95, 191; student support systems 42
student-teacher relationship 8, 83, 149–164; authority 161, 162; career development 157–159, 162–163; dependency 161, 162; identity 149, 151–152, 155–160, 163, 164; mindful followers 151–153, 155–156; and power relations 8, 186, 187; reflexivity 149, 155–160, 162–163, 164; role models 151–152, 155–156, 159, 164; trust 161, 163
sustainability 25, 94–95; and career development 163, 168, 170, 179
Sydney Conservatorium of Music (SCM) 106, 112

targeting 27–28, 54
Task Force on the Undergraduate Music Major (TFUMM) 7, 45, 56–57, 168, 180
taste, musical 68, 169
teachers: and curriculum 28, 117, 186–188; education of 28, 91, 202; instrumental 151, 153–5, 184–185, 195; of music 130, 139, 140; teaching skills 141, *142*; *see also* student-teacher relationship
technology: changes in 87, 169; Generation Z 87, 89; music 74, *75*, 76, 92–93, 145, 169, 173
tension, structural 195–196
territory 44–45, 47, 53, 56, 83

thinking: creative 131, 133, 136, 143;
    critical 8, 116, 122, 143,
    184–189, 192; *see also* policy
    thinking
Thomas, K. 119; and Mann and
    Reese 119
time factors 53, 194
Torgerson, D. 51
transculturalism 7, 122, 125–126, 193
transdisciplinary approach 115, 121,
    126
transformation, sense of 38, 105
Trede, F. and McEwen, C. 192
trust 39, 161, 163, 178
"truth" 120
Turner, V. 175

ubuntu leadership 121
United Kingdom 64, 88, 149–164
United States 88, 89, 90, 95–96, 130, 131
unity 120
University of Colorado, Boulder 170

value of musical experience 130,
    137–139, 145
van der Heijden, H. R. M. A. et al. 93
Van der Sandt, J. T. V. D. 116
variation 34, 35, 36–37, 38–39, 42
Vendler, H. 133

walls 11, 81, 85
Webster, P. 136
"we-centricity" 89, 91
Weick, K. E. 111
well-being 29–30, 204
Weller, Janis F. 7–8, 167–181, 185,
    191–192, 195
Wenger, E. 42
Wenig, Steve 55–56
Western music 63, 69, 120–121, 124,
    169, 172
Wildavsky, Aaron 11, 44, 50, 53, 57, 59
Wilfrid Laurier University 31, 32
William H. Buset Centre 31–32
Williams, Raymond 11, 81
women in the orchestra 119; *see also*
    gender equality
Wood, H. J. 119
Woodford, P. 123
working classes 70
working relations 34, 40
workloads 29
workplace practices 71, 72, 106

Yau, Christine Ngai Lam 8, 149–164, 195

Zappa, Frank 174–175
Zelinksy, W. et al 73
Zorn, John 174

CPSIA information can be obtained
at www.ICGtesting.com
Printed in the USA
LVHW081643030322
712560LV00003B/97

9 781138 587465